Studies in German Literature, Linguistics, and Culture:
Literary Criticism in Perspective

Studies in German Literature, Linguistics,
and Culture

James Hardin & Gunther Holst
Managing Editors

Editorial Board
Literary Criticism in Perspective

James Hardin (*South Carolina*), General Editor

Eitel Timm (*Waldorf School, Vancouver*), German Literature

Benjamin Franklin V (*South Carolina*), American and
English Literature

Reingard M. Nischik (*Freiburg i. Breisgau*), Comparative Literature

About *Literary Criticism in Perspective*

Books in the series *Literary Criticism in Perspective*, a subseries of *Studies in German Literature, Linguistics, and Culture*, trace literary scholarship and criticism on major and neglected writers alike, or on a single major work, a group of writers, a literary school or movement. In so doing the authors — authorities on the topic in question who are also well-versed in the principles and history of literary criticism — address a readership consisting of scholars, students of literature at the graduate and undergraduate level, and the general reader. One of the primary purposes of the series is to illuminate the nature of literary criticism itself, to gauge the influence of social and historic currents on aesthetic judgments once thought objective and normative.

The Critical Fortunes of a Romantic Novel
Novalis's Heinrich von Ofterdingen

Dennis F. Mahoney

The Critical Fortunes of a Romantic Novel

Novalis's *Heinrich von Ofterdingen*

Camden House

Published by Camden House, Inc.
Drawer 2025
Columbia, SC 29202 USA

Printed on acid-free paper.
Binding materials are chosen for strength and
durability.

ISBN:1-879751-58-5

Library of Congress Cataloging-in-Publication Data

Mahoney, Dennis F., 1950-
    The critical fortunes of a romantic novel : Novalis's Heinrich von
Ofterdingen / Dennis F. Mahoney.
        p., cm. -- (Studies in German literature, linguistics, and culture)
    Includes bibliographical references.
    ISBN 1-879751-58-5 (alk. paper)
    1. Novalis, 1772-1801. Heinrich von Ofterdingen I. Title. II. Series: Studies
in German literature, linguistics, and culture
    (Unnumbered)
    PT2291.H4M34 1994
    833'.6--dc20   94-11094
                                                                CIP

Acknowledgments

I would like to thank the University of Vermont for my sabbatical grant during the 1992-93 academic year, during which time I wrote the greater part of this book. With the help of Barbara Lambert, Patricia Mardeusz, and Daryl Purvee in the interlibrary loan office of the Bailey-Howe Library, University of Vermont, I have been able to provide accounts of more nineteenth- and early twentieth-century writings on *Heinrich von Ofterdingen* than I ever thought possible. Wolfgang Mieder (University of Vermont), who suggested that I pay close attention to the treatment of Novalis in German literary histories, provided me with such volumes from his personal library. There have been many colleagues and students, both within the Department of German and Russian at the University of Vermont and also at other institutions, who have been generous in their support. I think in particular of Beate Allert (Purdue University), Gerhart Hoffmeister (University of California, Santa Barbara), Alice Kuzniar (University of North Carolina, Chapel Hill), and Paul Michael Lützeler (Washington University, St. Louis), who have read my manuscript-in-progress and encouraged me in my efforts. Donald P. Haase (Wayne State University) first drew my attention to the French reception of Novalis during the first half of the nineteenth century. Charles Guignon (University of Vermont) helped guide me through the intricacies of twentieth-century literature theory; thanks to him and to students at the University of Augsburg with whom I discussed both Novalis and literary theory during the academic year 1989-90, the ideas in this book began to take shape. I likewise owe a debt of thanks to James Hardin and Eitel Timm, who not only encouraged me to undertake this project for Camden House but were exemplary in their prompt responses to questions I had along the way. Hope Greenberg (University of Vermont) was instrumental in introducing me to the world of word processing, and Janet Sobieski, the secretary of the German and Russian Department, was unfailing in providing those "final touches" that still eluded my grasp, while always displaying interest in the subject matter itself. Heartfelt thanks go to my beloved wife, Angelika Mahoney, and my friend and colleague David Scrase, who read the manuscript in its final stages and made many excellent suggestions for improving its style and substance.

Finally, I want to express my deepest appreciation to the individual who first provided me with the living inspiration to enter the teaching profession — namely my father, Justin Dennis Mahoney. I only hope that someday I will reach the level of concern and dedication for students that I witnessed in him as I was growing up. It is to him that I dedicate this book as a special token of love on the occasion of his eightieth birthday.

Dennis F. Mahoney
August 1994

To My Father:

Du hast in mir den edeln Trieb erregt
  Tief ins Gemüth der weiten Welt zu schauen;
  Mit deiner Hand ergriff mich ein Vertrauen,
  Das sicher mich durch alle Stürme trägt.

(Novalis, *Heinrich von Ofterdingen*)

Contents

Preface

SINCE THE POSTHUMOUS publication of *Heinrich von Ofterdingen* in 1802, German, French, British, and American critics have regarded this unfinished novel by Friedrich von Hardenberg (Novalis) as the epitome of German Romanticism. This judgment, however, has served as much to obscure as to highlight the precise nature of the work. The novel's title bears the name of a legendary medieval poet who reputedly took part in a song contest for life or death at the Wartburg castle in Eisenach against such luminaries as Wolfram von Eschenbach and Walter von der Vogelweide; in addition, the aura surrounding its author's name and artistic pseudonym, and the common understanding of the words Romantic and Romanticism conjure up visions of castles, minstrels, and the various trappings of romance. All this may lead the unwary reader to expect a tale somewhat in the manner of Sir Walter Scott's *Ivanhoe* and consequently to be disappointed by *Heinrich von Ofterdingen*'s relatively sparse plot, whose main function is to provide a framework for the interspersed tales and lengthy philosophical conversations. On the other hand, the novel has, at least for English and American readers, connotations of realism and sobriety that do not accord well with a work that begins with the dream of the Blue Flower and whose first part ends in a lengthy and immensely complicated fairy tale told by Klingsohr, Heinrich's poetic mentor.

Until relatively recently, however, those readers who might have found *Heinrich von Ofterdingen* attractive in spite of such confounding of initial expectations but who also desired authoritative guidance towards a greater understanding of the novel were not likely to have been well served by trust in the judgments of others. German literary critics, working on the paradigm of a fundamental difference between the fragmentary nature of German Romanticism and the measured Classicism of Goethe and Schiller, long tended to regard *Heinrich von Ofterdingen* and Goethe's *Wilhelm Meisters Lehrjahre* (Wilhelm Meister's Apprenticeship; 1795-96) as polar opposites rather than as early manifestations of self-reflective European modernism, which is how present-day scholars see them. And the rising reputation of Romanticism at the beginning of the twentieth century in Germany also coincided with a chauvinistic nationalism that led into Nazism, leaving behind a legacy of critical distrust toward German Romanticism after 1945, even though the Nazis themselves had little use for "bloodless" intellectuals such as Novalis. When one considers that even the author's own friends Friedrich Schlegel and Ludwig Tieck set the stage for more than a century of misconceptions by their slipshod edition of Novalis's reflections on philosophy and science — nowadays regarded as the intellectual foundations of his poetic output — the auspices for an informed appreciation of one of the most challenging works in German literature could not have been more unfavorable.

And yet, like the happy ending of so many fairy tales, the past three decades of *Ofterdingen* research have brought an ever increasing number and variety of substantive interpretations that have fundamentally altered our notions of what this Romantic novel aspired to accomplish and what it still can awaken in its readers. An investigation of the reception history of *Heinrich von Ofterdingen* thus provides an exemplary opportunity to examine how societal developments, combined with changing modes in scholarly criticism and editorial practice, can lead to striking differences of literary interpretation. As for fairy tales — and Novalis consciously designed *Heinrich von Ofterdingen* as a novel destined to make Heinrich's dream come true and Klingsohr's fairy tale come alive — the various critical readings of the Klingsohr tale throughout the past 190 years can serve as an indication of how close the critics in question come to understanding the inner logic of Novalis's novel, in which each unit amplifies the meaning of the other parts in a neverending progression.

As late as 1981, Ulrich Stadler could begin his interpretation of *Ofterdingen*, one of whose highlights is the discussion of Novalis's aesthetics of the fairy tale, by pointing out the lack of a reception history of this novel (Stadler 1981, 141) — although he acknowledges the preliminary work of critics such as Spenlé (1904), Haussmann (1911-12, 1913), Müller-Seidel (1953), Mahr (1970), and Kuenzli (1972). Herbert Uerlings has undertaken a giant step toward such a reception history through his detailed analysis of patterns of reception of Novalis in Germany, England, France, and the United States between 1800 and 1945 (1991: 1-104). Uerlings's treatment of major themes in modern and contemporary *Ofterdingen* research (398-519) and his extensive international Novalis bibliography (629-98) have been of enormous help to me in my own investigations. By focusing on a single literary work, *Heinrich von Ofterdingen*, and tracing its critical reception in chronological fashion from the date of its publication to the present, I hope to achieve the critique of literary historiography that Uerlings had originally intended as part of his project but then had to scale back in favor of concentration on Novalis and Novalis scholarship (5). Thus this book should meet a central goal of the series *Literary Criticism in Perspective*.

As to the time division of the individual chapters, my arrangement — from fifty-year segments at the beginning to a chapter detailing the scholarly highlights within the single year 1992 — illustrates in graphic terms the accelerating rate of scholarly interest in Novalis and *Heinrich von Ofterdingen*. While I will draw attention to the many estimable achievements during the first 160 years of criticism dealing with this novel and German Early Romanticism, I also maintain that not just the quantity but also the quality of research has improved dramatically in the past three decades. The results of my study, I would argue, contradict the notion that the publish-or-perish mentality within academia in recent years necessarily leads to a profusion of mediocre and repetitive publications. On the contrary, recent interpretations influenced by feminist, deconstructionist, and postmodernist methods suggest a real affinity between contemporary literary theorists and a writer like Novalis, who was a mining engineer by profession and whose philosophical and scientific interests find their most complete expression in the tales and conversations embedded within the plot of *Heinrich von Ofterdingen*. In my concluding remarks, I shall indicate areas in which significant work remains to be done.

Unless otherwise noted, all quotations from and references to Novalis's works and letters are taken from Novalis, *Schriften*, ed. Richard Samuel et al. (Stuttgart: Kohlhammer, 1960-), identified by volume and page number in parentheses. References to *Heinrich von Ofterdingen* come from the 1977 revised edition of volume one of the *Schriften*, supplemented by the corresponding pagination in the paperback reprint to Palmer Hilty's English translation of the novel in 1964 as *Henry von Ofterdingen* (Prospect Heights, Ill.: Waveland Press, 1990). For the benefit of scholars and students interested in tracing the reception of *Heinrich von Ofterdingen* but not fully conversant in German, French, and Italian, I have endeavored to summarize arguments rather than to quote directly. All references are included parenthetically in the text. The bibliography is arranged chronologically according to the date of first publication, and then alphabetically by author within any given year.

As much as my knowledge of other languages has allowed me, I have attempted to consider international scholarship on *Heinrich von Ofterdingen*. I can only hope that my efforts will inspire others to continue from where I leave off.

1: From Literary to Political Revolution —
1802–1850

AT THE TIME of its publication in 1802, Novalis's *Heinrich von Ofterdingen* bore the double burden of being an unfinished novel in an edition providing a severely truncated and often distorted record of its deceased author's reflections on poetry, science, and philosophy. More than many other challenging literary works, this novel was in need of critical interpretation that would help clarify its internal organization, indicate its ideal goals, and locate it within a particular literary school or movement. In the years immediately following 1800, though, the literary marketplace and forum for discussion were in a state of turmoil. Already apparent was the division between belletristic products catering to a mass market and that type of literature aimed at an small but elite leadership; indeed, Novalis and his literary associates had followed Goethe and Schiller's lead during the 1790s and even further increased the esoteric nature of their own journal, the *Athenäum* (1798–1800). In addition, because of the sheer mass of material published around 1800, the reviewing journals that had attempted to keep pace with the latest literary productions were obliged to be selective in determining what works to discuss. As a result, of the three reviews of *Heinrich von Ofterdingen* to appear in 1803, one of them was located in Friedrich Schlegel's journal *Europa*, a short-lived successor to the *Athenäum*, while the other two were contained in the principal organs of the reviewing trade, the *Neue Allgemeine Deutsche Bibliothek* (New General German Library) and the *Allgemeine Literatur-Zeitung* (General Literature Newspaper), which still attempted to survey the most important publications for the year. For the vast number of readers in the German-speaking world the appearance of *Heinrich von Ofterdingen* went unnoticed — particularly as the 3-thaler price of the two-volume Novalis edition was the equivalent of twenty-eight kilos of beef, putting it far beyond the means of most individuals (Hiller 1966, 95).

Given the high prices and sheer numbers of books available to German readers, journals such as the *Neue Allgemeine Deutsche Bibliothek* performed a valuable service in indicating to potential readers the nature and worth of new publications. Founded in 1765 and continuing until 1806, this journal attempted to exercise critical influence on educated readers in accord with the precepts of its editor, Friedrich Nicolai, the indefatigable leader of the Berlin Enlightenment (Berghahn 1988, 67–70). At the end of the eighteenth century Nicolai had engaged in acrimonious public disputes with both Friedrich Schlegel and the philosopher Johann Gottlieb Fichte on what he alleged to be their muddled style and modish jargon; in addition, he continued his feud with

Ludwig Tieck, who had begun his literary career as a writer for Nicolai before "deserting" to the party of the Schlegel brothers. Hence it is surprising to note the largely positive character of the review of *Heinrich von Ofterdingen* in Nicolai's journal. Indeed, it is the Schlegels and Tieck who receive the sharpest blows from the anonymous critic, who begins his review by observing that Novalis, had he lived longer and learned to gain control of his wild imagination, might have become an estimable poet and achieved far more than his friends. One notes here a tendency that was to become increasingly prominent in future criticism: the selection of Novalis as the principal poet and purest representative of German Romanticism.

As for *Heinrich von Ofterdingen*, the reviewer takes note of the originality and difficulty of the novel's theme, the development of poetic feeling from its first stirring until its conscious employment by the young hero. He suggests that many rough edges of the work might have been smoothed over, had the author lived to complete his task, and offers high praise both for the lyric poems embedded within the novel and for large portions of the text. On the other hand, he severely censures the fairy tale concluding the first part of *Ofterdingen*, which he accuses of soaring to the highest pinnacle of senselessness. For the reviewer this tale serves as proof of the immaturity of its young author, who has been led astray by the foolishness of Schlegelian transcendental aesthetics and induced to produce nonsense masquerading as profundity (Anon. 1803, 52). This latter remark also sets a precedent for future criticism of Novalis's novel, for which the understanding of his literary fairy tale often serves as either the barrier or the breakthrough to a comprehension of the work as a whole. What makes these words doubly ironic is that a central motif of what has become known as the Klingsohr tale deals with overcoming the type of reified, instrumentalist reason that Novalis and his literary associates saw as typified by the late Enlightenment; in fact, one could describe this review as a case in which the Scribe from the fairy tale writes a metacritique of the work that predicted his demise through the literary discourse of Romantic art.

Whereas the anonymous critic in Nicolai's journal displays an honest effort to comprehend a work that ultimately remains foreign to him, Johann Friedrich Delbrück, the reviewer of *Heinrich von Ofterdingen* in the September 12, 1803, issue of the Jena *Allgemeine Literatur-Zeitung*, goes so far as to say that this daring and original novel, had it been completed, would have represented an epoch-making development in the history of poetry; even in its incomplete state it occupies a high ranking among those works of Romantic poetry that express a sense of the mystical unity of the universe. As a friend of Friedrich Schleiermacher, Friedrich Schlegel's partner in the development of Romantic hermeneutics, Delbrück was in a position to offer the same sort of help in deciphering *Ofterdingen* that Schlegel had required from Novalis on his own first reading of the text (4: 655). In his review he admits that Klingsohr's allegorical fairy tale leaves him in the dark, but he also notes that most probably it would have received its elucidation through the completion of the second part of the novel, for which it acts as an outline. Even without this second part to the novel, Delbrück is able to identify key aspects of *Ofterdingen* such as the carryover of dream images into the plot, the interconnection between the tales told to Ofterdingen and his experiences on the journey to Augsburg, the reappearance of the same persons in different figures, and the humanization of nature (Delbrück 1803, 574-75). As Andreas Wistoff correctly observes, Delbrück's review is a far cry from the normative aesthetics of the Enlightenment; even where Delbrück criticizes the philosophical writings of Novalis for what he regards as their excessively mystical bent, he does not fail to praise the splendor of his poetic images (Wistoff 1992, 113-21). But for an explanation of the significance of these poetic transitions and transfigurations, one must turn to Friedrich Schlegel's discussion of contemporary developments in literature and philosophy in the first issue of his journal *Europa*.

Defining what he calls esoteric poetry as that which seeks to encompass humankind and nature alike, approaches the realm of science, and makes consequently higher demands on the recipient, Schlegel observes that ultimately this poetry has the goal of transforming everyday life as well. For those of his readers experiencing difficulty with the proposition that every novel should be constructed according to the model of a fairy tale, Schlegel offers the unfinished novel *Heinrich von Ofterdingen* as an example of what he means by the transition from novel to mythology (Schlegel 1803, 56). In part Schlegel's comment echoes a remark in the letter he received from Novalis on April 5, 1800, that announced the completion of part one of the novel and indicated that in its second part it would gradually turn into a fairy tale (4: 330); in part it provides an echo of Schlegel's own "Rede über die Mythologie" (Speech on Mythology, 1800) in the *Athenäum*, which calls for the creation of a new mythology linking the most disparate natural and human phenomena. More important than its origin is Schlegel's ongoing conviction that precisely that form of literature seemingly most remote from reality will be instrumental in changing our perceptions of reality. But although Schlegel here still upheld the Early Romantic belief in the transformation of the world through poesy, both it and the next phase of critical reception of *Heinrich von Ofterdingen* were soon to experience significant ideological modifications. In 1803 Schlegel was writing his remarks from Paris and emphasizing the pan-European notion of culture evoked in Novalis's yet unpublished essay *Die Christenheit oder Europa* (Christianity or Europe, 1826); by 1808 he and other Romantic writers would be engaged in a war of words against the Napoleonic occupation of German territory.

A transitional work in many respects was Adam Müller's *Vorlesungen über die deutsche Wissenschaft und Literatur* (Lectures on German Knowledge and Literature), held in Dresden in the winter of 1806 and published in 1807.

Concurrent with the growth of interest in German literature had been the institution of both university and public lectures on the subject, as demonstrated in August Wilhelm Schlegel's professorship in Jena from 1798 to 1801 and his 1802 Berlin lectures on literature, art, and the spirit of the age, which eventually brought the ideas of the Jena Romantics to a European and an American audience. In comparison with August Wilhelm Schlegel's groundbreaking work, Müller's highlighting of the term *deutsch* throughout his lectures indicates both a narrowing of focus and an attempt to mobilize German artists and intellectuals to patriotic and practical duty. In his lecture on the nature of German poetry, for example, Müller praises Goethe for his emphasis on the reconciliation of poetry and economy in *Wilhelm Meisters Lehrjahre* — precisely what Novalis had disputed in a letter to Ludwig Tieck during his work on *Heinrich von Ofterdingen* (4: 323) and which Tieck and Schlegel had included in the "Fragmente" (Fragments) of their deceased friend's notebooks and reflections (5: 233). Goethe's only weak point, Müller contends, is the absence of an appreciation for the spirit of Christianity permeating history, poetry, and philosophy. Müller therefore calls for a synthesis of the medieval Christian world of *Ofterdingen* with the sphere of contemporary life depicted by Goethe in *Wilhelm Meister*. As for Novalis, whose writings had been published in a second edition in 1805, Müller elevates him to the status of a prophet of future times whose works are destined to find fulfillment in German art and life alike (Müller 1807, 58). That Müller felt Novalis worthy of an expanded comparison with Goethe — *Wilhelm Meister* and *Ofterdingen* are the only two works discussed in this particular lecture — is a clear sign of the value Novalis was coming to hold among the later Romantics. This comparison of *Wilhelm Meisters Lehrjahre* and *Heinrich von Ofterdingen* quickly became a commonplace in literary criticism of the two works.

Müller's reference to "genuine successors" of Novalis was appropriate in that already evident on the literary scene were sickly-sweet imitators such as Otto Heinrich Graf von Loeben, whose novel *Guido* (1808) attempted to complete the tale of *Heinrich von Ofterdingen* but only earned the satiric scorn of foe and friend alike, including Joseph von Eichendorff, his erstwhile protegé in Heidelberg. Eichendorff, whose own poetic juvenilia written under the pseudonym Florens betray more than a little "Novalismus," in the meantime had come under the tutelage of Friedrich Schlegel, whose wife Dorothea was to suggest the title for Eichendorff's first novel, *Ahnung und Gegenwart* (Presentiment and Present, 1815), which contrasts the religious longings of its protagonist with the unpatriotic and materialistic present. Schlegel, who had moved to Vienna following his conversion to Catholicism in 1808, now repudiated his earlier belief in the autonomy of art and advocated a literature in the service of Catholicism and the Austrian empire in the struggle against Napoleon. In his 1812 Vienna lectures on the history of literature, which he dedi-

cated to Metternich upon their publication in 1815, Schlegel mentioned Novalis only once and in general terms, as one example among many of the recent
turn in German thought from Kantian error to the One True path (Schlegel
1815, 420).

What Schlegel was unable to provide in concrete detail Eichendorff later
attempted to supply through lengthy excerpts from Novalis in his *Geschichte der
poetischen Literatur Deutschlands* (The History of the Poetic Literature of Germany, 1857), the culmination of his work in literary history. Despite access to
Die Christenheit oder Europa, first published in 1826 in the fourth edition of
Novalis's writings, Eichendorff does not fail to point out the many places in
both this essay and *Heinrich von Ofterdingen* where Novalis deviates from or-
thodoxy and transforms Christianity into mere poetry (Eichendorff 1857,
305). Thus for Eichendorff Novalis becomes a symbol of the strivings, but also
of the shortcomings of a Romanticism without a firm religious base — a notion depicted in his story *Das Marmorbild* (The Marble Statue, 1819), in which
only the intervention of the pious poet Fortunato saves the young Florio from
falling prey to pagan, narcissistic entrapment.

Of much more immediate and long-term impact on the public perception
of Novalis as an individual and a writer, though, was Ludwig Tieck's biographical sketch in the introduction to the third edition of Novalis's writings,
published in 1815 and reprinted in ensuing editions. Tieck's account of the
probable continuation of *Heinrich von Ofterdingen* in the edition of 1802 had
already demonstrated his ability to add a Tieckian tint to Novalis — as the
reviewer in the *Neue Allgemeine Deutsche Bibliothek* had maliciously, but accu-
rately alleged (53) — but here his art reached new heights. Tieck, who had
known Novalis only from the summer of 1799, can be credited (or rather
charged) with the creation of the legend of Novalis as an ethereal poet whose
art was occasioned principally by the loss of his young fiancée, Sophie von
Kühn in the spring of 1797 (4: 560). In addition, by providing only vague references to Novalis's professional training as a mining engineer and alleging his
friend's virtual ignorance of developments in art and, indeed, all areas of intellectual life, Tieck contributed to the notion of Novalis as a poet whose mystical
utterances had little to do with empirical reality. August Koberstein's *Grundriss
der Geschichte der Deutschen Nationalliteratur* (Foundation of the History of
German National Literature, 1827), for example, already describes Novalis's
poetic efforts in *Heinrich von Ofterdingen* as dreamlike and foggy creations of
fantasy in which sometimes reality became a vision and sometimes the vision
became reality, but in any case everything more or less dissolved into mysticism
and allegory (Koberstein 1827, 4: 816).

It was not the least of Thomas Carlyle's achievements in his 1829 essay on
Novalis in the *Foreign Review*, which relied on Tieck for so much information,
that he decidedly called into question what German literary scholars unhesitat-

ingly regarded as the *Sophienerlebnis* (the Sophie experience) well into the twentieth century:

> That the whole philosophical and moral existence of such a man as Novalis should have been shaped and determined by the death of a young girl, almost a child, specially distinguished, so far as is shown, by nothing save her beauty, which at any rate must have been very short-lived, will doubtless seem to every one a singular concatenation. (172).

While confessing an inability to pass ultimate judgments on the worth of Novalis's philosophical speculations, Carlyle regards them as deserving repeated study. With respect to Novalis's fiction and poetry, he does not find them to be as striking as the fragments provided in Schlegel and Tieck's edition, but does translate the opening dream to *Heinrich von Ofterdingen* and Heinrich's later dream in Augsburg as examples of Novalis's poetic accomplishments. One might note that in his translations Carlyle has toned down the erotic nature of these dreams; for example, he renders "Die Flut schien eine Auflösung reizender Mädchen, die an dem Jünglinge sich augenblicklich verkörperten" (1: 197; 17) as "The flood seemed a spirit of beauty, which from moment to moment was taking form around the youth" (184).

Whatever Carlyle provided must have seemed enticing enough to American readers, who in 1838 gained access to Carlyle's review through Ralph Waldo Emerson's edition of *Critical and Miscellaneous Essays*, for in 1842 John Owen of Cambridge, Massachusettts, published *Henry of Ofterdingen: A Romance*. The anonymous translator — most probably the theology student F. S. Stallknecht — alludes in his brief preface to a remark by the German writer Jean Paul Richter that "translators were like wagoners who carry good wine to fairs — but most unaccountably water it before the end of the journey." A comparison of his translation of the above line from Heinrich's dream with that of Carlyle, however, suggests that he need not have been so diffident about his handiwork: "The flood seemed like a solution of the elements of beauty, which constantly became embodied in the forms of charming maidens around him" (*Henry of Ofterdingen* 1842, 20). Not only does he produce similarly faithful and felicitous renditions of the prose passages of the novel, but the verse translations also reproduce the rhyme and meter of the originals in an idiom that his readers would have recognized from English Romantic verse, as the following stanza from the song commonly known as the "Lied der Toten" (Song of the Dead; 1: 363) may suggest:

> Whispered talk of gentle wishes
> Hear we only, we are gazing
> Ever into eyes transfigured,
> Tasting nought but mouth and kiss;
> All that we are only touching
> Change to balmy fruits and glowing,

>Change to bosoms soft and tender,
>Offerings to daring bliss.

(220)

In addition to including Tieck's narration of the planned continuation to *Heinrich von Ofterdingen*, in which the above poem appears, and a "Life of the Author" drawn largely from Tieck's account, the translator provides his own notes to the novel and renditions of the first and third *Hymnen an die Nacht* (Hymns to Night). While finding both their sublimity and the religious fervor of the *Geistliche Lieder* (Spiritual Songs) by Novalis superior on the whole to his novel, he certainly presents his readers with an excellent opportunity to become acquainted with a poet whom he describes as "distinguished for extreme simplicity, both in style and language" and whose thoughts, "though lofty and sometimes vast, are yet fresh, chaste, and comprehensible" (232). In similar fashion, Frederic Henry Hedge — a key figure among the New England Transcendentalists and professor of German literature at Harvard from 1872 to 1882 — also included excerpts from *Heinrich von Ofterdingen* in his 1847 collection of *Prose Writers of Germany*, praising Novalis for his "purity of heart, religious fervor, deep poetic feeling, and mystic inwardness, combined with true philosophic genius and scientific attainments far above the standard of general scholarship" (489). Thanks to Carlyle's efforts and those of Novalis's American translators, New England Transcendentalists such as Emerson, Thoreau, and Margaret Fuller quickly recognized an affinity between Novalis's thoughts and writings and their own goals of promoting a nonorthodox religiosity and reverence for nature. (See Kuenzli 1972 for further information on nineteenth-century British and American reception of Novalis).

Had Carlyle's essay received similar attention in Germany, the critical understanding of Novalis might have taken a different turn. As it was, the admiration Carlyle displayed for German authors such as Novalis — but above all for Goethe — was decidedly absent in a Germany where what we today often call the Age of Goethe was perceived to be in its death agony. For liberal critics writing in the repressive Metternich era after 1815, remarks on literature served as an outlet for dissenting political views. Thus when writers such as Ludwig Börne or Wolfgang Menzel criticized the Romantics and Goethe alike for what they perceived as their distance from real life and lack of sympathy for republican ideals, they simultaneously renounced the concept of the autonomy of art developed in Weimar and Jena at the end of eighteenth century in favor of the earlier Enlightenment notion of literature as an instrument for political and moral progress (Hohendahl 1988b, 223). In *Die deutsche Literatur* (German Literature, 1828), Wolfgang Menzel condemns Goethe for possessing talent but not character and includes as support for this judgment a footnote containing the entire series of negative remarks on Goethe in the Tieck-Schlegel edition of Novalis's writings (Menzel 1828, 2: 210-11) This footnote

— the only one in the entire two-volume work — occupies more space in Menzel's study than that devoted to *Heinrich von Ofterdingen*, in which the standpoint for approbation is moral, not aesthetic: Menzel praises Novalis not for his poetic talents, but rather for his great heart and for the love he poured out on all that he saw as the god of his own immeasurably rich world (2: 138-39). In the second edition of this work, the evaluation of *Ofterdingen* has become decidedly more negative; here Menzel, in a clear rejection of Romanticism's goal of creating a world of the imagination as a means of transforming reality, describes Novalis as being crushed, like the Titan, by the mountains he had attempted to pile up in his own attempt to scale Olympus (Menzel 1836, 4: 160).

The truly crushing verdict delivered on Novalis in the year 1836, however, came from the pen of Heinrich Heine in his literary polemic *Die Romantische Schule* (The Romantic School, 1836). Heine, who had studied under August Wilhelm Schlegel in Bonn in 1819 and whose early poems clearly betray their indebtedness to the German Romantic tradition, here lashes out at the reactionary politics and morbid spiritualism of the Romantics. Writing from his self-chosen Paris exile, Heine was interested not in providing an objective account of a literary movement but rather in combating the political Catholicism he saw gathering strength in Germany and France alike. Jean Murat argues plausibly that Heine's portrait of Novalis — which first appeared in the May 10, 1833, issue of *L'Europe littéraire* and remained relatively unchanged in all subsequent French and German editions of Heine's collected writings on German Romantic authors — must be understood as the counterpart to Montalembert's 1831 essay on Novalis, which strove to claim him for an aggressive, antiliberal Catholic position (Murat 1985, 253-55). Yet so engagingly written is Heine's work that German readers and critics frequently took his polemics at face value, especially in the decades after 1830, when liberal and radical unrest became more pronounced and the Romantics seemed ever more distant from the concerns of the day. Jutta Hecker has determined that it was only after Heine that German literary critics began to regard the Blue Flower as the prototypical symbol of German Romanticism; Murat goes so far as to ascribe to Heine the birth of the clichéd image of Novalis as a sweet, consumptive poet with a touching but mediocre oeuvre (Hecker 1931, 78-81; Murat 1985, 256). For this reason it is important to examine carefully how Heine portrays Novalis and his Blue Flower, which I will here quote in the English translation by Helen Mustard included in The German Library volume edited by Jost Hermand and Robert C. Holub.

In contrast to Friedrich Schlegel, whose later writings Heine describes as the ideological counterpart to Metternich's Holy Alliance, Novalis receives censure neither for political nor for religious obscurantism. Heine does make clear, however, that he regards the art of Novalis as both the product and the cause of illness. Incorrectly stating that not only the poet but also his beloved had died of tuberculosis, Heine quotes the opening lines of *Heinrich von Ofterdingen* as far as the young Heinrich's longing to see the Blue Flower and then goes on to relate the account of a youthful acquaintance who was so enamored of this novel that she read it until she died of consumption herself:

> Mademoiselle Sophia was standing upstairs at the window, reading, and when I went up, I found once more in her hands a book bound in red morocco, with gilt-edged leaves, and it was again *Ofterdingen* by Novalis. So she had gone on and on reading this book and had caught tuberculosis from the reading and looked like a transparent shadow. But she was now of a spiritual beauty the sight of which moved me most grievously. (Heine 1836, 80)

In such a vignette one can observe how Heine has taken Tieck's stylized portrayal of Novalis and employed it for his own purposes. Heine, a Romantic in spite of himself, cannot suppress a certain painful attraction to *Ofterdingen* and its devoted reader, whom he gives the surname of Novalis's first fiancée. In the opening pages of *Die Romantische Schule* Heine compares German Romanticism, considered as a revival of the poetry of medieval Christianity, with the passion flower, "the sight of which even arouses in us an uncanny pleasure like the convulsively sweet sensations which result even from suffering itself" (3). In his account of Novalis, Heine transforms the passion flower, with its markings reminiscent of the crucifixion of Christ, into the Blue Flower, which according to Heine exudes an intoxicating but fatal fragrance on both the author and his readers. Comparing Novalis with E. T. A. Hoffmann, a late Romantic author who was already becoming quite popular in France, Heine observes that while Hoffmann's art is also born of illness, "in all honesty, Hoffmann was much more significant as a poet than Novalis. For the latter, with his idealized figures, always hovered above, his head in the clouds, whereas Hoffmann, with all his bizarre caricatures, still always clung firmly to earthly reality" (76). But beyond such qualified praise for Hoffmann at the expense of the febrile, poetically contagious Novalis, Heine lauds Goethe for his "pagan" appreciation of the delights of this earth, even though his poetic works do not inspire the emancipatory yearnings Heine views as essential to art's purpose (36-37).

For Georg Gottfried Gervinus — the German liberal and literary historian whose defense of academic freedom in 1837 led to his expulsion from the University of Göttingen along with that of other professors such as Jacob and Wilhelm Grimm — the standards of artistic perfection remain those of Goethe and Schiller: "While Heine reacted to the end of the age of art by demanding that literature fulfill a new function, the responsibility for this new function shifted for Gervinus from literature to politics. In this way he was able to bind a progressive conception of history with an aesthetic that remained essentially indebted to the period of Goethe" (Hohendahl 1988b, 238). Correspondingly, whatever good words Gervinus has to say about the Romantics have to do with their success in propagating the aesthetic doctrines of Goethe and Schiller and combating the attacks of Nicolai and his ilk. At the same time he condemns the Romantics for attempting more than they were capable of achieving and for giving undue praise to the mediocre accomplishments of poets such as Novalis (Gervinus 1843, 5: 645-49). Consequently, it is Novalis whom Gervinus first covers in any detail in the final chapter on Romanticism in his five-volume literary history. Rather than citing from *Heinrich von Ofterdingen* itself, however, Gervinus provides many direct and indirect quotes from Tieck and Adam Müller and disparages Novalis through ironic deflation of his admirers' words, as when he contrasts Müller's prophecy of Novalis's importance for posterity with the remark that in the following generation very few persons knows that there was a writer named Novalis or who he was (5: 655). Goethe's *Wilhelm Meisters Lehrjahre*, on the other hand, receives the praise withheld from *Ofterdingen* — a stratagem repeated in many succeeding liberal or leftist interpretations of Novalis, which likewise often distinguish themselves more by a critique of critics than by an understanding of or concern for the poetic works themselves. In this respect, a survey of the reception history of *Heinrich von Ofterdingen* makes amply clear that very often it is the so-called "secondary" literature that takes a primary role in affecting directions in literary criticism.

When Gervinus judged that Novalis was a largely unknown figure in the post-Romantic period, however, he took into account neither the British and American interest in Novalis nor the attention devoted to the poet in neighboring France. Although one still encounters the contention that it was Symbolist poets such as Baudelaire, Verlaine, and Mallarmé who first made Novalis known to the French reading public (Vordtriede 1963, Pfefferkorn 1988, 18), both Donald P. Haase and Jean Murat have documented an interest in Novalis among French writers, university scholars, publicists, and translators that effectively demolishes the myth that Heine's portrait of Novalis had destroyed whatever modest French awareness might have resulted from Madame de Staël's brief account of the poet in *De l'Allemagne* (Concerning Germany, 1813). In fact, the steady stream of essays and translations, including parts of *Heinrich von Ofterdingen*, following the Baron d'Eckstein's praise of the diaphanous purity of *Ofterdingen* in the first substantial assessment of Novalis by a non-German writer (Eckstein 1828, 129-44), suggest that the French critical reception of Novalis prior to 1850 may have surpassed in quantity and quality even that achieved in England and America (see Haase 1979 and 1981, Murat 1986). In 1847, for example, Saint-René Taillandier concludes his lengthy and appreciative discussion of Novalis and *Heinrich von Ofterdingen* with the observation that present-day German critics like Heine and Gervinus are not judging Novalis but rather revenging themselves upon him for having so long succumbed to a mysticism that may now be out of favor but whose nobility of spirit future, less partisan generations are more likely to recognize (Taillandier 1847, 36-39). Indicative of this lively French interest in Novalis is the republication of the fourth edition of Novalis's writings, in 1837, not only in Stuttgart but also in Paris.

Even within Germany things were not as quiet as Gervinus might have hoped and believed. In 1846 Tieck completed his editorial work on behalf of his long-dead friend with an additional volume of selected biographical information, letters, poems, and fragments, the latter being supplied by Eduard von Bülow, his new editorial assistant. In addition, a new generation of critics had begun to make themselves known, and their Hegelian training made them conscious of the philosophical elements in Novalis that had recommended themselves to Carlyle and the American Transcendentalists and had also received attention in the Novalis's French reception. Heine, himself a student of Hegel in Berlin, had already spoken of the effects of Schelling's philosophy of nature upon Romantics such as Novalis, but he had treated this influence more as a matter of sentiment, even to the point of fabricating an obituary that in no way corresponded to the actual date of death in March 1801: "Novalis saw everywhere only marvels, lovely marvels. He listened to the plants conversing with each other, he knew the secret of every young rose, in the end he identified himself with all of nature, and when autumn came and the leaves fell, he died" (Heine 1836, 76). By way of contrast, Arnold Ruge and Theodor Echtermeyer begin their 1839 essay on Novalis in the *Hallische Jahrbücher für deutsche Wissenschaft und Kunst* (Halle Yearbooks for German Learning and Art) with a general reflection on the progression from Fichte's abstract idealism, which they compare to a day without night, to the longing for the plentitude in nature found in Schelling's writing. It is in this transitional period that they locate the moonlit writing of Novalis, and then amplify this observation with an actual quote from *Heinrich von Ofterdingen* (1: 252):

> The night was clear and warm. The moon shone mild over the hills and evoked strange visions in all creatures. Itself like a dream of the sun, the moon hovered over the dream-world brooding within itself; and it led nature, divided into countless separate entities, back to that mythical primeval age when every bud and germ still slept by itself, lonely and untouched, yearning in vain to unfold the obscure wealth of its own immeasurable existence. (*Henry von Ofterdingen* 1964, 77)

But whereas in the continuation of this passage from the fifth chapter of the novel Heinrich actually receives a sense of the unity of nature, Ruge and Echtermeyer choose to place their interpretive emphasis on the vain longing for totality that they ascribe to Novalis in particular and to pre-Hegelian thought in general (1839, 1-2).

This essay, the fourth installment of Ruge and Echtermeyer's manifesto *Der Protestantismus und die Romantik* (Protestantism and Romanticism), concerns itself mainly with Novalis's *Die Christenheit oder Europa* and *Hymnen an die Nacht*, but *Ofterdingen* also comes in for its share of discussion. Ruge and Echtermeyer cite with approval the words of the Graf von Hohenzollern in the first part of *Ofterdingen* when he distinguishes between the accidental existence of individual figures and the great, simple soul of the times that becomes visible in the fables of the poet (7). Their main criticism of *Ofterdingen* has to do with its attempt to make manifest this spirit pervading the world with the help of allegorical figures such as those found in the Klingsohr tale or in the depiction of Astralis, the spirit of poetry whom they call the "siderische Wechselbalg," or sidereal changeling, replacing the flesh-and-blood child of Heinrich and Mathilde, his beloved, that they would have preferred (16-17). Quoting fragments from Novalis's own writings wherein children are described as love made visible or human beings are called God's sole temple on earth, they argue that the form of Novalis's poetic writings does not accord with the depth of his philosophy or with the depth of true poetry evident in works such as *Wilhelm Meister* (17-18). Spirit, in the Hegelian sense of the word, has not found its proper manifestation. For Echtermeyer and Ruge, then, Novalis is an important figure for their own times precisely because he illustrates a tendency within German culture for longing to remain caught within itself, rather than penetrating and intermingling with concrete phenomena. This criticism can be traced back to a brief remark about Novalis in Hegel's posthumously published lectures on Aesthetics (Hegel 1835, 12: 221), but Ruge and Echtermeyer exemplify it in a wealth of detail that makes their essay stand out amid the many German discussions of Novalis in the first half of the nineteenth century. Regardless of whether or not one ultimately agrees with Ruge and Echtermeyer's criteria for judging Novalis, one can not overlook the seriousness with which they take the poet at his own words.

Like the comments of such critics as Menzel and Heine, who had to contend with the strict German censorship regulations, Echtermeyer and Ruge's remarks have a political meaning once literature and religion are understood as code words for politics. What is the proper manifestation of the spirit at the moment, they ask: is it the Catholic hierarchy proclaimed in Novalis's essay *Die Christenheit oder Europa* or rather a free spirit of Protestantism? Today we are likely to know Echtermeyer and Ruge only in conjunction with Benno von Wiese's continuation of the Echtermeyer anthology of German lyric poetry or with the young Karl Marx's coeditorship of Ruge's *Deutsch-Französische Jahrbücher* (German-French Yearbooks, 1844), but both of these projects were undertaken in the hope of stimulating the emancipation of the German national spirit, very much in the same way that Romantic writers such as Achim von Arnim, Clemens Brentano, and Joseph Görres had used folk-song collections and journals as rallying points during the Napoleonic era.

In his *Geschichte der Literatur der Gegenwart* (History of the Literature of the Present, 1842), in fact, Theodor Mundt draws explicit attention to the contributions of the German Romantics in first having promoted a national consciousness and a sense of the importance of literature as an expression of popular spirit. Listed on the title page as a continuation of Friedrich Schlegel's *Geschichte der alten und neuen Literatur* (History of Ancient and Modern Literature, 1815) — whose "elevated point of view" Heinrich Heine wittily situated in "the belfry of a Catholic church" (Heine 1836, 49) — Mundt's literary history shifts Schlegel's late Romantic religious perspective to one more akin to the latter's Early Romantic origins, namely that of revolutionary emancipation. In the introduction to this work, Mundt identifies revolution as the myth of modernity; whoever can interpret it and reconcile its self-contained contradictions will thereby thrust the old Sphinx into the abyss and place the free man upon the throne of humanity (2). Such an opinion also indicates that Mundt, one of the principal Young German critics of the 1830s, and Young Hegelians such as Ruge and Echtermeyer were not as far from Romanticism as one might at first surmise, since they too view a proper understanding of literature as a revolutionary step in itself.

Like Echtermeyer and Ruge, Mundt believes that the topic of religiosity, understood as the search for a centralizing point of existence, is the proper approach to Novalis's works, and like them he finds in Novalis genuine philosophical depth that, however, falls short of full realization. Whereas Heinrich Laube, a Young German compatriot of Mundt, had described Novalis in his history of German literature as a footless bird of paradise who therefore always had to hover in the air (1840, 3: 152), Mundt takes a different metaphorical direction by drawing upon an image from *Heinrich von Ofterdingen* and calling Novalis the miner who got lost in his own shaft and was found there buried amidst all of his riches (1842, 75). For Mundt, *Ofterdingen* is the work in which Novalis most notably lacks the ability to provide any concrete expression of his dream of reconciling vision and reality. On the other hand, Mundt finds the *Geistliche Lieder* and *Hymnen an die Nacht* successful as lyrical outpourings. Unclear, however, is what his own remarks have to do with unraveling the mystery of revolution, which Mundt had proclaimed so resolutely as the main task of the age.

Far more explicit in this regard were the *Vorlesungen über die deutsche Literatur der Gegenwart* (Lectures on German Literature of the Present), which Robert Prutz published in Leipzig in 1847 after he had been prohibited from presenting a series of twelve lectures on that subject in the Prussian capital earlier that winter. In the lengthy preface to this work, Prutz states that many of the ideas in these lectures are not new and that a principal reason for their publication is to enable the public to judge whether his thoughts are as dangerous as the Prussian authorities maintain. Prutz, a friend of Arnold Ruge who was denied the chance to become a professor or even hold private lectures at the University of Halle because of his radical political views, offers these published lectures as a document of the times similar to Fichte's *Reden an die deutsche Nation* (Speeches to the German Nation, 1808): pointing out that Fichte could give his speeches in Berlin even during the height of the Napoleonic occupation, Prutz finds the decline of freedom in contemporary Prussia all the more striking (xi).

In his first lecture — the only one to be held publicly before the Prussian authorities decried the intermingling of politics and literature and forbade any further continuation of the series (lxxiv) — Prutz explains Romanticism as the unfortunate result of political repression in Germany at the time of the French Revolution: just at the point when German literature and art had reached a maturity that would have allowed them to proceed from beauty into freedom, the wretchedness pervading rulers and ruled alike forced writers to turn away from reality in favor of an artificial art that became increasingly isolated from the foundation of national life (52-53). In the lecture devoted to specific Romantic authors it is once again Novalis who is the first to be treated in detail as exemplifying Romanticism at its purest, and once again the judgments are less harsh than one might expect from Prutz's programmatic assumptions. Prutz is correct in reemphasizing that many of his ideas are not new (114) — the description of Novalis as the pale, sick moon hovering above the magical night of Romanticism (117), for example, is a compilation of images from Heine, Laube, Echtermeyer, and Ruge — but he does indicate why he believes Novalis will continue to have a significance for the German nation long after Romanticism's ideals and goals will have faded away. Prutz sees Novalis's fragile health, which caused his early death, as justification for what he considers the poet's abstention from active participation in life and his choice of a world of art, thinking, and theory (118). According to Prutz, Novalis and his poetic works — in particular "der großartige Entwurf seines Ofterdingens" (the grand design of his *Ofterdingen*, 119)— will serve as living monuments to an epoch of German history when high promise was blighted early. But Prutz also makes it amply clear that the task of the present lies in the foundation of a free national state. Then, and only then, he maintains, will great literature be possible in Germany: the sun of freedom must rise before the flower of beauty can unfold (24-25).

By the time revolutions broke out across the length and breadth of Europe in the winter of 1848, the Romantic era, when writers such as Novalis hoped that literature would transform reality, seemed a thing of the past. Hermann Hettner — a literary historian who, like Prutz, became actively involved in the struggle for a new constitution for Prussia and Germany — wrote a study entitled *Die romantische Schule in ihrem Zusammenhange mit Göthe und Schiller* (The Romantic School in its Connection with Goethe and Schiller, 1850) which presented a more balanced comparison between Goethe and Novalis than Gervinus had been able to give. Hettner calls *Heinrich von Ofterdingen* an apotheosis of poetry as remarkable in its own way as the realism of Goethe's *Wilhelm Meister*. He regrets that Novalis did not live to complete his novel, in which Romanticism would have found its *Erfüllung* (Fulfillment — the title of the second part of *Ofterdingen*), although he also expresses the opinion that this would have involved the complete dissolution of reality into a bottomless allegory and fantastic dreamland (82-84). On the other hand, Hettner also makes it clear that no sort of art can serve as the substitute for a complete re-vamping of German political life. As he states in the conclusion to his study, there were only two possibilities for the future: either Germany would become a great and free nation and its poetry would outstrip even that of Goethe and Schiller in quality; or the political struggle would fail, and with that failure would come a calamitous decline in art and culture (206-7). The outcome of such a struggle, as mirrored in new directions of *Ofterdingen* criticism, will be the subject of the next chapter.

2: A Candidate for Canonization — 1851-1900

BY 1850 IT was apparent that the revolutionists were not going to succeed in their struggle for a liberal constitutional monarchy in a unified Germany. Indeed, in the tide of reaction that followed the failed revolution, critics like Gervinus and Prutz found themselves in danger of being tried for treason or dismissed from their state positions. In the years leading to 1871, liberals learned that national unity was to be imposed through the efforts of Prussian chancellor Bismarck and that they would have to accommodate themselves to this development if they wished to partake of the economic and political gains promised as a result. In correlation to these developments, liberals who were literary historians put more stress on the promulgation of a *national* German culture; by the latter decades of the nineteenth century the pantheon of German culture was already being erected, with Goethe and Schiller serving as the chief representatives of the glory that was Germany, but with their Romantic contemporaries now being seen as allies rather than rivals.

The various editions of Julian Schmidt's *Geschichte der Deutschen Literatur im neunzehnten Jahrhundert* (History of German Literature in the Nineteenth Century) illustrate this gradual shift in literary cultural politics in the years after 1850. In the 1853 preface to the first edition Schmidt indicates that a work of literary history, in order to be of use for the present age, must deliver a remorseless critique of those aspects of German poetry that have exercised a harmful effect on the nation's ethical foundations, instincts, ideals, and history. Schmidt — who used his influential journal *Die Grenzboten* (The Border Messengers) to promulgate a normative notion of realism whereby the ideal is contained in the depiction of everyday conditions of the home and workplace — here criticizes the widespread tendency to postulate an enmity between the ideal and the real. In the preface to the second edition of his literary history, published in 1855, Schmidt allows that the gulf between the level of cultivation of writers such as Goethe and Schiller and that of the public at large made their idealistic preconceptions more understandable. All the same, he feels obliged to point out the seeds of future dissolution in the literature written in Weimar and Jena between 1794 and 1806 (Schmidt, 1856, x); in so doing, Schmidt follows Hettner's lead in further diminishing the qualitative distinction between German Classicism and Romanticism that Gervinus had postulated in his literary history from the pre-1848 era. The fact that a third edition of Schmidt's work had appeared by 1856, to be followed by further revised editions in the course of the century, demonstrates the extent to which his diagnoses helped shape the judgments of the educated elite.

In his chapter on Novalis, Schmidt makes use of the biographical account by Hardenberg's friend and supervisor August Coelestin Just first included in the 1846 Novalis edition in order to draw positive attention to Novalis's solid training in the natural sciences and his expertise as a mining engineer and state official. It is as a writer that Schmidt finds Novalis beset by an absolute lack of formative and critical judgment, which consequently negates his undoubted richness in ideas and perceptions. In *Heinrich von Ofterdingen*, he notes, one encounters now and again characters who might have caught our interest had they not disappeared so soon into the prevailing mist (Schmidt 1856, 410). Signs of an enchanting realism all too quickly lose out to intimations of a metaphysical realm shimmering through the stories and character descriptions. Schmidt correctly notices the correspondence between the figures in the novel proper and those in the interpolated stories, but he proves unable to explain it. By the beginning of part two of *Ofterdingen*, Schmidt concludes, it becomes impossible to make sense of the otherworldly atmosphere, which has become fragmentary, disjointed, and incomprehensible (413).

The explanation of that metaphysical atmosphere, which had escaped the comprehension of the previous fifty years of writing on Novalis, was the stated task of Wilhelm Dilthey's essay of 1865 for the *Preussische Jahrbücher* (Prussian Yearbooks), excerpts of which appeared in an article on Novalis for the popular journal *Westermanns Monatshefte* (Westermann's Monthly) in 1868 and in Dilthey's monumental life of Schleiermacher in 1870. Above all, though, it was the republication of this essay in Dilthey's frequently reprinted volume *Das Erlebnis und die Dichtung: Lessing — Goethe — Novalis — Hölderlin* (1906) that was to make it the most influential treatment of Novalis until the appearance of the historical-critical edition of the 1960s. The book's explicit linkage of writers from the periods of the Enlightenment, Classicism, and Romanticism under one unitary framework — "experience and poetry" — is already implicit in Dilthey's Novalis essay. Not only are the comparisons between *Wilhelm Meisters Lehrjahre* and *Heinrich von Ofterdingen* (by now obligatory) freed from the polemical undertones characteristic of so many previous discussions of Novalis's works, but Dilthey also draws on analogies from Lessing's and Schleiermacher's writings in providing an explanation for the metaphysical realm in *Ofterdingen* that Schmidt had regarded as incomprehensible: the novel documents its author's belief that the transmigration of souls links together people from previous existences. Dilthey emphasizes the experiential nature of this idea by drawing attention to Novalis's sketch of his first fiancée, Sophie von Kühn, that incidently notes her belief in the transmigration of souls [Novalis, 4: 25]; from there it is but a short step to the speculation that Novalis might well have been tempted to employ conversations with Sophie on this matter as a foundation for the unity of his novel (Dilthey 1865, 339-40). This surmise is one of the passages that Dilthey incorporates into his volume on the life of Schleiermacher, though he makes the instructive mistake of substituting the name of Mathilde, Heinrich's beloved in the novel, for that of Sophie (Dilthey 1870, 450) — thereby indicating the extent to which life and poetry have become indistinguishable elements in his view of Novalis.

The notion that Novalis's experiences in loving and losing Sophie might be the clue to his poetic existence was not new — Tieck had established this idea in his 1815 account of Novalis's life and works — but Dilthey here links it with suppositions that were to characterize his intellectual and philosophical studies throughout his career. At the very beginning of his essay Dilthey states that it is the personality of Novalis that speaks to us through his works and hence allows a more personal relationship with him than one can have with the great objective poets Homer, Shakespeare, and Cervantes (Dilthey 1865, 268). Through an exacting study of Novalis's writings, allied to his empathy with the personality of the author, Dilthey hopes to regain for the present the most important thoughts of the generation of German writers and thinkers following Goethe, Kant, and Fichte. Dilthey has little use for Novalis's speculations on nature and mathematics — an understandable reaction, considering the desolate state of their transmission in the Tieck and Schlegel editions — but regards his thoughts on the human sciences as extraordinarily original, on the same level as those of Friedrich Schlegel and Schleiermacher (304-5).

In his attempted renewal of Romantic hermeneutics, however, Dilthey has no room for politics and only limited interest in Novalis's attempts to integrate the natural sciences into the "progressive universal poesy" that had been the essence of Friedrich Schlegel's definition of Romanticism. In his discussion of the fairy tale at the end of part one of *Heinrich von Ofterdingen*, Dilthey observes that for Novalis the unity of poetry and science was the fundamental feature of his view of the world; he remarks that whoever is familiar with the magnetic and galvanic theories of Romantic natural philosophy will find this tale easily comprehensible (345). But it is left to future scholars to puzzle out the exact meanings of the many details in the Klingsohr tale, which Dilthey refrains from doing on the grounds that this would transform the graceful fairy tale into a frosty allegory. As the founder of the discipline of *Geistesgeschichte*, Dilthey developed a concept of intellectual history that encouraged the ever-growing gap between the humanities and the natural sciences in the latter half of the nineteenth century and that certainly discouraged any attempt to understand Novalis's poetry with the help of his studies in natural philosophy.

Of all Dilthey's observations, however, perhaps the most influential was his treatment of German novels written around the year 1800 as Bildungsromane, or novels of individual development. In the chapter of his biography on Schleiermacher devoted to the latter's Romantic comrades, Dilthey precedes his discussion of Novalis by defining the novels in the school of *Wilhelm Meister* as Bildungsromane, to which he adds the further term Künstlerromane, or novels about artists, to characterize *Heinrich von Ofterdingen* in particular (Dilthey 1870, 299-300). In both instances he provides little more than the terms themselves, which later found their fuller definition in the Hölderlin chapter of *Das Erlebnis und die Dichtung*. But by 1870 Dilthey had laid the groundwork for understanding *Heinrich von Ofterdingen* as a novel about the individual development of a young poet. And by the time his thoughts reached new audiences at the beginning of the twentieth century, the notion of Germany as the nation of poets and thinkers had acquired an ideological stridency only implicit within the affirmative concept of culture contained in Dilthey's words at a time when it was the force of Bismarckian "blood and iron," not that of poetry, which was to unite the German principalities (for a discussion of the history of the term Bildungsroman see Mahoney 1991; for a critique of ideological components of Dilthey's and Julian Schmidt's writings in the context of their times, see Peschken 1972).

Yet another monumental work of literary scholarship devoted to German Romanticism appeared in 1870, Rudolf Haym's *Die romantische Schule: Ein Beitrag zur Geschichte des deutschen Geistes* (The Romantic School: A Contribution to the History of the German Spirit). Though the work has a title identical with that of Heine's and Hettner's critiques, Haym's subtitle and introduction indicate a historical rather than polemical treatment of Romanticism. But this does not mean that Haym views his work as detached from the immediate present. A professor at the University of Halle and founder of the *Preussische Jahrbücher* who had served terms in both the Frankfurt Parliament of 1849 and the Prussian legislature, Haym states his interest in clarifying national tradition and presenting an objective study of a literary movement at a time when political unity has made obsolete the shadow battles against Romanticism from the 1840s (Haym 1870, 4-5). After giving due praise for the earlier literary histories by Gervinus, Hettner, Schmidt, and Koberstein, Haym makes clear the need to study developments in philosophy, religion, and the theoretical pronouncements of the Romantics to do justice to their poetic output (5-9); in the footnote to his extensive chapter on Novalis, Haym refers to the studies of Ruge, Echtermeyer, and Dilthey as well. Such exactitude in his research has gained for Haym's work the reputation as the first work of literary scholarship on Romanticism that still merits consideration today. The fact alone that Haym's treatment of *Heinrich von Ofterdingen* was reprinted in the 1966 collection of interpretations edited by Jost Schillemeit — the only nineteenth-century treatment of a novel to be included — indicates the authority his work still possessed almost a century after its publication.

Haym's desire for a measured approach causes him to reject both Tieck's reverential worship of *Heinrich von Ofterdingen* and the opinion of a more recent, unnamed critic that a study of this novel is fit more for the annals of visionaries and dreamers than for the history of poetry (Haym 1870, 372; the work in question is Karl Goedeke's *Grundriß zur Geschichte der deutschen Dichtung aus den Quellen* [Outline of the History of German Poetry from the Sources, 1859], 6: 50). Making clear that he regards *Heinrich von Ofterdingen* as a highly imperfect work of art and a doubtful model for aspiring young writers, Haym at the same time stresses its importance in the history of German literature. Nor does he fail to acknowledge the magic of the poetic language of the novel and lively scenes, such as the feast in Augsburg and the betrothal with Mathilde, that in his opinion have the makings of novellas in them. Rather than simply decrying the lost opportunities for literary realism, however, as had Julian Schmidt, Haym undertakes an explanation of the aesthetic convictions of this Romantic novelist in the hope of uncovering the reasons behind his thoroughly idealistic outlook and accompanying poetic form.

Idealism is not completely divorced from common sense in the case of Novalis, Haym contends, citing with approval Klingsohr's words to Heinrich regarding the poet's need for clarity of thought and purpose (1: 280-87; 108-16). Seeing in Klingsohr a portrait of Goethe, Haym uses the expanded, more philologically correct notes on Goethe from Novalis's unpublished studies, available only since the 1846 edition of his works, to demonstrate for the first time the extent to which the poetics of *Heinrich von Ofterdingen* were gleaned from extensive studies of *Wilhelm Meisters Lehrjahre*. As a proof of Novalis's critical acumen, Haym points out that a number of these latter observations coincide with central remarks from Schiller's analysis of *Wilhelm Meister* in his correspondence with Goethe, such as that *Wilhelm Meister* begins with a dissonance between art and business that is eventually resolved in the character of Natalie (375).

All the same, Haym contends, this study of Goethe's formal artistry had ruinous consequences for Novalis in that it encouraged him to overly accentuate and carry over into his writings an innate tendency towards introspective spiritualization of the outer world. Whereas the key word in Dilthey's view of Novalis was *Erlebnis*, or experience, Haym's contribution to future catchphrases of Novalis scholarship was *magischer Idealismus* — a term from Novalis's notebooks from 1798 that Haym employs again and again to characterize the mystical subjectivism of Novalis's thought and poetry. Just as the phrase magical idealism occurs in the notebooks, so too could Haym point to an aesthetics of the fairy tale that culminates in the poetic practice of *Heinrich von Ofterdingen*, although his characterization of Novalis's fairy-tale outlook on the world (378), makes it clear that his description is a value judgment as well. But he observes that, given this poetics of the fairy tale, form and content stand in perfect correlation to one another in *Heinrich von Ofterdingen*; it is logical that part one of the novel should end in a fairy tale and part two should have been intended to repeat the pattern of this tale enacted by the novel's characters (383).

Haym, the editor of the journal in which Dilthey's essay on Novalis had appeared, not only makes use of his younger colleague's study but also offers alternate accentuation of key points. Whereas Dilthey had refrained from an extensive interpretation of the Klingsohr tale, Haym observes that this key to the meaning of *Heinrich von Ofterdingen* is itself quite hieroglyphic in nature and hence requires deciphering. After having recorded repeated readings of this tale, much rumination, and no small amount of boredom, he announces his conclusion: the Klingsohr tale narrates the overturn of the realm of prosaic utility and the return of a kingdom of love and poetry, told within the framework of the resolution of a magic spell. Haym provides an allegorical explanation of the major figures in the tale — father, mother, Ginnistan, Eros, Fabel, Sophie, and the Scribe — in accordance with clues given in Novalis's notebooks and letters and observes that the allegorical fairy tale contains the main theme of the novel in concentrated form (384-85). In like manner, Haym takes issue with Dilthey on the latter's theory of metempsychosis as the key to the character interrelationships in *Ofterdingen*: for a writer such as Novalis, who held that eternity was within us, the transmigration of souls could be only a temporary and secondary matter (386). Rather, it is the soul of Heinrich in which the differences between this world and the next resolve themselves; the transformation of the world into a fairy tale is implicitly present within him.

Where Dilthey and Haym fundamentally agree, however, is their grounding of *Heinrich von Ofterdingen* in the actual experiences of its author. For Haym, the one thing that gives this metaphysical story any human interest is its experiential quality as an *erlebtes Gedicht*: the hero of this apotheosis of poetry is Hardenberg himself (387). All evidence of formal artistry in the novel does not alter his initial contention that *Heinrich von Ofterdingen* is a dreamy and tangled construction, but at least it is consistent with the personality and worldview of its author. When one compares this chapter in *Die romantische Schule* with Haym's remarks about Tieck and Friedrich Schlegel — whom he finds morally lax and whose novels he condemns on ethical and artistic grounds alike — it appears to represent a comparative upgrading of Novalis's literary reputation.

Haym wrote in the conviction that German Romanticism had become a merely historical phenomenon. The first sentence of *Die romantische Schule* stresses that one hundred years have passed since the birth of those authors whose first literary activities will be the subject of this study (3). Centenaries, of course, can also serve to reawaken interest in past personages, works, and events, particularly when they happen to coincide with an event such as the establishment of the second German Empire in 1871. And so, in an era addicted to monumentalizing the German past, Novalis received on May 2,

1872, the hundredth anniversary of his birth, his own graveside memorial, consisting of a highly idealized bust by Friedrich von Schaper and the engraving of a stanza from one of his *Geistliche Lieder* extolling faithfulness and thankfulness (1: 165). Sophie von Hardenberg, a grand-niece of the poet, published a biography of Novalis in 1873 containing an extensive number of previously unpublished letters; in 1883 a second, expanded edition appeared. Anxious to protect her ancestor from the charge that he had converted to Catholicism or at the very least turned away from his Lutheran and Pietistic upbringing, she describes *Heinrich von Ofterdingen*, with its medieval setting, as an imperfect first attempt at writing (Hardenberg 1883, 152) and shifts her attention to the *Geistliche Lieder*. In the latter half of the nineteenth century, it was principally through these spiritual songs, a number of which Schleiermacher had succeeded in introducing into Protestant hymnals, that German and non-German critics alike came to perceive Novalis as primarily a religious writer, even if they had difficulties in defining the precise nature of his religiosity (see Uerlings 1991, 80-81).

In his study of German Romanticism, volume two in his survey of the main currents of nineteenth-century literature, the Danish critic Georg Brandes explores what he believes to be the source of Novalis's religiosity: the recesses of the German Romantic *Gemüth*, or soul — although Brandes hastens to add that no other language can render directly the essence of this mystic word (Brandes 1873, 229). Drawing upon ideas from Ruge and Heine, Brandes sees in Novalis's writings a love of inwardness and illness derived from his Pietistic background and then magnified into a religion of death, night, and sensual delight that finds its height in the song of the dead in *Heinrich von Ofterdingen* (241-42). This mystical inwardness, Brandes claims, leads Novalis from the praise of a life of vegetative inactivity in his poetic works to the advocacy of political reaction in *Die Christenheit oder Europa*. In an extended comparison of Novalis with Shelley, Brandes finds them equal in poetic talent, but he awards the laurels to the English Romantic poet for his love of freedom and condemnation of clerical hypocrisy, as opposed to the quietism of Novalis.

Brandes does, however, allow the Romantic *Gemüth* one outlet for its inwardness, namely *Sehnsucht*, or Romantic longing, as exemplified in the symbol of the Blue Flower. If it was Heine who first linked Novalis and Romanticism inextricably to the Blue Flower, the chapter Brandes wrote on "Die romantische Sehnsucht; die blaue Blume" (265-303) certainly assured its continuation; by 1900 his volume was in its seventh German edition and served as a chief source of information on German Romanticism for Thomas Mann, among others (see Cerf 1981 and Reiss 1987). While Brandes turns a rather jaundiced eye to the Klingsohr tale and the plans for the continuation of *Heinrich von Ofterdingen* as outlined by Tieck, like Haym finds poetic worth in the novel to the extent that it reflects the experiences of its author (278). Regarded as a work that might inspire activity, however, Brandes finds it sorely wanting; for him *Heinrich von Ofterdingen* remains the epitome of self-consuming longing. All the same, the mere fact that so influential a critic as Brandes discussed *Ofterdingen* as extensively as he did shows that this novel was beginning to emerge from the comparative obscurity into which it had fallen.

In 1876 Julian Schmidt issued the first separate edition of *Heinrich von Ofterdingen* since 1802 — yet another indication that Novalis's works were now attracting the attention of more than just a small circle of literary historians. In his introduction Schmidt characterizes *Heinrich von Ofterdingen* as the most influential and long-lasting of the literary works from the beginning of the nineteenth century; according to him, the "Blue Flower" is still a popular term for Romantic poetry. Taking a historicizing approach similar to that of Haym, Schmidt suggests that contemporary readers enjoy a changed perspective on a work he describes as *merkwürdig*, or peculiar: whereas seventy-five years earlier the novel met with either enthusiastic involvement or rationalistic ridicule, at this point he says it is not likely to win new adherents to its beliefs, but cultured readers may find it a charming work of art, even when the meaning remains obscure (Schmidt 1876, v).

In a partial revision of his judgments on *Ofterdingen* from the 1850s, Schmidt now endeavors to clear up the mysteries, at least to some extent, by explaining the novel's genesis in the light of its author's thought. Quoting from newly available letters to Schiller and Reinhold, Hardenberg's teachers in history and philosophy at the University of Jena, Schmidt places particular emphasis on Novalis's attraction to the mystical side of Kantian philosophy, namely its stress on the notion of freedom in the realm of ideas. He furthermore maintains that Schiller's poem "Das Reich der Schatten" (The Realm of Shadows) — later renamed "Das Ideal und das Leben" (The Ideal and Life) — contains ideas we encounter in the song destined for the second part of *Ofterdingen* in which spirits sing of the beauties of the world beyond the grave. Schmidt provides but a brief recapitulation of Tieck's account of the projected continuation of Novalis's novel, no doubt in an attempt to tone down its more incomprehensible aspects, but this editorial decision also allows him to excerpt only those verses from the song commonly known as the "Lied der Toten" that support its supposedly Schillerian derivation. Had Schmidt, for example, printed the following stanza in its entirety, rather than only lines 5-7 in his paragraph of verses cited as if they were prose, it might have been more difficult to come to the conclusion that in Novalis's vision of the life to come there exist no passions but only serene contemplation (xxi-ii):

> Alles was wir nur berühren
> Wird zu heißen Balsamfrüchten
> Wird zu weichen zarten Brüsten

Opfer kühner Lust.
Leiser Wünsche süßes Plaudern
Hören wir allein, und schauen
Immerdar in selge Augen
Schmecken nichts als Mund und Kuß.

(1: 352)

It is in such bowdlerization of "improper" verses — which the first American translation of *Ofterdingen* of 1842 handled quite easily, as we have seen in chapter one of this study, but which disappear completely from the heavily-edited excerpts contained in M. J. Hope's 1891 edition of *Novalis (Friedrich von Hardenberg): His Life, Thoughts, and Works* — that one realizes that the Victorian era existed on both sides of the Atlantic. But Schmidt's linkage of Novalis with Schiller, as well as the reprint of *Heinrich von Ofterdingen* itself, also documents that influential critics were now integrating Novalis ever more firmly into the German poetic canon.

Dr. A. Schubart's voluminous study of Novalis's life, works, and thought is an attempt at canonical interpretation in the full sense of the word, as the date at the conclusion of its introduction attests: Weimar, Christmas 1886. Written in an effort to affirm Novalis's status as a Christian (more specifically, Protestant) poet, Schubart's study also does not shrink from quoting passages from Goethe's *Faust* in its explication of *Heinrich von Ofterdingen*. Whereas Haym had noted affinities between Goethe and the depiction and poetic doctrine of Klingsohr, Schubart goes so far as to assert that Klingsohr's wise words to his Heinrich, his poetic apprentice, could easily be passed off to the unsuspecting reader as selections from Goethe's conversations with Eckermann; he compares Klingsohr's truly fatherly benevolence with that of the Lord in the Prologue in Heaven to Goethe's *Faust* (Schubart 1887, 356-57). Such comparisons suggest that Schubart, while proudly advertising his doctoral title and including scholarly notes at the end of each chapter, has a cultured but nonacademic audience in mind as the target of his proselytizing efforts on behalf of Novalis; so too does the heading for his lengthy section on *Ofterdingen* (291-440), which identifies it as a retelling and analysis of the novel. Even Dilthey's and Haym's discussions of Novalis's philosophical speculations often consist of little more than citations and paraphrases of the texts in question, but in the case of a novel with so simple a plot one is tempted to lay this book aside quickly as a deservedly forgotten exercise in redundancy.

Schubart's discussion of the Klingsohr tale, however, contains elements that confirm the virtues of scholarly patience as well as other parts that provide a type of comic relief for the long-suffering reader. To begin with an example of the latter sort: Schubart quotes an earlier scholar who understands the seduction of Eros by Ginnistan as an allegorical representation of the lassitude

(*Verweichlichung*) of the Roman church in its idolatrous and superficial cult of Mary (375). Why such an interpretation could even be cited becomes clearer a few pages later when Schubart becomes uncomfortable about the moral implications of a seduction undertaken by a figure in the guise of Eros's mother, let alone the prior bliss that the father has enjoyed in the arms of the seductive Ginnistan (381-83); once again the erotic passages in *Heinrich von Ofterdingen* provoke unusual interpretive contortions on the part of nineteenth-century critics.

To Schubart's credit, however, he does not excise such passages from consideration, as did Schmidt. On the contrary, in his discussion of the Klingsohr tale he cites in full the prophetic poem near its beginning — a poem veritably charged with erotic impulses — as the key to its interpretation (372):

> Nicht lange wird der schöne Fremde säumen.
> Die Wärme naht, die Ewigkeit beginnt.
> Die Königin erwacht aus langen Träumen,
> Wenn Meer und Land in Liebesglut zerrinnt.
> Die kalte Nacht wird diese Stätte räumen,
> Wenn Fabel erst das alte Recht gewinnt.
> In Freyas Schooß wird sich die Welt entzünden
> Und jede Sehnsucht ihre Sehnsucht finden.
>
> (1: 292; 122)

While Novalis's fusion of sexuality and speculations on natural philosophy — which Haym had noticed but dismissed as empty fantasizing (Haym 1870, 366-67) — here escape Schubart's ken, he does recognize Novalis's use of one section of the text to interpret other parts. Here it may well be Schubart's theological bent that allows him an insight into an essential feature of *Heinrich von Ofterdingen*; one should not forget that literary hermeneutics, particularly as practiced by figures such as Schleiermacher and Dilthey, grew out of the tradition of biblical exegesis familiar to Novalis as well. In any case, Schubart devotes attention to the Klingsohr tale as if it were a product of revelation, and many of his findings are still worthy of notice.

For example, Schubart recognizes the parallel between Ginnistan's journey to the realm of the moon, her father, and the reunion in Augsburg between Heinrich's mother and her father Schwaning (386-87) as an indication that novel and fairy tale are interacting with one another as early as part one of *Ofterdingen*. With respect to Fabel's journey into the underworld, Schubart notes that the sphinx's response to her question as to the whereabouts of love — "In der Einbildung" (1: 301; 132-33) — indicates the fatal error made by Eros: by losing itself in the imagination, love has abandoned the path to its true longing, namely Freya (395). Likewise, he points out stylistic similarities between question-and-answer passages in Goethe's *Märchen* and the Klingsohr tale (396). Here Schubart's reference to Goethe's works does more than merely convey literary authority upon the corresponding text by Novalis; it makes evident how the careful study of Goethe's writings played a crucial role in the development of Novalis's literary craft.

Finally, Schubart interprets the turning point of the fairy tale, namely the death of Eros's mother and the dissolution of her ashes, with the help of the poem spoken by Astralis at the beginning of the second part of *Ofterdingen*, and recognizes, albeit disapprovingly, the correspondence between this sacrifice and Christ's redemptive death (404-6). In similar fashion, he notices other references in Astralis's poem to scenes in part one — such as the feast in Augsburg, the kiss Heinrich and Mathilde exchange, or their morning walk before the gates of the city — and takes these as evidence of how clearly Novalis had planned to establish interconnections throughout the entire course of the novel (415). Had Schubart gone one step further and identified Astralis as the embodiment of poesy coming to self-understanding through the medium of love, he would have produced the first significant interpretation of the beginning of part two. Instead, however, he literally rewrites Astralis's address to the readers of *Ofterdingen* to suit his own conception of what should have been said, namely that Astralis and the readers of the novel have had the delight of encountering one another, without realizing it, in the scene where Heinrich and Mathilde exchange their first kiss:

> Ihr kennt mich nicht und saht mich werden.
> Wart ihr nicht Zeugen, wie ich, noch
> Nachtwandler *euch* [mich] zum ersten Male traf
> An jenem frohen Abend? Flog euch nicht
> Ein süßer Schauer der *Entzückung* [Entzündung] an?
>
> (1: 317; 151)

Readers of this study may find it ironic when Schubart complains that he has found the senseless wording "I encountered myself" even in Julian Schmidt's edition of *Ofterdingen* (413); in 1876 editorial revisionism apparently had not yet progressed to the point of actual substitution of wording. Likewise, it is peculiar that the attention he had given to the poem from the Klingsohr tale, where the verb *entzünden* is used in the closing rhymepair, should not have "sparked" his attention regarding its repetition as a noun in the passage just quoted. All in all, though, Schubart deserves credit for major advances in the interpretation of *Heinrich von Ofterdingen*, even though he was not quite capable of providing an overall framework for his insights.

The honor for this achievement belongs to Just Bing for his 1893 study. As Schubart did, Bing leaves to Dilthey and Haym the discussion of philosophical aspects of Novalis and concentrates instead on his life and works. Long quotes and extensive plot narrations are common to both studies, but Bing does not explain everything biographically. For example, he regards the description of the feast at Augsburg in chapter six of *Heinrich von Ofterdingen* as so lively and explicit not because Novalis could call to mind happy days of celebration with the family of Sophie von Kühn but rather because this episode is of crucial importance in Heinrich's development as a poet (134-39). Here the adoption of Dilthey's classification of *Heinrich von Ofterdingen* as a Bildungsroman and Künstlerroman (117) bears fruitful results in that Bing looks for clues within the novel as to how individual scenes and remarks bear upon its overall conception. In like fashion, he understands Klingsohr's comment that the depiction of a poet who is simultaneously a hero lies beyond the current scope of representational ability (1: 285; 114) not as a reflection of Goethean poetics but rather as a clue that it is precisely such a hero-poet that Novalis had planned for the second part of his novel (141).

Bing's most original remarks, though, involve his discussion of the transition from the conclusion of the Klingsohr tale to the beginning of part two of the novel. The final verses of Fabel had sung of the foundation of the realm of eternity; now this realm is to be realized in part two of *Ofterdingen*, once Heinrich recognizes the eternity of love and the world-transforming power of poetry — precisely what the opening poem sung by Astralis depicts (150-51). Bing, like Schubart, quotes Astralis's words "Ihr kennt mich nicht und saht mich werden," but he provides an interpretation, not a rewriting, of the verses that follow, observing that the change from blank verse to irregular rhymed couplets — the "Knittelvers" of Goethe's *Faust* — suggests the difference between the measured pace of the first part of the novel and the ascent into the realm of wonder planned for part two. Bing's interpretation of the genesis of Astralis (173-74, footnote 30) presages many of the points I later make in my discussion of this scene as a recapitulation of part one of the novel (Mahoney 1980, 63-65), although he does not consider those studies in natural philosophy that play a major role in determining the poetic imagery Novalis employs. All the same, when one compares Bing's words on Astralis with Ruge's and Echtermeyer's earlier rejection of this "sidereal changeling" (1839, 16-17), it is evident that a major shift in interpretation has taken place.

This is not to suggest, however, that the reception of *Heinrich von Ofterdingen* in the latter half of the nineteenth century consists of an unbroken progression in interpretive sophistication. By the 1890s Novalis's works had sufficiently increased in academic respectability as to become grist for the dissertation mill developing in Wilhelmine Germany, and the ensuing products were not always of particularly high quality. In an 1893 dissertation on the influence of Goethe's *Wilhelm Meister* on the novels of the German Romantics, for example, Joakim Donner provides little more than a listing of residual prejudices in the many opinions of earlier critics he cites in lieu of his own interpretation of *Heinrich von Ofterdingen*.

Nor were negative evaluations wholly a thing of the past. In his essay "Novalis and the Blue Flower," Hjalmar Hjorth Boyesen, a professor of German at Columbia University, relies heavily on Heine and Brandes and hence portrays Novalis as a regressive, consumptive artist whose praise of the Middle Ages reveals an enthusiasm for feudalism and Catholicism. As for *Heinrich von Ofterdingen*, Boyesen acknowledges the beauty and clarity of its poems, but calls the novel itself a labyrinth without beginning or end (1892, 323-24); clearly his own aesthetic allegiances lie more with Goethe and Schiller, to whom he devotes the greater half of his *Essays on German Literature*. And in a book on social forces in German literature, Kuno Francke, professor at Harvard University and founder of the Busch-Reissinger Museum of German culture, delivers in "The Disintegration of Classicism" a critique of the novels of Tieck, Friedrich Schlegel, and Novalis that far exceeds Rudolf Haym's strictures against these same authors:

> In studying these fantastic ravings of an eccentric and uncontrolled imagination one understands how a generation whose reason and will had been benumbed by their influence, should have become unfit for discharging the simple duties of the citizen and the patriot; one comprehends Napoleon's contempt for these "German ideologists"; and one sees the inner justice for the political humiliation of Germany in 1806. (1895, 428)

Although Francke was writing far away from his native Germany, his aesthetic standards were fully consonant with current Wilhelmine notions of literature as an educative force: works that did not contribute to individual development within the framework of the social whole deserved condemnation. On the whole, though, by the end of the nineteenth century both Novalis and *Heinrich von Ofterdingen* had escaped from the opprobrium of characterizations such as those offered by Francke and had assumed a respectable if yet not prominent position in the literary canon. In the conclusion to his study of Novalis's lyric poetry, which — like Boyesen's essay — rated the individual songs within *Ofterdingen* much more highly than the novel as a whole, Carl Busse observed that Novalis would never become a leader (*Führer*) for his readers but that he could serve as a quiet and friendly companion from time to time, provided that one were willing to come under his poetic spell (Busse 1898, 134).

Busse noted in addition, however, that a wave of neo-Romanticism appeared to be under way in Germany as well as abroad — an observation confirmed by the appearance of a new, three-volume edition of the complete works of Novalis. In an article for the influential periodical *Deutsche Rundschau* (German Review), Wilhelm Bölsche attempts to explain why the Diederichs publishing house should have issued not only such an elegantly bound and typeset edition but also the first complete edition of Novalis in over fifty years: perhaps, he speculates, people finally had begun to realize that Novalis's goal of romanticizing the world was in essence an early expression of the will and capacity to transform the globe that had become manifest at the end of the nineteenth century (1899, 190). And so Bölsche predicts a bright future for Novalis in the new century, once the outmoded clichés about him have been discarded and his modernity and philosophical depth have become more widely recognized.

The same year that Bölsche's article appeared, Ricarda Huch published her *Blüthezeit der Romantik* (Golden Age of Romanticism, 1899), which had a second edition in 1901. Huch, herself a novelist, has high words of praise for *Heinrich von Ofterdingen*: if one could only merge the merits of this work with those of Goethe's *Wilhelm Meister*, she says, there would be no more beautiful novel. She likewise notes the clear organization of *Ofterdingen*; Novalis has fashioned his novel on the model of the Christian Bible, with the second half intended to serve as the fulfillment of the first (316). And she understands Novalis's use of the term *Gemüth* more precisely than did Brandes: *Ofterdingen* differs from the other Romantic novels in that Novalis was in search not of himself, but rather of the world (317). With such sympathetic interpreters emerging on the critical scene, the future appeared bright for "Novalis und das neue Jahrhundert" (Novalis and the New Century) — the title Bölsche had given to his article. Some further reasons for this renaissance of interest in German Romanticism, as well as its effects on interpretations of *Heinrich von Ofterdingen* in the opening decades of the twentieth century, are treated in the following chapter.

3: Neo-Novalicism — 1901-1933

MORE THAN THE mere centenary in 1901 of the poet's death brought about the Novalis renaissance at the beginning of the twentieth century. Within the context of a general, international revival of interest in German Romanticism, readers and critics alike saw Novalis and his fellow poets as alternatives to the empty materialism of industrialized society. As Wolfdietrich Rasch has observed in his survey of salient characteristics of German literature around 1900, the bombastic optimism of the Bismarckian and early Wilhelmine years had been succeeded by a sense of anxiety about the loss of values and vitality in a civilization without a spiritual foundation, while poets, philosophers, and scientists alike concerned themselves ever more with a search for an underlying unity in life whose very vocabulary betrayed the heritage of Goethe and the Romantics (Rasch 1967, 41-45). Once again poets such as Hofmannsthal, Rilke, and Trakl attempted to evoke through language a sense of the mystical unity of creation, while authors like Hermann Hesse and Thomas Mann addressed the theme of opposition between the poet and prosaic society that was implicit in the contrast between Heinrich and his father in the first chapter of *Heinrich von Ofterdingen* and whose dissonances had been further developed by authors such as Clemens Brentano and E. T. A. Hoffmann. Hesse's early plans to write a popular introduction to German Romanticism were aborted by the publication of Ricarda Huch's monograph, but he later praised Novalis as a profound mystic in works such as *Demian* (1917) and also coedited a volume of documents on the poet's life and death published by S. Fischer in 1925 and reissued in paperback by Insel Verlag in 1976, following the Hesse wave of the 1960s. While speaking of Novalis's work as the most marvelous and mysterious known to German cultural history, Hesse makes it clear that for him it was the poet's life and love affair with death that turned him into a figure to be ranked with Hölderlin and Nietzsche (Hesse, 1925, 160; for a discussion of Hesse and Novalis, see Ziolkowski 1987).

Hesse here was following a trail marked by Maurice Maeterlinck, the Flemish poet and enthusiast for the Middle Ages who in 1895 had published a French translation of *Die Lehrlinge zu Sais* (The Apprentices at Sais), Novalis's other incomplete novel, as well as selections from the fragments — many of which now seemed to be theoretical anticipations of Symbolist aesthetics, such as the notebook entry that envisioned dreamlike tales bound together only by association, and merely euphonious poems without sense or connection (3: 572). In the lengthy introduction to this volume, which was reprinted in French and English collections of his essays and hence reintroduced the name of Novalis into countries where it had sunk into relative obscurity since the mid-nineteenth century, Maeterlinck follows Tieck's example and depicts Novalis as a quasi-saint eminently worthy of emulation. He refers positively, albeit only in passing, to *Heinrich von Ofterdingen*, which in his view does not possess the same astonishing audacity as the fragments and *Die Lehrlinge zu Sais* but whose crystal-clear prose seems to him to have been written by an angel descending from a paradise of ice and snow (Maeterlinck 1895, li). In images such as these, Maeterlinck contributed to the repopularization of Novalis as the mystic poet whose oracular utterances gave glimpses of a world beyond the ken of most mortals.

Adolf Bartels gives this notion a Nietzschean twist in his influential, frequently reprinted, and ever more aggressively nationalistic *Geschichte der Deutschen Literatur* (History of German Literature) by maintaining that most members of the new cult of Novalis focus only on the mystical voluptuousness of his writings and use his great but fragmentary ideas as an excuse for their own inability to penetrate reality; such weaklings fail to fathom Hardenberg's truly aristocratic spirit (Bartels 1909, 653). And whereas in earlier editions of this work Bartels finds only the poems in *Heinrich von Ofterdingen* to be of lasting value, by 1919 he describes the novel as a mystical and magical book of worldviews (*Weltanschauungsbuch*) such as possessed by no other nation (Bartels 1919, 242). In like manner, Arthur Moeller van den Bruck — the right-wing irrationalist perhaps best known for *Das dritte Reich* (The Third Reich, 1922) — includes Novalis in the third volume of his compendium entitled *Die Deutschen: Unsere Menschengeschichte* (The Germans: Our Human History, 1910). Here he extols him as a modern-day representative of the mystical spirit found in such figures as Meister Eckhart, Paracelsus, and Jakob Boehme, whose fragments point toward the only possible religion for the present, namely the worship of nature (Moeller 1910, 191-92). The relatively short space both Bartels and Moeller allot to discussions of Novalis's literary works suggest that for them Novalis was important more as a figurehead for displaying their own convictions than as a writer whose presuppositions might not coincide with theirs.

A particularly crass example of the disregard for factual detail in the stylized portraits of the artist as a young mystic may be found in the volume on Novalis for a typographically elegant series on literature edited by Georg Brandes. Here the neo-Romantic poet Franz Blei, who had published an edition of Novalis's poetry for Reclam Verlag in 1898, begins by comparing Novalis to a sleepwalker who could pass through life without stumbling because he heard, not the calls of those around him, but rather the music of the spheres (Blei 1904, 1-3). If so, even during his life Novalis must have accomplished a remarkable triumph over conventional chronology, because, according to Blei, he spent happy months with Sophie von Kühn in the summer of 1798 before she was brought to Jena for medical treatment in July 1797, where she died in

March of that year (22-27). Blei uses lines from the feast at Augsburg in *Heinrich von Ofterdingen* (without identifying their source) to depict the period of first bliss between Novalis and his fiancée as a seamless coincidence of life and poetry. For his few remarks on the novel itself, Blei observes that its sense may not be fully clear to us but that its beauty provides more than mere understanding ever could (59). For Blei, the life and death of Novalis were the supreme work of art, so he closes his slim volume with a fulsome image of Novalis pouring out his blood upon the altarstone of the temple of the Third Reich while uttering the words "Dies ist mein Wein" (This is my wine; 62-63). In such an account, Blei turns poetry into an aestheticist pseudo-religion devoid of the intellectual substance that lies behind, for example, Novalis's daring speculations on the connections between the eucharist and sexual commingling (1: 166-68; 2: 620-21).

Fortunately there were studies of Novalis at the beginning of the twentieth century that did more than simply exploit a passing phase of interest — a prime example being Ernst Heilborn's 1901 biography. As Herbert Uerlings has observed, Heilborn's discussion of Novalis's personality does not conform to the standard sentimentalizing portraits of his predecessors and contemporaries; instead, Heilborn emphasizes the hectic, restless, "modern" side of the author as well as the coincidence of opposites in his psyche such as religious devotion and a highly sensuous nature (Uerlings 1991, 96-97). In the same year that this biography appeared, Heilborn published a new three-volume edition of Novalis's works based on manuscripts in the von Hardenberg family archives that doubled the number of "fragments" made accessible in previous editions, and he also made a first attempt at arranging them in chronological order. Although the scope of his biography did not permit an intensive treatment of *Heinrich von Ofterdingen*, Heilborn's approach gave an inkling of the benefits to be gained from employing the theoretical notebooks, fragments, and letters of Novalis as an aid to understanding the poetic works. In resisting the temptation to criticize the figures in *Heinrich von Ofterdingen* for their lack of distinct individuality, Heilborn points out that in his fragments Novalis had described the mysterious as an essential feature of poetic characters and that he had no intention of individualizing the figures in his novel; it is rather the atmosphere conveyed in *Heinrich von Ofterdingen* that is so compelling (187). Heilborn likewise notes that for all of Novalis's polemics against *Wilhelm Meisters Lehrjahre*, he also made productive use of Goethe's configuration and variation of character traits by incorporating this stylistic feature into his own novel (175-76) — an insight that Oskar Walzel was to develop in more detail some fifteen years later.

As a further indication of the escalating interest in Novalis among the cultivated reading public, hardly had Heilborn's edition appeared when a fourth, supplementary volume to the Meissner and Wille edition of Novalis's complete works was issued by Diederichs Verlag — a publishing house whose cultural politics during the period around 1900 included the championing of mysticism and the critique of modernist rationality (see Hübinger 1987). To these two editions was joined a 1903 collection of selected works edited by Wilhelm Bölsche. In his introduction to *Heinrich von Ofterdingen*, Bölsche does not hesitate to label this a work belonging to world literature by virtue of a combination of lyrical form and philosophical depth that made it a living example of its chief theme: the power of poetry. For Bölsche it no longer matters whether the medieval minstrel Heinrich von Ofterdingen had been a great poet or had even existed; thanks to Novalis, Heinrich von Ofterdingen has become a figure of archetypal human significance like Hamlet or Faust (8; for a discussion of the figure of Heinrich von Ofterdingen in German literature, see Riesenfeld 1912).

This latter claim, bolder than Bölsche's remarks on the occasion of the 1898 edition of Novalis's works, faced critical examination when foreign scholars began publishing extended studies of Novalis's work. In France, the renewed attention accorded to Novalis and his contemporaries also meant that the German Romantics began to be read in the schools — and to appear on the national university examinations for certification in foreign language instruction at the secondary level. In 1901, Novalis's *Hymnen an die Nacht* were among the works to be tested, and students preparing for their exams were advised to consult the studies by Schubart, Bing, and Heilborn as well as the most recent editions (see Glorieux 1972, 134). In 1903, Jean-Édouard Spenlé received the distinguished *docteur és lettres* degree for his dissertation on Novalis and Romantic Idealism and a complementary thesis on Novalis's critical reception that far surpassed in thoroughness both Heilborn's introductory chapter on this subject and Haussmann's subsequent survey of nineteenth-century German estimates of Novalis. Both theses appeared in printed form in 1904 and still stand as monuments of lively and lucid scholarship.

In his introductory remarks, Spenlé cites with approval Arnold Ruge's remark that Novalis exemplifies in concentrated form all the aspirations of the German consciousness. Spenlé likewise calls Novalis the key to German Romanticism but also a profoundly enigmatic writer whose cryptic works have been misappropriated by predisposed critics of various religious and ideological persuasions; he announces his goal, on the contrary, to be an impartial explication of the writer's ideas even where they differ from his own (1-4). All the same, Spenlé brings to bear on his subject a critical perspective owing much to Hippolyte Taine's theories on the effects of heredity and environment on the individual, which results in a tendency to psychologize what he regards as the more pathological aspects of the artist. Unlike previous critics such as Carlyle, Schmidt, and Schubart, Spenlé does not gloss over the voluptuary elements in his accomplished translations of selections from *Heinrich von Ofterdingen* (52-

54) but rather explains Novalis's fascination with the erotic nature of water, as well as the confluence of love and death in his writings, as products of the poet's hypersensitive, tubercular nature. Citing in support of his theories the findings of the German psychiatrist Krafft-Ebing (64), Spenlé makes a case study out of his investigation of the poet and his writings — in effect providing a modern restatement of Goethe's dictum that all that is Classic is healthy, and all that is Romantic is diseased.

With respect to *Heinrich von Ofterdingen*, Spenlé not only makes use of the Heilborn critical edition for his translations but also provides a detailed commentary on the action and symbolic meaning of the Klingsohr tale that draws upon Novalis's references to alchemy and cabalism in his fragments, notebooks, and letters. As for its evaluation, however, Spenlé finds this to be a bizarre tale containing a delirium of abstractions and an overuse of allegory (218-30). It is instructive that Spenlé includes his discussion of the Klingsohr tale in the chapter dealing with Novalis's development of a magical, symbolic philosophy of nature during his studies at the Mining Academy of Freiberg, which makes sense thematically but divorces the tale from its function in *Heinrich von Ofterdingen* as a whole. Spenlé defends this procedure in a footnote by interpreting Klingsohr's remark that his tale is an immature product of his youth (1: 287; 115-16) as a confession on the part of Novalis that the story to come had been composed long before the novel was written and was merely appended to the main text (233); here we have one of the instances in which Spenlé's biographical and chronological approach to his study has the effect of reinforcing his central notion that Novalis was a fertile but immature thinker who provided intimations of ideas but lacked the time or patience to execute them fully. In many regards, Spenlé's thesis represents a philologically more developed version of Hegelian criticism of Novalis; indeed, in the conclusion to his work Spenlé quotes with approval Hegel's remarks on the "consumption of the spirit" that the systematic philosopher had found in the poet's fragmentary writings (345).

Nonetheless, Spenlé observes that Novalis presents an organic conception of the universe not as a philosophical thesis but rather as an artistic reality to be not so much comprehended as sensed; what for Georg Brandes and Franz Blei was only effusion becomes linked here with Novalis's notion of poetry as *Gemütherregungskunst* (3: 639), which Spenlé translates as "l'art du dynamisme psychique" — the art of psychic dynamism (356). Referring to the 1898 publication on Richard Wagner as poet and thinker by Henri Lichtenberger, his principal doctoral advisor, Spenlé glimpses in Novalis the schematic beginnings of a new aesthetics that not he but rather Wagner was later to put into practice (359). In view of the extraordinary international prestige that Wagner enjoyed at the beginning of the twentieth century, such a concluding judgment is actually more positive than it may appear at first sight, although Spenlé makes it clear that he does not regard Novalis as belonging to the highest ranks of thinkers and artists.

Spenlé's dissertation was only the most prominent of a flood of French publications dealing with Novalis at the turn of the century (for further information, see Glorieux 1972 and 1982). The next step in the acclimatization of Novalis in France occurred in 1908 with the appearance of an annotated translation of *Heinrich von Ofterdingen* by Georges Polti and Paul Morisse with a preface by Henri Albert, who had written about and translated Novalis prior to Maeterlinck's edition of 1895. Albert's introduction makes heavy and derivative use of ideas from Georg Brandes's remarks on Novalis and is not always reliable in its presentation of biographical and literary information — he regards the early Romantics, and Novalis in particular, as devotees of the Middle Ages to the exclusion of classical antiquity, the Enlightenment, and practical activity (Albert 1908, xix-xv) — but Morisse and Polti not only render the novel into crystal-clear French but also provide explanations of potentially obscure passages in annotations drawing upon the studies by Schubart and Bing. One can also speak of a successful "translation" with regard to the portrait of Novalis adjacent to the title page. German books on Novalis during this period often printed reproductions of the engraving by Eduard Eichens that Tieck and von Bülow had included in the 1846 supplement to their edition and that in the opinion of Gerhard Schulz turned the physiognomy of a spirited young man into that of a dreaming, girl-like youth (Schulz 1969b, 7). For their engraving, however, the editors returned to the original portrait owned by the von Hardenberg family; the result, more an interpretation than a reproduction, provides a fuller-faced, firm-chinned, more mature-looking individual with distinctly Gallic features, whose attire and free-flowing hair have the effect of identifying him as the contemporary of the French Revolution that he was. (For a survey of the history of Novalis portraits, see Weissenberger 1987.)

The crowning glory of international research on Novalis in the early decades of the twentieth century, though, was undoubtedly Henri Lichtenberger's 1912 monograph. Its inclusion in the series *Les Grands Écrivains Étrangers* (Great Foreign Writers) signals the esteem that Novalis had come to enjoy in France, as does the fact that Lichtenberger's book went through six editions within its first year of publication (Glorieux 1972, 158). Such success was well deserved, for in this work Lichtenberger combines the ability to engage the interest of an educated general public — as had earlier writers on Novalis such as Carlyle, Heine, and Huch — with the scholarly depth of Spenlé. Making additional use of findings from Heilborn's biography and other recent critics, Lichtenberger modifies a number of Spenlé's principal points without explicitly criticizing his former student. In his concluding remarks, he observes that Novalis has been freed from the legends that earlier marred his reputation and now stands not as a "case" of psychological interest but rather as an exemplary figure in German Romanticism who was at once a mystic and a lover of life, a delicate epicurean yet a model civil servant. Likewise, his remark that "*Ofterdingen* annonce *Parsifal* et *Zarathustra*" is meant as unqualified praise, for he follows it with the declaration that Novalis's magical idealism need not fear comparison with the beauty of Wagner's doctrine of regeneration and Nietzsche's hypothesis of eternal return (Lichtenberger, 256-58).

Lichtenberger provides the proof for such assertions in his discussion of *Heinrich von Ofterdingen*, which he treats as the high point in Novalis's poetic oeuvre — yet another difference from Spenlé, for whom the *Hymnen an die Nacht* represent the best that Novalis had to offer. Previous critics had been prone to praise the poetic beauties of *Heinrich von Ofterdingen* while displaying an increasing degree of helplessness or even hostility the closer they got to the Klingsohr tale and the fragmentary beginning of part two, but Lichtenberger demonstrates that the poetic logic of Novalis's novel is meant to make evident the illusory nature of what people normally term real life. For this reason he begins his analysis of the novel with a discussion of the "prehistory" of Heinrich's father, who had spurned the presentiment of a superior life granted him by his own dream in favor of a worthy albeit unfulfilling mode of existence as a craftsman (199-200), and only then contrasts this existence with the dream of the Blue Flower that decides the course of Heinrich's life (199-202). Tracing succinctly the various stages of Heinrich's journey with his mother to her native town of Augsburg, Lichtenberger does not fail to emphasize that beneath the simple contours of this story may be glimpsed intimations of a higher realm in the various dreams, tales, and déja-vu experiences that punctuate the narrative. In such a context, it is only natural that the first part of the novel should conclude with a tale in which the realm of earthly reality gives way to that of mythological fiction. Drawing upon Fritz Strich's discussion of the Klingsohr tale in his voluminous study on mythology in German literature from Klopstock to Wagner (Strich 1910, 2: 62-70), Lichtenberger summarizes the message of this tale in one felicitous phrase as the triumph of magnetism over polarity and the arrival of the reign of unity (218).

In his treatment of the Klingsohr tale Spenlé had taken recourse largely to Novalis's interest in alchemy and cabalistic thinking. By way of contrast, Lichtenberger begins his interpretation of this tale by reminding his readers of the intense excitement generated by Galvani's experiments in animal electricity at the end of the eighteenth century, when thinkers such as Schelling saw in galvanism the vital force linking chemistry, electricity, and magnetism. In Schelling's system of natural philosophy, the One must divide in order to manifest itself, and so Novalis's tale opens with a polarity between spirit and nature; but as these two phenomena ultimately are one, so must not only such figures as Eros and Freya, Arctur and Sophie, but also the realms of heaven, earth, and the nether world be brought together by poetry in the conclusion

(218-21). In place of a final judgment on a tale praised by some critics and damned by others, Lichtenberger diplomatically observes that its allegorical nature might not be of sufficient taste to a French audience for it to become popular, but endeavors to show its place in the general plan of the novel, which was something that Spenlé had seen no sense in trying: in part two of *Heinrich von Ofterdingen*, the ties between "reality" (Heinrich's life) and "fiction" (the Klingsohr tale) become ever more intertwined (227-29). While Lichtenberger wonders whether *Heinrich von Ofterdingen*, here too like Nietzsche's *Zarathustra*, might not have remained a fragment even had its author lived longer, he regrets that Novalis did not have the chance to attempt the poetic realization of his grandiose plan (237-38). But it is principally thanks to Lichtenberger, building as he did on the individual insights of previous critics, that readers finally had the opportunity to appreciate *Heinrich von Ofterdingen* as a successful work of art even in its embryonic state. Novalis's observation that the true reader must be the extended author, through whom the raw material becomes a essential component of effective intellect (2: 470), receives an exemplary illustration in Lichtenberger's book, which still deserves consideration by anyone seeking insight into Novalis's work.

Francophone writers may have been at the forefront in promoting an international interest in Novalis, but they were by no means alone in their efforts. In the wake of Maeterlinck's work, in 1905 Giuseppe Prezzolini published an Italian translation of *Die Lehrlinge zu Sais* and selections from the fragments and *Die Christenheit oder Europa* in a series dedicated to poets and minor philosophers. By 1911 Novalis's prestige had increased so dramatically in Italy that Arturo Farinelli began the second of his introductory lectures on German Romanticism by referring to Novalis as a mystic and very great poet whose destiny he did not hesitate to compare to that of Dante's (Farinelli 1911, 37-41). Ludwig Tieck had already begun the practice of linking Novalis with Dante (4: 559), but such a statement gained greater authority when spoken by a established scholar of German, French, Spanish, and Italian literature. In 1914, readers of Italian had the opportunity to draw their own conclusions from such comparisons when the first Italian translation of *Heinrich von Ofterdingen* appeared in print.

In the bibliographic notes to his series of lectures, Farinelli had noted the lack of a profound and conscientious study dealing with *Heinrich von Ofterdingen* (159), which suggests that he was looking for a student of his to fill the gap. In any event, by 1916 Giovan Angelo Alfero had published *Novalis e il suo "Heinrich von Ofterdingen"* as the fourth volume in a series on modern literature edited by Farinelli. Alfero's tripartite study begins by providing a review of Novalis's life and thought before proceeding to a discussion of topics including Novalis's response to Goethe's *Wilhelm Meisters Lehrjahre*, the nature of romantic longing, Heinrich's journey, the birth of poetry upon his arrival in

Augsburg and his encounter with Klingsohr and Mathilde, and the advent of a new Golden Age in the second part of the novel. The concluding section of Alfero's work deals with more general considerations such as the relationship between "novel" and fairy tale, the characters and major motives of the novel, the New Mythology envisioned by the Romantic theorists and artists, and the function of the lyrical passages in *Heinrich von Ofterdingen*. Impressive in its careful consideration of previous scholarship, Alfero's study lacks any single distinguishing feature other than a peculiarly hermetic quality in its reflections. Indeed, considering that his book appeared in the midst of what was then the most ferocious and destructive war ever fought, it may at first seem surprising that Alfero neither criticizes what he understands to be Novalis's enthusiasm for the Crusades as a war of ideas (187-91) nor reflects on the capacity of propagandistic art like the bloodthirsty Crusading song (1: 231-33; 55-57) to inspire and justify all manner of atrocities, such as the fate suffered by the unfortunate Saracen maiden Zulima and her family at the hands of the marauding Crusaders (1: 235; 59). But in view of the hysteria for war that swept over all of Europe in 1914 and left traces even in the writings of authors like Thomas Mann and Robert Musil, Alfero's critical nearsightedness becomes all too symptomatic of an entire generation of European intellectuals.

The war years may have reduced the interest in German culture outside of central Europe, but some Novalis studies of note by German-speaking authors appeared during that time, such as Paula Scheidweiler's chapter on *Heinrich von Ofterdingen* in her book on the German Romantic novel. Interested in contrasts between the "plastic" depiction of the world in works of Goethe's Classical period and the "musical" evocation of feelings and sensations in the Romantic novel, Scheidweiler often extends the meaning of the term *musical* until it loses all concrete significance, as when she posits timelessness as the essential characteristic of the musical novel (Scheidweiler 1916, 71), though music is the art most dependent upon time and rhythm for its realization. Scheidweiler's belief in a fundamental dichotomy between Classicism and Romanticism causes her to interpret Novalis's extensive analyses of graduations in character among the figures in Goethe's *Wilhelm Meister* as another sign of a lack of interest in outward depictions in favor of inner feelings (58-59). But whenever Scheidweiler concentrates on textual analysis of *Heinrich von Ofterdingen*, she has new insights to bring, as when she points out how Zulima's song and ensuing praise of her native Arabia counteract the one-sided depiction of the Saracens by the Crusaders (64). Scheidweiler regards the juxtaposition of figures, scenes, and motives as a prime characteristic of Novalis's poetic style, and she makes a good case for her distinction between the terms *plastic* and *musical* — in their Schillerian and Hegelian sense — when she demonstrates how for the opening scene in part two of *Heinrich von Ofterdingen* Novalis rejected his comparatively detailed initial sketch of a mountain landscape for an evocation of Heinrich's inner desolation after the death of his beloved Mathilde, for which the landscape serves at best as an echo (81-82). At a time when the emerging critical school known as *Geistesgeschichte* favored increasingly more general schemes of interpreting literary movements — the term's literal translation as "history of the spirit" provides a far better indication of this movement's character than does its Anglo-American development as "intellectual history" — Scheidweiler's study illustrates both the potential pitfalls of such an approach and the benefits of close readings of literary texts.

Even more ambitious than Scheidweiler's book in its systematic aesthetics is *Die Theorie des Romans* first published by Georg Lukács in 1916, which draws on Hegel's distinction between the totality of the classical epic and the subjectivity of the modern novel and develops from it an entire philosophy of history. According to Lukács, the times are past when people felt at home in the world and expressed this in literature: he understands the "transcendental homelessness" (32) of modern society as finding its expression in the alienation between self and world that is the subject of so many novels from *Don Quixote* onward. This formulation — like the quote from Novalis on the opening page of *Die Theorie des Romans* defining philosophy as *Heimweh*, or longing for home (21) — indicates Lukács's familiarity with and affinity for the theoretical writings of the Early Romantics at this stage of his career. Indeed, the young Lukács had at one point intended to write a book on the philosophy of Friedrich Schlegel, and, like Schlegel, his initial response to war and turmoil throughout Europe was a turn toward aesthetics, not social praxis (for more information on the neo-Romantic roots of Lukácsian aesthetics, see Kruse-Fischer 1991).

In an essay on Novalis written in 1907 and published in 1911 as part of his essay collection *Die Seele und die Formen*, Lukács cites Schlegel's 216th *Athenäum*-Fragment on the French Revolution, Fichte's *Wissenschaftslehre* (Science of Knowledge, 1794-95), and Goethe's *Wilhelm Meister* as a concentrated expression of the greatness and the tragedy of German cultural developments: individuals who would have become tragic heroes in revolutionary France had recourse only to poetry in Germany (Lukács 1911, 21). In pronouncements that remind one of Robert Prutz and his judgment on the Romantics, Lukács describes Novalis as the one true poet of the Romantic school, able alone to turn life into poetry, and even this poetry was sufficient only for a beautiful death (34-35). Such interest in "life" and the person of the poet, as opposed to the poetic work itself, which receives not a single word of treatment in this essay, was characteristic of the neo-Romantic reception of Novalis in the first decade of the twentieth century; but the subordination of individual works to an overarching systematic construct is also evident in the theory of the novel that Lukács developed in the Hegelian, pre-Marxist phase of his thinking, as he confessed in the preface to its reissue in 1962 (6-8). In his attempt at a typology of the novel, Lukács distinguishes between those works featuring an abstract idealism in the main character, which could be treated in either a comic or a tragic fashion, and those novels in which the discrepancy between harsh reality and subjective inwardness becomes even more brutally and radically unmasked. As a possible synthesis between these two forms Lukács offers Goethe's *Wilhelm Meisters Lehrjahre* — that novel which Dilthey had understood as the classical Bildungsroman because of its depiction of the reconciliation of the individual with society and whose canonical importance had reached new heights in Wilhelmine Germany. In this sense it is ironic that Lukács, who wrote his essay as a protest against the chauvinistic patriotism of wartime German society, should pick as a model for aesthetic orientation precisely that work whose culturally affirmative significance had never been greater, as attested by Max Wundt's 1913 book on Goethe's *Wilhelm Meister* and the development of the modern ideal for living. In addition, like those nineteenth-century critics whose praise for *Wilhelm Meister* went hand in hand with a condemnation of *Heinrich von Ofterdingen*, Lukács includes in his typology of the novel a critique of Novalis's conscious attempt to reconcile world and individual through the medium of the fairy tale (124-26). This standpoint, which Lukács maintained and even accentuated in all future writings on Goethe, Novalis, and the Romantics, was to have a significantly dampening effect on orthodox Marxist interpretations of *Heinrich von Ofterdingen* well into the 1960s and 1970s.

Given the heightened interest in Goethe's *Wilhelm Meisters Lehrjahre* in the early twentieth century, it is not surprising that Lukács was only one of many literary scholars who once again turned their attention to Novalis's remarks on this novel, now available in more philologically correct form in the Novalis editions supplied by Heilborn in 1901 and Jakob Minor in 1907. In 1911 Georg Gloege categorically denied the influence of Goethe's novel on *Heinrich von Ofterdingen*, and in 1914 Käte Woltereck emphatically maintained it, but neither of them provided any essentially new insights into the interrelationship between these two works. Oskar Walzel did this in his investigation "Die Formkunst von Hardenbergs *Heinrich von Ofterdingen*," which appeared in 1919, after the end of the First World War and the resumption of the recently founded *Germanisch-romanische Monatsschrift*. Walzel's persistent use of the name Hardenberg, as opposed to the poetic pseudonym Novalis, in his analysis of the formal artistry of *Heinrich von Ofterdingen* is indicative of a major shift of emphasis in his study. Rather than entering into a renewed discussion of the mystical world view of "Novalis," Walzel attempts to break through old clichés by looking at the poet's notebooks in their original wording — as opposed to their heavily manipulated form in the Tieck and Schlegel editions — for clues to the poetological considerations determining the composition of *Heinrich von Ofterdingen*. Thanks to the expanded, improved edi-

tions initiated by Heilborn and Minor, the popular image of Novalis as moon-
struck poet no longer enjoyed a philological basis, but it remained for Walzel
to demonstrate the remarkable extent to which *Heinrich von Ofterdingen*, the
archetype of the German Romantic novel, was the product of extensive study
and calculation.

Walzel begins by taking a fresh look at Hardenberg's notebook sketches for
part two of *Heinrich von Ofterdingen* and ascertaining that Tieck had carelessly
combined them for purposes of his own construction of how the novel would
have continued (Walzel 1919, 36-38). This might seem a minor observation
had it not to do with one of the most hotly contested controversies in Novalis
scholarship since the writings of Dilthey, Haym, and Schmidt: namely
whether or not Novalis's linkage of characters from the novel with the inter-
woven tales and the uncanny resemblances between persons from parts one and
two of the novel signified his belief in a metaphysical union and transmigration
of souls. Walzel shifts the focus of the entire debate by arguing that state-
memts like "Klingsohr ist der König von Atlantis. Heinrichs Mutter ist Fanta-
sie. Der Vater ist der Sinn" (1: 342) correspond grammatically and functionally
with Hardenberg's extensive analyses of the configuration of characters in
Wilhelm Meisters Lehrjahre (3: 312); in other words, in his own novel Hardenberg consciously applied the technique of variation of characters that he believed to have discovered in Goethe's work. While not claiming that this
discovery makes irrelevant a discussion of how to interpret the technique, Walzel contends that a good portion of the interrelationships between characters in
Heinrich von Ofterdingen needs to be understood as a matter of artistry rather
than of worldview (Walzel, 42-45). Haym had led the way in investigating
formal similarities between the two novels, but his understanding of Novalis as
an overly introspective individual had prevented him from pursuing the matter
very far, whereas Walzel could cite the newly available Goethe essay that had
been plucked apart by Tieck and von Bülow in which Novalis praised not only
praised Goethe's sense of form but also his powers of observation and his de-
scriptive abilities as a natural scientist (2: 640-42); as a result, Walzel shows a
rational, scientific side to Novalis that the more serious critics had come to
realize was true of his character in everyday life but that many people had been
unable to recognize in the artist.

While not neglecting to cite Novalis's familiar reproaches against *Wilhelm
Meister*, Walzel observes that they were written during the first stage of work
on *Heinrich von Ofterdingen* and in that regard could be understood as the
author's attempt to free himself from a revered model in order to be able to
produce his own work, even while continuing to gain from years of careful
study of an artistic predecessor. In this regard, Walzel draws attention to the
same antithetical arrangement of characters and sequences that Scheidweiler
had discussed in her treatment of *Heinrich von Ofterdingen*, and he traces them

also back to Hardenberg's notes on *Wilhelm Meister* (49-53). In fact, in the third section of his study, Walzel provides an analysis of *Heinrich von Ofterdingen* in terms of its "musical" composition — a wording that Friedrich Schlegel had employed in his masterful essay on Goethe's novel. Here too, though, one observes the difference between a conscientious and a masterful treatment of the same notion. Referring back to Spenlé's discussion of musical aspects of Novalis's art of psychic dynamism, Walzel notes that precisely because Novalis strove for musical effects in his poetry he also took care to exercise a particularly careful control over his arrangements of words, sentences, chapter divisions, and entire parts of *Heinrich von Ofterdingen* (74-75). Walzel proceeds to demonstrate these assertions in detail. Without disputing the major differences in outlook between Goethe and Novalis in their respective novels, he establishes the great extent to which the simplicity of style in *Heinrich von Ofterdingen* was the result of its author's extensive and exacting analysis of *Wilhelm Meisters Lehrjahre*, and he thereby initiates a new and important direction in Novalis scholarship, the form studies of *Ofterdingen* that continued well into the 1970s.

In 1919, Walzel's student Walter Benjamin wrote a doctoral dissertation on the concept of artistic criticism in German Romanticism that demonstrated the philosophical foundations of the aesthetic thinking of Friedrich Schlegel and Novalis. In the early 1920s there was another dissertation by an author who today is best known for his idiosyncratic approach to Marxism and cultural theory but whose training had prepared him for a career as a professor of literature, until the increasing anti-Semitic bias of German academia obliged him to explore more unorthodox paths of scholarly work. Herbert Marcuse's 1922 doctoral thesis at the University of Freiburg, where he later became an assistant under Martin Heidegger, has to do with the Künstlerroman, or novel about artists. Building on key ideas from Hegel and Lukács in determining why the artist should become so prevalent and so problematic a figure in German novels from the late eighteenth century to Thomas Mann, Marcuse also remains remarkably independent of their normative aesthetics in his analyses of individual novels; in fact, one is tempted to discern a foreshadowing of his later pronounced opposition to "One Dimensional Man" and sympathy for the student rebels of the 1960s in his interest in marginal heroes, whose longing for art signifies an estrangement from their self-satisfied surroundings (for further information on Benjamin and Marcuse, see Jay 1973).

Though he notes Scheidweiler's remarks on Novalis's admiration for the form of *Wilhelm Meister*, Marcuse chooses to concentrate his attention on Novalis's reversal of that novel's dialectical direction, in which Heinrich's role as artist is to dissolve the ossified, illusory polarities of the real world and to restore the Golden Age whose latent presence humanity needs only to recognize (Marcuse 1922, 110-11). Just as Novalis pursued an "unartistic" career as a mining engineer with diligence and devotion, so too his hero has the task of making manifest in all walks of life the world of wonder that he first glimpsed in his dream; thus Heinrich neither literally nor figurally disappears over the hills but rather penetrates into the mountain with the help of the miner and discovers the presence of the eternal within earthly reality (114-15). Even the experience of the death of his beloved Mathilde does not rob him of hope; it reveals to him that while we will never fully possess the ideal world of our dreams — hitherto one of the greatest problems of the artist — we are always proceeding in that direction. In his explication of the most famous quote from *Heinrich von Ofterdingen* — "Immer nach Hause" (always homeward bound; 1: 325; 159) — Marcuse himself becomes almost poetic in his differentiation of Novalis's marvelous poetic certitude from the restless longing of other Romantic artists (119). Marcuse maintains that Novalis achieves in *Ofterdingen* the same level of thematic resolution that Goethe does *Wilhelm Meisters Lehrjahre*, although in the one case reality triumphs over the protagonist's dreams of artistic longing and in the other the ideal world becomes reality (120). Marcuse's sympathetic yet evenhanded treatment contrasts favorably with the comparison offered by Lukács, for whom — as in his future decisions for Thomas Mann in favor of Kafka or for "realism" as opposed to expressionism — there could be only one choice. For this reason it is regrettable that Marcuse's dissertation went unnoticed by other scholars and was not published until 1978, as part of the philosopher's complete writings.

Another work from the year 1922 — and one that rightly received immediate recognition — was Paul Kluckhohn's magisterial survey of the concept of love in the literature of the eighteenth century and German Romanticism. Kluckhohn maintains that the ideas of German thinkers at the end of the eighteenth century cannot be properly appreciated unless one understands the intellectual context from which they developed, so he devotes the first two chapters of his work to a discussion of the concept of love in England and France during the Enlightenment before turning to a discussion of specifically German developments. But as Dilthey's concept of *Erlebnis*, or experience, plays the principal role in determining Kluckhohn's exploration of how writers and thinkers came to their personal understanding of love, it is not surprising that he allots the first half of his lengthy treatment of Novalis to the poet's experiences with Sophie von Kühn and his second fiancée Julie von Charpentier (464-91) and only then proceeds to an exploration of areas in which previous and contemporary writers had been of importance to Novalis (491-511). Kluckhohn understands *Heinrich von Ofterdingen* primarily as a symbolic depiction of Novalis's inner development. For this reason he chooses to emphasize the biographical foundations of the Klingsohr tale, as expressed in the concern Novalis voiced in a letter to his friend Just that Sophie's death might cause his intellect to tyrannize over the heart (476-77) — even though in this same letter of March 29, 1797, Novalis also speaks of a renewed interest in the sciences from what he terms a higher viewpoint (4: 215). It was perhaps inevitable that the force of Dilthey's fundamental distinction between the human and the natural sciences made it almost impossible for Kluckhohn even to consider possible links between "love" and "science" in Novalis's thought, but this blind spot in a scholar whose significance in the development of Novalis scholarship in the twentieth century is incontestable indicates how the self-imposed limits of a critical methodology served to curtail its own goal of studying individual thought within a greater intellectual context.

This shortcoming, however, does not negate the considerable merits of Kluckhohn's study, among which are his linking of the erotic components of the Klingsohr tale with ideas in Hardenberg's notebooks (478) that he ascribed to the writings of Jakob Böhme and other mystics and theosophists (498-99). In his 1922 dissertation on the influence of Jakob Böhme on Novalis, Walter Feilchenfeld had observed the presence of images derived from Böhme beginning in the fifth chapter of *Heinrich von Ofterdingen*, only to confess ultimately that what he regarded as Böhmean in nature also could be found in Novalis's thoughts and writings prior to *Ofterdingen* (74-75). In contrast to this study of "influences," Kluckhohn devotes more space to interpretation of the relevant passages in Novalis's own work, and often with significant results, as when he observes that in their initial encounter Heinrich and Mathilde display their inner affinity for one another through gestures, not words, and that their mutual declaration of love emphasizes the ideal being that each of them sees shining through the other's features (Kluckhohn, 480). Kluckhohn's intimate familiarity with Novalis's thoughts and writings enables him to interpret this scene with the help of the *Blüthenstaub* (Pollen) fragment in which Novalis developed a theory of the necessity of a mediator to link us with divinity (483-84; 2: 441-45). In this regard Kluckhohn makes a significant contribution to advancing the understanding of the internal coherence of Novalis's thoughts and poetry. An example of *Geistesgeschichte* at its best, Kluckhohn's study also signaled that German literary scholarship was rapidly becoming synonymous with studies of German Romanticism, which made up the latter half of this particular work.

The cultural prestige now accorded Novalis and his Romantic contemporaries may be gauged in Thomas Mann's attempt to use Novalis's political writings as a proof for the contention in his October 15, 1922, speech, "Von deutscher Republik" (On a German Republic), that a heritage of democratic thought did exist in Germany; but equally significant was the disappointed reaction by conservative scholars, who until then had regarded not only Novalis but also Mann as belonging to their ideological camp (see Reiss 1987). Whereas the June 24, 1922 assassination of Walter Rathenau, the German Jewish industrialist who had become foreign minister of the Weimar Republic, shocked Mann into a proclamation of loyalty to the struggling republic, in his essays on Hölderlin and Novalis Karl Justus Obenauer continued to stress the alleged dichotomy between an overintellectualized Western "civilization" and a German "culture" of poets and visionaries (Obenauer 1925, 85-90) that Thomas Mann had postulated in his wartime essays and the *Betrachtungen eines Unpolitischen* (Observations of an Unpolitical Person, 1918). Not that Obenauer necessarily regarded Novalis as the paragon of German manhood; on the contrary, in his essay on the Blue Flower Obenauer criticizes the images of water and fluidity in Novalis's writings as symptomatic of what he terms a lack of masculine firmness and fortitude in the writer's Romantic soul, which could feel at home only in the boundless fluidity of its dream world (112-13). On the other hand, Obenauer finds in Novalis's dreams and fairy tales an expression of cosmic unity that he contrasts positively with the psychological interpretation of dreams as repressed and primitive eroticism (271-72). Obenauer glosses over the erotic components of these same tales and dreams as quickly as possible. As interesting and useful as his interpretation of the astral myths in the opening section of the Klingsohr tale may be (245-54), his attempts to give it a chaste, "Christian" interpretation necessitate serious misreadings of plot elements, as when he assigns Novalis's transformation of the tale of Cupid and Psyche to Eros and Freya (245) rather than to Eros and Ginnistan, who seduces Eros in the course of his search for his beloved.

Given the nationalistic and irrationalist tendencies in Obenauer's writings in the mid-1920s, it is hardly surprising that during the Nazi years it was he who as dean of the philosophical faculty at the University of Bonn took away the honorary doctorate bestowed on Thomas Mann because of the latter's allegedly unpatriotic criticism of the Nazi regime (Schulz 1986, xiv-xv). But even the sober and scholarly treatises on Friedrich von Hardenberg's theories of the state and history that Paul Kluckhohn and his future coeditor Richard Samuel published in 1925 exhibit signs of the prevailing trend to claim Novalis as an ancestor of the Conservative Revolution of the 1920s. In Samuel's brief discussion of the depiction of the Middle Ages in *Heinrich von Ofterdingen*, he is principally concerned with demonstrating how Novalis idealized this period, including the Crusades, in the style of a medieval legend, and he wonders aloud why the Crusades had not been the midpoint of Novalis's essay *Die Christenheit oder Europa* (262-72; for a discussion of Novalis and his conservative reception, see Kurzke 1983 and Uerlings 1991, 523-41). Julius Petersen, Samuel's doctoral advisor, further illustrates the symptomatic nature of such developments in a lecture held in November 1924 in which he claims that present-day man, while no Romantic himself, possesses characteristics such as anti-intellectualism and an opposition to rationalism, mechanism, and materialism that signal an essential affinity with Romanticism (Petersen 1926, 2-3). When one considers that Petersen was no unknown figure but rather the occupant of the prestigious chair in German literature at the University of Berlin, the increasingly reactionary character of academic German scholarship becomes evident. But even Petersen's words were mild compared with Alfred Bäumler's evocation of the cult of blood and soil he discerns in the writings of the Heidelberg Romantics and finds wanting in Jena Romantics like Friedrich Schlegel and Novalis, who for him represent the end of the eighteenth century, not the beginning of a new age. It speaks well once again for Thomas Mann that he reacted immediately to Bäumler's words by asking whether it was a good idea to propagate values such as earth, folk, nature, the past, and death as if they were the wave of the future. Bäumler provided an answer to this question by becoming one of the most prominent academic proponents of Nazism; hardly had he given his inaugural lecture as professor of political education in Berlin when he marched with his students to the May 1933 bookburning ceremony at the university (Bäumler 1926, clxvii-clxxi; Mann 1926, 11: 48; see also Conrady 1967, 102-3 and Ritchie 1983, 68).

Despite such disturbing developments, scholarship on Novalis during the final years of the Weimar Republic continued to build upon the advances of the preceding decades. In a volume entitled *Romantik-Forschungen* (Romantic Research, 1929) that also included significant studies on Novalis by Käte Hamburger, Richard Samuel, and Benno von Wiese in the respective areas of mathematics and philosophy, biography, and religion, Kurt May furthered the tradition established by Oskar Walzel by calling into question the distinction between Classicism and Romanticism as represented by *Wilhelm Meisters Lehrjahre* and *Heinrich von Ofterdingen*; indeed, May goes so far as to suggest that with respect to form Novalis's novel is even more perfect than that of Goethe, in that the conclusion to *Ofterdingen* is visible from the start and becomes increasingly more evident, whereas Wilhelm Meister's years of apprenticeship end on a note of uncertainty that requires clarification in a further novel (170-72). Rather than remaining within the typological polarities proposed by Scheidweiler and Strich, May alludes to the Goethean poetics expressed by the figure of Klingsohr and concludes his essay by wondering whether German Romanticism originated less as an antithesis to Goethean Classicism than as an attempt at a greater synthesis (175-77) — an idea that Hermann Korff was to develop in depth in his multivolume opus on *Der Geist der Goethezeit* (The Spirit of the Age of Goethe).

Also in 1929, Kluckhohn and Samuel published a four-volume edition of Novalis that further responded to Heilborn's call for a chronological arrangement of the greatest available number of fragments and studies; it also contained an expanded volume of letters, diaries, and biographical documents for which Richard Samuel supplied the commentary. In addition, Kluckhohn contributed an introductory essay on Friedrich von Hardenberg's development and poetry that Samuel later reprinted in the historical-critical edition of Novalis with only slight modifications and corrections. A definite product of its times, Kluckhohn's essay shares the same essential presuppositions as his earlier remarks on Novalis. With regard to *Heinrich von Ofterdingen*, like Spenlé some twenty-five years before him Kluckhohn discusses the Klingsohr tale separately and argues that it was composed before other parts of the novel — a contention made untenable by subsequently discovered drafts of this tale. Kluckhohn's designation of its ideas as partially frozen into allegory also suggests an adherence to the Goethean concept of symbol that permits him to accept the tale only to the extent that it reflects the personal experiences of its author or can be understood as a eschatological prophecy reflecting the divinatory powers of the poet (*Schriften* 1: 53-54). And Kluckhohn's sharp distinction between the poet and the scientist or philosopher and his continuing emphasis on the *Sophienerlebnis* as the key incident in Novalis's life serve to perpetuate in more subtle form the neo-Romantic clichés about Novalis from the turn of the century (see Uerlings 1991, 83-84). On the other hand, in his demonstration of how the short, simple sentences and the plentitude of adjectives beginning with *un-* or *wunder-* reflect not a poverty of resources but rather a conscious attempt to weave a spell on the reader (*Schriften* 1: 60-61), Kluckhohn paves the way for the investigations of the language, structure, and style of *Heinrich von Ofterdingen* later conducted by Wolfgang Kayser and Richard Samuel.

In 1931 Jutta Hecker published her Munich dissertation from the previous year on the symbol of the Blue Flower in its Romantic context as well as its post-Romantic reception. Maintaining that it is mistaken to search for a botanical model for this flower, she points instead to such possible sources of inspiration as the saga of the flower on the Kyffhäuser (to which the dream of Heinrich's father alludes); a dream flower in Jean Paul's first novel, *Die unsichtbare Loge* (The Invisible Lodge, 1793); and similar mystical flowers in Tieck's dramatic scene "Die Sommernacht" (The Summer Night) and his allegorical poem "Der Traum" (The Dream). As for its color, she alludes to the blue haze of mountains in the distance, the color of the sky, and Goethe's later description of the restless longing this color produces upon the human psyche. But Hecker devotes only a few pages to a discussion of the actual function of the Blue Flower in the novel itself. Once again, the idea that poetry is the product of *Erlebnis* and can best be appreciated in an awe-filled reliving of this original experience provides a barrier to understanding.

Of considerably greater subtlety than Hecker's thorough but not profound study was the investigation of Novalis's allegorical fairy tales that Max Diez, a professor of German at Bryn Mawr College, included in the eight-article series "Metapher und Märchengestalt" (Metaphor and the Fairy-Tale Form), which appeared in the 1933 issues of *PMLA*. Unlike Kluckhohn, Hecker, and scholars before them, Diez considers allegory not inferior to the symbol but rather a particular variant of the combination of image and thought contained within each metaphor. In his discussion of figures from the Klingsohr tale, he pays particular attention to Freya, Fabel, and the Scribe. Whereas this latter figure's attributes move him from a human dimension to the plane of despotic abstract reason that typifies his nature, a multivalence of metaphors associates Freya in unceasing combinations with the notions of goddess, longing, peace, maiden, and natural phenomena such as galvanism and magnetism (143-51). Of similar fundamental importance for an understanding of the Klingsohr tale is Diez's discussion of Fabel's metaphorical genealogy, childlike wisdom, successful combat of the Scribe's machinations, and function as a exemplification of Heinrich's poetological conversations with Klingsohr and Sylvester on either side of this tale. At a time when the exodus of artists and intellectuals from Nazi Germany had already begun, the publication of this article by Max Diez in an American scholarly journal was a fortuitous sign that the suppression of reason in one country did not spell its extirpation everywhere.

Just as one cannot say that the Weimar Republic ended with Hitler's chancellorship in January 1933 — the death agony of democracy had begun earlier and continued well into the 1930s before the Nazis had established total control over German society — so too no fundamental change in Novalis scholarship suddenly occurred in 1933. But there is enough correlation between politics and scholarship to warrant a separate chapter on the reception of *Heinrich von Ofterdingen* during the darkest years of German history.

4: Dark Times for Freya — 1933-1945

IN THE KLINGSOHR tale, the onset of the long night of darkness in the heavens is signaled by the separation of Sophie, or wisdom, from the ruler of a frozen realm, whose daughter Freya — apostrophized at various points throughout the story as peace and longing — awaits her delivery through the arrival of Eros, her prince and lover. Critics such as Karl Justus Obenauer had made much of the figure of the Scribe in this tale as representative of an Enlightenment at war with true German culture. With Hitler's accession to the chancellorship in January of 1933 and his rapid acquisition of dictatorial powers in the wake of the Reichstag fire, it should have been clear to Germans of all walks of life that the real threat to German culture came from a rabidly irrational and militaristic ideology that vaunted its alleged Aryan supremacy. Among the professorial class, however, the prevailing response to Nazism was acquiescence, compliance, or even enthusiastic support, and scholars writing on Novalis and *Heinrich von Ofterdingen* proved no exception to this general rule. The worst excesses of Nazi "scholarship" are to be found elsewhere; an esoteric work like *Heinrich von Ofterdingen* was largely impermeable to the type of ideological *Gleichschaltung* (coordination) practiced on the writings of Goethe, Schiller, and Hölderlin (see Zeller 1983). But a survey of those instances in which German academic critics discuss Novalis documents a disturbing and often debasing readiness to howl with the singularly ignoble wolves of National Socialism.

Hardly had Julius Petersen returned to the University of Berlin in the fall of 1933 from a guest professorship at Columbia University when he assumed coeditorship of the newly renamed journal *Dichtung und Volkstum* (Poetry and Nationality). It was symptomatic of the times that Petersen, who was also the president of the Goethe Society, would sign his name to an editorial statement describing the earlier title *Euphorion* as signifying the overemphasized dependence of German culture on humanistic learning now being replaced by literary learning in service to the Folk. But whereas Novalis brought together Eros and Freya — the Greek and the Norse deities of love — at the conclusion of his tale of the marriage of heaven and earth, and Goethe's Euphorion had Faust and Helen of Troy as his parents, Petersen's 1934 essay in *Dichtung und Volkstum* on the longings for the Third Reich in German legend and poetry represents the offspring of scholarship and servility. After commenting on the recent use of the term *Third Reich* by writers such as Moeller van den Bruck and Spengler, Petersen traces the mythical, religious, imperial, humanistic, economic, and social history of the term in a lengthy two-part essay that posits National Socialism as the culmination and realization of these age-old longings. Throughout his essay, Petersen seems to have succumbed to what he claims to find in Novalis's theory and practice of poetic representation, namely a magical idealism that attempts to pass off its dreams and visions as existing reality (160). Such is his interpretation of the Klingsohr tale as a prelude to the realization of hopes for a kingdom of poetry, love, and freedom planned for the second half of *Heinrich von Ofterdingen*. Not only does Petersen overlook the obvious fact that the depicted "fulfillment" of such expectations would have remained "expectation" for its readers; his linkage of such dreams to the present-day Third Reich also suggests a profound inability to recognize reality as it was developing around him. His fellow editor Hermann Pongs displayed a better premonition of things to come in his own two-part contribution to the premiere issue of *Dichtung und Volkstum*, which bears the title "Krieg als Volksschicksal im deutschen Schrifttum" (War as the Fate of the Folk in German Writing), opens with a quote by Joseph Goebbels, and frequently cites Hölderlin as the poet who glorifies death on the battlefield. When one considers that ever since the 1840s critics frequently had mentioned Hölderlin and Novalis in one breath, it is instructive that during the Nazi years Novalis's poetry proved decidedly more resistant to such ideological manipulation.

At a May 28, 1933, commemoration of the ninetieth anniversary of Hölderlin's death, Paul Kluckhohn — by this time a professor at the University of Tübingen — stressed that the idea of a united people was once again alive in Germany and that an inner spiritualization as evoked by Hölderlin should accompany the outward rebuilding of a German fatherland (cited in Zeller 1983, 1: 80). As coeditor of the highly regarded *Deutsche Vierteljahrschrift für Literaturwissenschaft und Geistesgeschichte* (German Quarterly for Literary Studies and Intellectual History), Kluckhohn also published an article on the social responsibility of the German poet throughout the ages as a summation of his courses on this theme at Tübingen. For Kluckhohn it is Hölderlin who incorporates most purely the ethos of poetic responsibility and service to the people, but after Hölderlin he sees Romantics such as Novalis and Friedrich Schlegel coming closest to this same ideal of the poet (Kluckhohn 1936, 13). In Kluckhohn's view, Novalis regards poets as priests and magicians, guides and interpreters through life.

At first it may appear a matter of oversensitivity based on hindsight to stress Kluckhohn's choice of the word *Führer* to describe the type of leader Heinrich von Ofterdingen was destined to become in the second part of the novel (14). After all, in 1928 Max Kommerell had published a book entitled *Der Dichter als Führer in der deutschen Klassik* (The Poet as Leader in German Classicism) that promoted Stefan George's notion of the poet as prophetic visionary, and Kluckhohn had described Novalis in similar words that same year in the introduction to his edition of the poet's works. But an examination of the names Kluckhohn now lists as "responsible" poets of the present age indicates how his understanding of the role of the poet — which seems harmless enough, albeit overly effusive, when applied to writers like Hölderlin and Novalis — becomes deeply suspect once he links it to archconservative, reactionary, and even openly fascistic writers like Paul Ernst, Hans Grimm, Erwin Guido Kolbenheyer, Hanns Johst, and Will Vesper or welcomes the new opportunities now provided for public choral recitation (25-29). At a time when the Nazi Party rallies were already amply demonstrating what Walter Benjamin was to call the aesthetization of politics, Kluckhohn's apotheosis of the socially committed poet of the present transgresses the merely naive and approaches the reprehensible.

At the conclusion of a lengthy report in *Dichtung und Volkstum* on recent publications dealing with Romanticism, Benno von Wiese asks whether the affinity between Thomas Mann and (Early) Romanticism discerned by Käte Hamburger in her 1932 monograph on this subject does not confirm Alfred Bäumler's hypothesis that Early Romanticism was the end of an era and not the beginning of another. He goes on to suggest that both Mann and the Jena Romantics are part of a history of Western decadence in which individualistic, self-gratifying art represents the final medium for understanding life, as opposed to a specifically German Romanticism that progresses through art to a grasp of fate, myth, and community (Wiese 1937, 84). Considering that in 1936 Thomas Mann had been stripped both of his German citizenship and of his honorary doctorate from the University of Bonn, Benno von Wiese's opportunistic remark also indicates the relative disfavor accorded the Early Romantics during the Nazi era. In the sixteenth edition of the history of German literature by Adolf Bartels, whose foreword closes with a May 1, 1937, statement from Hitler awarding Bartels the Eagle Emblem of the German Reich for his work as crusader for racial and cultural renewal (ix), Bartels likewise discerns an air of decadence among the Early Romantics, which he contrasts unfavorably with what he considers the truly Romantic German youth after 1806 (Bartels 1937, 229), and deplores the presence of clever young Berlin Jewesses in this circle (242); already in the 1919 edition to his work he had described the participation of Rahel Varnhagen and Dorothea Veit-Schlegel in the discussions of the Early Romantics as the beginning of an unbroken and often highly dangerous influence of Judaism upon German poetry. But as for Novalis, the vaguely worded, mild appreciation of *Heinrich von Ofterdingen* from earlier editions also remains unchanged: apparently Novalis's life and poetry had been sufficiently mythicized in previous decades to shield them from Bartel's criticism and comprehension alike.

In the fourth, revised edition of his literary history of the German people, Josef Nadler provides an explanation of the difference between Friedrich von Hardenberg and the intellectualizing Schlegel brothers: thanks to his inherited eastern German mystical traits, Hardenberg articulated a vision of folk rebirth in *Die Christenheit oder Europa* that dismayed the Schlegels when they first read this essay. Likewise, when Nadler discusses the importance of Abraham Gottlob Werner, Novalis's teacher in geology at the Mining Academy of Freiberg, he suggests that it is not Werner's scientific knowledge, but rather his mystical affinity with rocks and minerals that helped raise his student above and beyond Friedrich Schlegel (Nadler 1938, 2: 378-84). In her discussion of Nadler's undertaking, Gisela von Busse correctly observes that for Nadler, poetic works such as *Heinrich von Ofterdingen* are incidental to an understanding of Novalis and Romanticism; rather it is the place of origin that determines the nature of a writer (Busse 1938, 265). Nadler had been developing his idea of a literary history of Germany organized according to regional and tribal subdivisions since 1912, but its affinity to the "blood and soil" ideology of the Nazis was apparent; nor was it coincidental that Nadler gave the title *Reich* to the concluding volume of this fourth edition, covering the years 1914-1938.

The third volume of another massive literary history, Hermann August Korff's *Geist der Goethezeit* (Spirit of the Age of Goethe), appeared in 1940, but this was a work begun during the heyday of *Geistesgeschichte*" in the 1920s that continued with only marginal concessions to the "spirit" of the Age of Hitler. In the preface to the second edition, published in 1949 under the license of the Soviet military administration, Korff speaks of the nearly unaltered republication of the original volume. While it is technically correct, Korff's statement elegantly evades mention of his June 1940 dedication of this volume to "Den Helden unseres Freiheitskampfes" (the heroes of our war of liberation), his citation of a stanza from Hölderlin's ode "Der Tod fürs Vaterland" (Death for the Fatherland), and his explicit linkage of the German capture of Paris to the day on which he ended writing this earlier preface (see Zeller 1983, 1: 292). Such details exhibit both Korff's attempted actualization of German Romanticism and the refusal to admit that there might be material differences between the wars of the Napoleonic period and contemporary German aggression against France.

In his interpretations of literary works, Korff proceeds with a Hegelian notion of thesis, antithesis, and synthesis that interprets the German Classicism of Goethe and Schiller as the reaction to their "Sturm und Drang" (Storm and Stress) period and German Romanticism as the result of a second generation of poets in the Age of Goethe who brought to a higher level the achievements of their somewhat older contemporaries. Korff regards Hölderlin, Tieck, and Novalis as the three most significant poets of the Early Romantic period, with Hölderlin representing a Romantic Classicism, Tieck the emergence of the Romantic world, and Novalis the culmination of Early Romanticism in the realms of the Blue Flower: nature, night, Christ, and poetry. In many respects Korff's discussion of Novalis resembles that of Dilthey and Haym from the previous century, with an understanding of *Heinrich von Ofterdingen* as a dreamlike novel taking place in a fairy-tale Middle Ages in which the Golden Age is not sought but rather already found (589). In his emphasis on the fairy-tale nature of the novel, Korff regards everything that does not pertain to this conception, such as the many philosophical conversations, as a break in style (595). He nowhere refers to the work of any critical predecessors, and his interpretations of the words of Astralis and the constellation of figures in the novel could have benefited from the insights already provided by scholars such as Bing and Walzel. But in his discussion of the Klingsohr tale Korff does not fail to include the now familiar notion of the Enlightenment and so-called civilization as the eternal enemy of Romanticism and poetry, which however is predestined to be overcome by fate's decree; the figures of the fairy tale carry out the roles already written out for them in the stars, and the redeeming kiss that Eros gives Freya is merely the final stage of a set ceremony (619-20). Korff maintains that it is this feeling for a supernatural, transrational unity of life that characterizes the essence of Romanticism and the poetic purpose of *Heinrich von Ofterdingen*. In such an interpretation, any aspects of the novel that might remind one of rationality and calculation disappear in a mystic mist. Korff arrives at a positive evaluation of the novel by discerning in it all the elements that Bäumler had claimed were foreign to the work of Novalis. As Korff's work was to have near-canonic importance among students and scholars alike for decades after its appearance, this "rescue" of Novalis was in many ways a mixed blessing, as it codified in authoritative and readable form almost every imaginable cliché about Novalis and Romanticism. In considering the allergic reaction of East German Marxist critics to Romanticism after 1945, one should not forget that in large part they were responding to the images that scholars like Korff had articulated.

It would be an injustice, however, to dismiss all scholarship written in Germany during the Nazi years. In his edition of Novalis research for the *Wege der Forschung* (Paths of Research) series, Gerhard Schulz includes Max Kommerell's 1942 essay on the *Hymnen an die Nacht*, calling it not only the most significant work ever written on these poems but also an expression of Kommerell's "inner emigration" following the painful recognition that poetry was not an ordering force for his own day and age (Schulz 1986, xvii). While not on the same high plane as Kommerell's essay, Albert Reble's "Märchen und Wirklichkeit bei Novalis" (Fairy Tale and Reality in the Work of Novalis) is a solid piece of scholarship that explicates Novalis's poetics of the fairy tale by elaborating on theoretical observations contained in the Kluckhohn and Samuel edition of 1929 and also demonstrating the intricate interplay between the fairy tales in *Heinrich von Ofterdingen* and Heinrich's journey into the depths of his inner being. Alluding to an editorial remark by Kluckhohn, Reble cites the text of a letter Novalis wrote immediately after the death of his fiancée Sophie von Kühn in which expressed the fear that this loss might cause his reason to exterminate the heart that Sophie had restored to its proper place within

him (4: 215; Reble 1941, 103-4). By emphasizing the personal mythology Novalis built into the Klingsohr tale, Reble provides a counterpoint to those interpretations in which the Scribe is demonized as a representative of mechanis-
tic Enlightenment science and philosophy; as soon as one realizes that Novalis
saw the Scribe as being very much a part of himself, the tale takes on a more
complex individual as well as universal significance.

It may seem like faint praise to emphasize that in his footnotes Reble gives
due recognition to the work of previous scholars such as Richard Samuel and
Fritz Strich, but one must consider that this essay appeared in 1941, when
German Jews were required to wear a yellow star of David as a sign of their
rapidly increasing ostracization from their place of birth. The "scholarly"
equivalent of this vicious practice can be found, of all places, in the published
version of a Tübingen dissertation by Irmtrud von Minnigerode on the view of
Christ in the works of Novalis, where the following remark appears at the beginning of the bibliography: "Die mit einem * versehenen Namen weisen auf
die nichtarische Abstammung des Verfassers hin" (The names marked with an
* designate the non-Aryan descent of the author) (Minnigerode 1941, 126).
One can only wonder how Minnigerode and the series editors, Ernst Benz and
Erich Seeburg, could have accepted such a practice in a series dedicated to religious and church history without at least stipulating that an asterisk be placed
in the text each time after the word *Christ*. It is only slight comfort to realize
that today the intended infamy does not rest on the names of scholars such as
Richard Samuel and Käte Hamburger, whose timely emigration saved them
from the death met by millions of innocent victims of Nazism, but rather on
those who initiated and tolerated such practices.

In the preface to his 1942 edition of selections on wisdom and love from
the writings of Novalis, Waldemar Bonsels provides his explanation of why it
is necessary for good Germans to recognize from afar the dangers that Jewish
writers and critics present. Bonsels turns what at first sounds like praise of Judaism's three thousand years of history as a people, compared with the relatively recent development of the German language and culture, into a
confrontation between an old, overly sharp Jewish intellect and the mysterious,
inchoate forces still evolving in the soul of a young people like the Germans.
With respect to Novalis and Romanticism, he charges Heinrich Heine as being the skeptical, negative critic who first drew Novalis and Romanticism into
the backwaters of sensationalistic intellectuality and so attempted to poison the
movement whose source Novalis guarded so passionately; as one might expect,
Bonsels sees the German *Gemüt* (soul) shining through the writings of Novalis
as proof that the poetic preservation of true sentiment is a manly responsibility
(10-18). At a time when German soldiers went into battle with government-
issue editions of Hölderlin's poetry, Bonsels no doubt understood his own
compilation as a spiritual contribution to the war effort; in any case he did not
fail to include snippets from Klingsohr's and Heinrich's remarks from chapter

eight of *Heinrich von Ofterdingen*, in which war is described as a poetic incitement for creation out of chaos (70-71). By 1943 this edition had already gone through a third printing, and Bonsels promised a companion volume containing a more complete discussion of the life of Novalis together with the best of his lyric and epic works. One can only be glad that such a volume was never published, as opposed to Ewald Wasmuth's 1943 edition of Novalis, which surpassed in completeness even the Kluckhohn and Samuel edition of 1929, albeit with the return to an arrangement of "fragments" according to categories of content such as that imposed by Tieck and Schlegel (and Bonsels).

Fortunately for Novalis, wartime Germany was not the only country where his works were read and edited. In 1942 G. A. Alfero and Vincenzo Errante translated into Italian selections from Novalis for which Alfero also provided introductions. Returning to the poet on whom he had devoted his first scholarly studies and with whom he associates the springtime of his life, Alfero observes that whoever is too immersed in the reality of life and wants to find in poetry an echo of our human earth will not seek out Novalis, but that those who have a sense for the exquisite harmony of the soul will find in him a confidant and friend (Alfero 1942, x). This comment suggests that Italians as well as Germans were in need of a respite from the grim reality of wartime Europe. But whereas Korff had seen *Heinrich von Ofterdingen* as a repository for the poet's longing for a past Golden Age, Alfero stresses that Novalis desired to transfigure his own world through the dream of a new Golden Age (x-xii; xvii). In his selections from the novel (71-170), Alfero provides what he considers the most significant and characteristic sections, such as the dream of the Blue Flower, Heinrich's conversation with the merchants about poetry in chapter two, and the encounter with Zulima in chapter four, and he summarizes what he does not translate. In short, Alfero provides enough material and information to whet the appetite of any Italian not conversant in German but interested in acquiring an initiation into the poetry and thought of Novalis.

In his bilingual edition of *Heinrich von Ofterdingen*, on the other hand, Marcel Camus supplies notes and an introduction designed for Francophone students of literature who might wish to read Novalis in the original German but also desire explication and orientation in their native tongue. Building on the worthy tradition established by French scholars such as Spenlé and Lichtenberger, Camus's commentary far outshines anything written on *Heinrich von Ofterdingen* in Germany during the Third Reich; indeed, the second half of his introduction contains insights on the ideal message and poetic form of the novel that warrant scholarly consideration even today. Camus emphasizes the great deliberation involved in the construction of the novel, with simultaneous antitheses within chapters and a gradual progression through its course. Likewise he finds it deliberate that the landscapes in the dreams are more vivid than those in the novel as a whole. Camus's intimate acquaintance with the text in the course of its translation into French enables him to discern its weak and strong points: so deliberately written are the dialogues and so packed full of ideas, he contends, that they have lost the quality of natural speech (1942, 41-43). Like Spenlé and Lichtenberger before him, Camus finds the Klingsohr tale overladen with ideas, as much as he appreciates them; but he also acknowledges the verbal mastery of the poetic prose and the lyric inserts throughout the novel.

In the section dealing with Novalis's gospel of universal harmony, Camus directs attention to concrete details of the present-day discord intruding between the primitive unity of humanity and nature postulated by German Idealistic thinkers and the future triumph of poetry and love: the initial episodes of the Klingsohr tale — in which strife, egotism, and evil reign — are the symbolic representation of conditions that Heinrich encounters in part one of the novel. The Scribe's hatred of poetry, love, imagination, wisdom, and the heart and his imprisonment of the outer senses correspond in the human realm to the paralysis found within nature and the fatal activity of the Fates in their underworld realm (28-29). Turning to young Heinrich, Camus observes how Novalis regularly places him in contrast to essentially decent individuals like his father, the merchants, crusaders, and peasants — whose actions, however, are motivated by principles of utility and whose innate perceptions of poetry are dimmed by habitude. And whereas Alfero in his 1916 study had glossed over the treatment of war and the crusades in *Heinrich von Ofterdingen*, while Bonsels had included excerpts but not commented on them in his introduction, here Camus takes care to highlight Klingsohr's remark to Heinrich in chapter eight that human madness takes full form in wars of religion (1: 285; 113-14). Just as Novalis used the Crusades as the foil for metahistorical reflections on the war and chaos of his own day, it seems all but impossible to regard Camus's discussion of war in *Heinrich von Ofterdingen* as anything other than an indirect commentary on conditions in Europe in 1942. In contrast to critics who have stressed the unproblematic nature of Novalis's optimistic idealism, Camus emphasizes how Novalis wrestled with the problems of evil, war, and death before coming to understand them as painful but necessary stages along the way to an awakening of the heavenly conscience slumbering within us. Camus thus sees the love between Heinrich and Mathilde as their initial breakthrough to the deepest level of being, which, however, is not yet fully present in transitory reality; in that regard, the death of Mathilde is the precondition for Heinrich's birth as a poet and their reunion at the end of the novel. Camus notes that while Novalis did not live to complete this depiction, he did outline its ideal form in the conclusion to Klingsohr tale — where Eros delivers Freya in a marriage of human love and cosmic forces and where a freedom now tempered by wisdom becomes the guiding principle of a world renewed (37).

When Novalis began writing his novel in December 1799, such hopes were the stuff of which dreams are made, and they seemed more illusory than ever at a time when the Nazi death camps made manifest the Klingsohr tale's Brueghelian tableaux of universal annihilation. But it was no accident that Novalis began *Heinrich von Ofterdingen* with a dream. At the beginning of his unfortunate 1934 essay, Julius Petersen cited (19) but did not discuss a quote from Novalis describing the search for eternal peace and the perfect state as a continuously frustrated and continuously renewed expectation (3: 296); by the time he died, in 1941, blackmailed by former students like Franz Koch who decried his attempts to provide shelter for Jewish colleagues in research projects under his control, Petersen had come to experience Hitler's Third Reich not as a dream but rather as a nightmare come true. But the perversion and betrayal of ideals proclaimed by poets such as Goethe, Schiller, Hölderlin, and Novalis did not destroy them either: at the height of Nazi terror there were also students in Germany, more clear-headed than many of their professors, who not only shared Novalis's dreams of universal love and reconciliation among peoples but were willing to die for them. Walter Jens has discovered the use of thoughts from Novalis's essay *Die Christenheit oder Europa* in leaflets the German resistance group *Die Weiße Rose* distributed at the university of Munich:

> "Blood will flow over Europe until the nations become aware of their madness and … a great love feast will be celebrated with hot tears in the name of peace on the smoking battlefields. Only religion can reawaken Europe and visibly install Christendom with new splendor on earth in its old peacemaking office." This was written in 1799, with a view toward an age of universal emancipation, centered around a church of peace. It was quoted in 1942, under the banner of the Nazi politics of extermination, by the conspirators from the circle of the "White Rose." (Jens 1991, 182)

Novalis's Blue Flower and the White Rose may not have been able to stem the tide of Nazism, but neither were they engulfed by it; while they should not serve as an alibi for the moral degradation of a nation, neither should they be condemned as irrelevant and immaterial. A study of the reception of *Heinrich von Ofterdingen* during the Nazi period reveals not least the power of words for good and for evil; and scholars incredulous of the depths to which the critical mind can sink should recall both Joseph Goebbels's doctorate in German literature and their present-day responsibility to prevent a recurrence of such dark times in any form.

5: Gathering the Ashes — 1945-1959

AFTER THE IMMOLATION of the mother in the Klingsohr tale, Fabel had to gather the ashes before a regeneration of the earth was possible. In the case of Novalis scholarship in Germany after the end of the Second World War, the transformation from desolation to regeneration was also a laborious process that did not occur overnight. While the Western Allies undertook a process of denazification and trial of the most obvious criminals and collaborators, they also recognized the necessity of reestablishing structures of society such as the school and university system, and many of the professors who had taught during the Third Reich remained in their positions. In the Soviet-occupied zone, the victors brought with them not only an ideology of antifascism that turned a blind eye to Stalin's temporary partnership with Hitler between 1939 and 1941 but also a core of functionaries who had survived the purges of the 1930s and were willing to implement Soviet policy throughout Eastern Europe.

Among the latter group was Georg Lukács, whose *Fortschritt und Reaktion* (Progress and Reaction), published by Aufbau Verlag in 1945, helped establish the contours of literary politics in East Germany for the next two decades. Lukács had no doubt as to German Romanticism's place in the dichotomy indicated by his book's title; in the essay "Die Romantik als die Wendung in der deutschen Literatur" he makes unmistakably clear that for him Romanticism is the great turning point in German literature against the Enlightenment and German Classicism. In addition to providing a polemic against the unbridled individualism and libertinism of the young Friedrich Schlegel that suggests a bad conscience about his earlier interest in this writer, Lukács also sharpens his longstanding condemnation of the *Wilhelm Meister* critique of Novalis, which he now understands as a complete break with Goethe and the initiation of a flight of fantasy in *Heinrich von Ofterdingen* that ends in a cult of night and death in the *Hymnen an die Nacht* (47-48). It is ironic that Lukács, coming from an ideological position almost diametrically opposite to that of Alfred Bäumler, arrives at a nearly identical verdict as to the decadence of Schlegel and Novalis and shares with Bäumler a preference for the later Romantics because of their interest in the people and in popular forms of art. Above all, though, Lukács is staking claims for a Marxist appropriation of the Classical humanism of Goethe and Schiller, which the Romantics allegedly rejected in favor of an irrationalism that led inexorably to Nazism.

In the opening talk for a lecture series on German Romanticism held at the University of Tübingen in the summer semester of 1947, Paul Kluckhohn disputes any such antinomy between German Classicism and Romanticism, but only because he sees them both as part of what he calls the "Deutsche Bewegung" (German movement) against the Enlightenment's excessive emphasis on reason. Kluckhohn takes care to laud the Enlightenment's achievements in the areas of science and political thinking and in the spread of tolerance and the idea of freedom; after surveying the various centers of Romanticism in Jena, Dresden, Heidelberg, Halle, Berlin, and Vienna, he disputes Nadler's contention that German Romanticism was a cultural movement from east of the Elbe and Saale rivers (Kluckhohn 1948, 25). But anyone looking for a critical reexamination of scholarship on Romanticism from the previous two decades will be sorely disappointed; both in this lecture and in the following one, on Romantic poetry, Kluckhohn echoes his positions from the 1920s, also with respect to *Heinrich von Ofterdingen*, without the slightest indication that anything had occurred in the meantime that might call them into question. As Klaus Peter observes, throughout this entire lecture series on Romanticism the consideration of past glories in art, music, and literature serves as a means of escape from more recent, less pleasant memories (Peter 1980, 9-10). The only lecture that explicitly evokes the Nazi years is the one by Adolf Köberle on Romanticism as a religious movement. After citing Karl Barth's difficulty in distinguishing a clear line between human and divine love in the thought and poetry of Novalis, Köberle calls Romanticism the German illness and observes in the German soul a permanent and dangerous tendency to mistake Eros for Ethos, intoxication for belief, and "Sieg-Heil" for "Gottes-Heil" (God's salvation); Köberle warns that the repetition of such errors is bound to lead to the total destruction of German society and culture. Nonetheless he regards the values of inwardness cultivated by the Romantics as a necessary complement to technical training at the university (83-85). His statement on this matter foreshadows the nostalgic, restorative cultural climate that was to characterize the early years of the Federal Republic of Germany, during which vaguely theological or existentialist interpretations of literary works served as one type of response to the literary scholarship practiced under National Socialism.

The 1947 dissertation by Antonius Bus on the myth of music in *Heinrich von Ofterdingen* represents a much more productive development of earlier directions in Novalis scholarship. Unfortunately, it has not received the attention it deserves; even Herbert Uerlings does not discuss this study in his thorough review of research on *Heinrich von Ofterdingen*, although he does list it in the bibliography. One possible reason for its neglect may lie in the title, which suggests both a mystifying approach and a return to Paula Scheidweiler's typology of the "musical" Romantic novel. Not Scheidweiler, however, but Oskar Walzel is the source for the insight that a truly musical style requires a strict sense of form. Continuing the discussion of the variation of figures in *Heinrich von Ofterdingen* that Walzel had initiated, Bus dismisses Tieck's contention that Mathilde, Zulima, and Cyane are the same person and instead calls their configuration a

Dreiklang, or accord of characters related to one another by an acoustics of the soul: in the vision at the beginning of part two of the novel it is significant that Heinrich recognizes Mathilde by the sound of her voice (Bus 1947, 118-21). Bus displays a well-developed sense for the fine points of the text, as when he notes how the opening sentence of the novel emphasizes the ticking clock, soughing wind, and rattling window panes as Heinrich lies restlessly in bed and thinks of the Blue Flower (41); the reference to this scene in the poem on the marriage of the seasons that Novalis intended as the conclusion to *Heinrich von Ofterdingen* indicates the extent to which the individual parts of the novel appear and reappear like motifs in a musical composition (111-12).

The frequent association of poets and maidens with music, as in the tales the merchants relate to Heinrich, causes music to be a theme in the content of the novel as well, particularly with regard to Heinrich and Mathilde. Contrasting the overdone use of music in Tieck's novel *Franz Sternbalds Wanderungen* with the more subtle treatment preferred by Novalis, Bus demonstrates how the singing of the loud, intoxicated Crusaders and the tender, elegiac Zulima not only illustrates the fundamental difference in their respective natures but also makes evident Heinrich's preference for peace over war when he chooses to remain with Zulima rather than return to the carousing knights (78-81). As was true for the commentary on *Heinrich von Ofterdingen* written by Marcel Camus during the Second World War, it is perhaps not entirely coincidental that a citizen of Holland like Bus had more sensitivity to such features of the novel than did German commentators during the same period.

Wolfgang Kayser, a student of Julius Petersen whose early scholarship contain its share of National Socialist literary vocabulary, later developed an approach to literature similar to that of Anglo-American New Criticism in that it eschewed all extraliterary considerations and directed its full attention upon the work of art as a self-contained linguistic structure. In his programmatic work *Das sprachliche Kunstwerk* (The Verbal Work of Art, 1948), which became the introduction to literary studies for a whole generation of German university students after the Second World War, Kayser provides exemplary analyses of poems and prose texts; two passages from *Heinrich von Ofterdingen* serve as models of a unified style of writing, namely Heinrich's departure from Eisenach at the beginning of chapter two and the episode in chapter six in which Heinrich and Mathilde exchange their first kisses. Kayser remarks that regardless of whether we read the reflections of the narrator upon the phenomenon of first parting or observe how Heinrich and Mathilde are drawn to one another gently but irresistibly, in either case the text imparts a quiet confidence in the presence of an abiding world unaffected by changing circumstances; the narrator knows the inner feelings of the characters and imparts these in adjectives that do not describe visual impressions but rather express psychic dispositions (303-8).

Kayser falls behind Walzel's analyses when he maintains that the narrator and the characters in the novel all speak indistinguishably from one another; his contention that evil, meanness, base striving, and desire never cross Heinrich's path (309) likewise does not do justice to the nuances discerned by critics such as Camus and Bus. As much as Kayser attempts a strict adherence to textual analysis, such preconceived notions of Novalis continue to affect the overall outcome of his interpretations. But when one compares Kayser's approach with that offered by Hans Heinrich Borcherdt in his 1949 monograph on the novels of the Age of Goethe, which follows Kluckhohn and Korff in viewing *Heinrich von Ofterdingen* as an attempted synthesis of the classical Bildungsroman and the Romantic Künstlerroman and which emphasizes content almost exclusively over style, Kayser's methodological advances become more readily apparent. At the conclusion of his interpretation, Kayser observes that when literary studies of the old school of *Geistesgeschichte* cite pronouncements by Heinrich or Klingsohr isolated from their context and then admire them for their deep philosophical content, the reader is likely to be struck by the immaturity and lack of profundity of the alleged revelations: it is in the placement of his thoughts in the poetic text and more particularly in its narrative flow that Novalis weaves his magical spell upon the reader (310). In a period of German literary scholarship when the prevailing mode was one of effusion rather than explication, Kayser's concentration on close reading was a welcome change.

A further contrast to Kayser's methodological sobriety are the two books on Novalis by Frederick (Friedrich) Hiebel that employ Rudolf Steiner's anthroposophic merge of esoteric Christianity and Goethean thought. Steiner, a great admirer of Novalis, drew upon many of the sources from which Novalis derived his own images. As we shall see, Florian Roder's 1992 study of Novalis demonstrates the value of a judicious use of anthroposophy in illuminating the mystical sides of Novalis's thought that undoubtedly do exist. But Hiebel's *Novalis: German Poet, European Thinker, Christian Mystic* — a condensed version of his 1951 study *Novalis, der Dichter der Blauen Blume* for an English-speaking audience — contains many of the same flaws present in both that volume and its 1972 revised edition in that it too does not so much analyze as proselytize. In his discussion of the Klingsohr tale, for example, Hiebel interprets the flame that immolates the mother as none other than Christ, who puts an end to the chaos of sensual love she earlier represented and transforms her into the heart that is the true mother of love (Hiebel 1951, 137-38; Hiebel 1959, 63-65; Hiebel 1972, 333); why it is the mother rather than Ginnistan who is burned does not seem of particular import. In his survey of problematic aspects in recent Novalis scholarship, Walter Müller-Seidel criticizes Hiebel's work for such interpretive reductionism and for the imposing but empty references to the "word fugues and symphonic movements" within the tale and in *Heinrich von Ofterdingen* as a whole (Hiebel 1951, 7; Müller-Seidel 1953, 282, 290-91). Even more disturbing in Müller-Seidel's view, though, is Hiebel's underestimation of the interpenetration of poetry and thought in Novalis's work. Noting that Novalis, like Kleist and Hölderlin, was dissatisfied by the philosophy of his day but arrived at his mature poetry only through intensive study of this same philosophy, Müller-Seidel calls for a stronger consideration of the thought formations in his work if scholars wish to progress beyond the concentration on "experience" and "worldview" in the previous fifty years of Novalis research. As a model for future work he praises a recently completed Heidelberg dissertation by Jurij Striedter (281).

Striedter's *Die Fragmente des Novalis als "Präfigurationen" seiner Dichtung* (The Fragments of Novalis as a "Prefiguration" of His Poetry, 1953)— a dissertation written under the direction of Paul Böckmann and Hans-Georg Gadamer that was first published in book form only in 1985 — in many respects prefigures the best Novalis scholarship of the 1960s and 1970s. Striedter devotes to the philosophical aphorisms of Novalis the same close attention that Kayser brought to passages in *Heinrich von Ofterdingen* and thereby demonstrates that these are not the "fragmentary" jottings that previous scholarship had regarded them to be, but rather well-formed, dialectical presentations of positions Novalis gained from his intensive readings of Kant, Fichte, and Schelling. After demonstrating that *Die Lehrlinge zu Sais*, the novel Novalis began while studying at the Mining Academy of Freiberg in 1798 and 1799, contains all the essential themes and forms of the fragment collections published during Novalis's lifetime, Striedter devotes the final chapter of his dissertation to the implications of his findings for *Heinrich von Ofterdingen* as well. Seeing in this novel a productive development of the medieval Christian tradition of the *figura* in the light of Kantian and Fichtean thought, Striedter maintains that truth for Novalis is no longer immediately present in divine revelation but rather is developed by the individual's active comparison of signs and figures. Thus it is Heinrich's task to interpret the dreams, stories, and conversations he experiences in the course of his way to Augsburg, Klingsohr, and Mathilde. It is no coincidence that the hermit's illuminated manuscript at the end of book five is incomplete; as such it remains a fiction and a postulate that Heinrich has to make real and comprehensible (227-29). Striedter likewise understands Novalis's project of romanticizing the world as the intent to develop active readers who in turn will act upon their surroundings. He also notes, however, that once the presuppositions underlying such an idealization of the world came into question, it was no wonder that people misunderstood the poetry as fantastic and illusory in a negative sense (102-4). In the context of the early 1950s in West Germany, where the only miracles taking place were economic ones and where reflections on the transformation of society were few and far between, it is regrettable, although not surprising, that Striedter's doctoral thesis remained unpublished for so long; but given the development of reception and reader-response criticism during the 1960s and 1970s, it is also not surprising that Striedter and Hans-Robert Jauss were partners in critiquing each other's dissertation work, as Striedter relates in the preface to his book.

In comparison with Striedter's insights, the other books and articles published on Novalis during the 1950s register incremental advances on previous scholarship but no dramatic breakthroughs. An article by W. J. Fries, "Eros und Ginnistan: Ein Beitrag zur Symbolik in *Heinrich von Ofterdingen*" (Eros and Ginnistan: A Contribution to the Symbolism in *Heinrich von Ofterdingen*), corrects Hiebel's misconception that Ginnistan is made immortal through immolation by pointing out that this occurs through the hours she spends in the arms of Eros (1954, 36). Fries also draws attention to correspondences between Heinrich's erotic immersion in the waters of his initial dream and the scene in the Klingsohr tale in which Ginnistan seduces Eros in the guise of his mother — a scene that had scandalized critics ever since the late nineteenth century. Fries observes that Novalis frequently associates the idea of lover with mother and that after her seduction of Eros Ginnistan assumes a motherly attitude toward him; thus he sees in Ginnistan the development of a "hearty fantasy" that Novalis had described as characteristic of his own religiosity and that becomes the prerequisite both for the positive conclusion to the fairy tale and for Heinrich's own development (34-35). But once again the unsettling aspects of sexual attraction, particularly with respect to mother-son pairings, remain unexplored or else banished to a footnote, as had been the case for Armand Nivelle's discussion of the sexual content of Heinrich's dream (Nivelle 1950, 406-7); it is not until the early 1980s that Friedrich Kittler explores in immeasurably more detail the wanderings of Eros.

In the 1956 volumes on the German lyric edited by Benno von Wiese, Hans-Joachim Schrimpf investigates the poem whose union of death and love had been the other major source of embarrassment for Victorian critics, namely the song of the dead contained in the plans for part two of *Heinrich von Ofterdingen*. Schrimpf's rather conventional remarks on Novalis's life and concepts of history and poetry, which occupy the first third of his essay, finally give way to an extended, virtuosic analysis of the poem's organization, technique, and content that far surpasses Walter Rehm's discussion of "Das Lied der Toten" in his 1950 monograph on Orpheus, the poet, and the dead. Schrimpf shows how the unbounded praise of the delights of death, where love is unending and the sands of time flow unceasingly, finds expression in fifteen eight-line stanzas whose trochaic verses, varied rhyme schemes, and changes of cadence in the fourth and eighth lines evoke an eternal ebb and flow of the elements (422-23). Although on occasion Schrimpf imputes to Novalis a renunciation of life, he also makes clear that this particular conception of the afterlife combines Christian spirituality with a Dionysian hymn to heightened delight that culminates in the central three stanzas of the poem — whose content we may recall from the discussion of Julian Schmidt's bowdlerized edition. In the song's concluding stanzas, the grateful dead flow out from the heart of God with an invitation to their living lovers to help them bind the earth spirit, learn the meaning of death, and find the word of life. Schrimpf ends his interpretation by connecting this message with the onset of the Golden Age proclaimed in the verses sung by Astralis at the beginning of part two of *Heinrich von Ofterdingen*.

Schrimpf's critical achievements would have been even more considerable had he investigated connections between these two poems and their references to motifs from the Klingsohr tale or had he been able to trace the poem's dynamics back to the "Hin und her" (back and forth) direction that Striedter had documented as so central an element to the thought processes of Novalis. And while Schrimpf did point to erotic imagery in the praise of the primeval fluid in the *Lehrlinge zu Sais* that parallels the images in the central three stanzas of the "Lied der Toten" (425-26), it would be another twenty years before scholars would investigate their source in the natural philosophy of Novalis. But Schrimpf's close reading of this poem represents an advance on Wolfgang Kayser's analysis of passages from *Heinrich von Ofterdingen* in that he begins to consider the poem's integration into the context of the novel rather than discussing textual subsections and drawing general conclusions from them.

It is precisely such fidelity to Kayser's model that leads to the questionable results of Eberhard Haufe's style analysis of the dream concluding chapter six of *Heinrich von Ofterdingen*, published as a contribution to the 1957 festschrift honoring Hermann August Korff. Haufe convincingly argues that the gliding rhythm of the prose conveys the gentle flowing of the stream that at the end of the dream envelops not only Mathilde but also Heinrich in eternal, indissoluble bliss. The syntax likewise suggests not action but rather duration — yet another correspondence between form and content in the dream, as when Mathilde reacts passively to her death by drowning, and Heinrich's attempt to swim to her or follow the sound of her voice only carries him away from his beloved. It is the word *heiter* (bright, cheerful), which characterizes not only the heavens in the dream but also Mathilde's expression as she contemplates the vortex that pulls her under, that signals the fundamental lyric oneness between self and world that is the ultimate ideal of the novel. Haufe observes that a fluid, lively peace predominates both in Novalis's poetry and in his view of life, pointing to the *Hymnen an die Nacht* and the "Lied der Toten" as further evidence for this contention. He quotes an observation by Novalis that paradise is strewn all over the earth and therefore unrecognizable — all that needs to be done is to gather together these scattered parts (3: 447); but he also argues that it is this latent presence of paradise that removes from *Heinrich von Ofterdingen* any sort of the dramatic confrontation that one expects from the Bildungsroman and the historical novel. As for the novel's characters, they are figures, persons without personality because they are also without development (179-86).

Haufe comes to these conclusions without reproaching Novalis for artistic incompetence; on the contrary, he regards these features of the novel as a perfect expression of the longing for the *Aufhebung der Zeit* (abolition of time) that for him is the inner essence of *Heinrich von Ofterdingen*. But *Aufhebung* is a notoriously multifaceted word in German, and the understanding of time that Haufe brings to the text is inadequate to deal with those notions that Novalis developed in his philosophical studies and put into practice in his poetry: the poem that was planned for the conclusion to *Heinrich von Ofterdingen*, after all, is entitled "Die Vermählung der Jahreszeiten" (The Marriage of the Seasons; 1: 355). As of 1957 Hans-Joachim Mähl's groundbreaking study on the image of the Golden Age in the works of Novalis had not yet appeared, nor had Striedter's investigation of the figurations in Novalis's thought and poetry become well known among Novalis scholars. But had Haufe considered the integration of this second dream into the plot of *Heinrich von Ofterdingen*, which, like the dream of the Blue Flower, is interrupted before it reaches a conclusion and hence inspires the continued search for enlightenment, he might not have been so absolute in his pronouncements. Looking for confirmation of his theses in other passages from the novel, Haufe refers to the mysterious book Heinrich finds in the cave of the hermit in chapter five and comments, "Nicht nur sein vergangenes Leben sieht er darin, auch seine Zukunft ist schon im Bilde gezeichnet, nur das Ende fehlt" (Not just his past life does he see there, also his future is already contained in the picture; only the end is missing; 189). Haufe had displayed great insight in his analysis of adverbial expressions in Heinrich's dream, but the oversight of that tiny word *only* marks the crucial blind spot of his interpretation.

The following year another piece of Novalis scholarship appeared in Leipzig: the dissertation by Gerhard Schulz on the professional activity of Friedrich von Hardenberg (Novalis) and its significance for his writing and thought. In 1951 Heinz Dieter Schmid had written for Paul Kluckhohn in Tübingen a dissertation on Novalis and his geology teacher in Freiberg, Abraham Gottlob Werner. Both this dissertation and the one by Schulz were never published, but their findings provided a basis for the new consideration of the interplay between science and poetry in the work of Novalis that came to fruition in the following two decades. With respect to the landscape depictions in *Heinrich von Ofterdingen*, Schulz demonstrates that these are not flights of fancy but rather observations of reality that have been generalized until all superfluous individual elements have been removed and only the typical remains (Schulz 1958, 105-6). And as for the idealized portrayal of the miner and mining life in chapter five of the novel, Schulz ascribes this neither to Hardenberg's ignorance of the harsh life of the miners in the Saxony of his own day nor to a desire to sweeten oppression by masking true conditions; rather, he sees it as a protest against capitalistic exploitation and a longing for conditions as they existed in the Middle Ages (112-20). Schulz interprets the caves that appear again and again throughout the novel as symbols of refuge from a world that has turned evil, though he notes that No-

valis, like the miner in this respect, does not remain in the depths but rather aspires to the light of day (132-36). All the same, in his conclusion Schulz echoes
the thesis of Lukács that Romanticism represents a break with the Enlightenment and German Classicism, although he attempts a more differentiated view
of Novalis (171-76). The placement of this critique at the end of his dissertation
suggests that Schulz may have been performing an obligatory bow here to prevailing modes of Marxist criticism; what he regarded as central to his dissertation
are rather the analyses of the miner's songs in *Heinrich von Ofterdingen*, which
appeared the following year in the mining journal *Der Anschnitt*, and the 1963
account of Novalis's professional career he later included in his edition of land-
marks in Novalis scholarship.

However, investigations such as those by Schmid, Schulz, and Hans-Joachim
Mähl, whose 1959 dissertation on the image of the Golden Age in the work of
Novalis did not appear in print until 1965, proved exceptions to the rule. The
prevailing trend in Novalis scholarship on both sides of the Atlantic was to study
works like *Heinrich von Ofterdingen* in isolation not only from the poet's liveli-
hood but also from his philosophical and scientific speculations. Hiebel's monographs may represent the most extreme trend in this direction in that they
attempt to disqualify such thoughts as the immature exercises of the student who
then passed on to poetic mastery, but in 1959 Bruce Haywood and Peter Küpper
both express similar reservations about considering external, "nonpoetic productions" (Haywood 1959, 3) when investigating the imagery or the experience of
time in the work of Novalis. For large stretches of Haywood's discussion of
Heinrich von Ofterdingen, textual analysis amounts to little more than plot recapitulation, and his interpretation of the transformation of Eros into the love of
Christ seems more beholden to Hiebel than the imagery from the tale that he
cites, but he does point out links between the Klingsohr tale and other parts of
the novel (133-36). As for Küpper, he provides many examples of how Novalis
unites what is normally separated by time and space, and he notes the fact that
Novalis has deliberately chosen the Middle Ages in its capacity as *Übergangszeit*
(transitional age) for the setting of *Heinrich von Ofterdingen*; but the objections
already noted for Haufe's essay largely apply here as well. Even after citing Walzel's warning against any attempt of a reconstruction of the notes to the second
part of the novel, Küpper concludes his chapter on *Heinrich von Ofterdingen* by
sketching out what he presumes would have been a great synthesis in which all
individual contours dissolve (105-19). Such a conclusion is symptomatic of those
studies that attempt to take a close look at Novalis without considering the
greater intellectual and social context of his work and consequently fill the void
with their own preconceptions of who or what Novalis was. What began in the
late 1940s as an understandable reaction against the excesses of *Geistesgeschichte*
had reached the point of stasis and redundancy a decade later.

In his 1953 survey of literature on Novalis, Walter Müller-Seidel, observing that no complete edition of his works had yet appeared in Germany after 1945, saw little likely evidence of a Novalis renaissance. Klaus Peter notes that, during the 1950s, critics who defended the works of other Romantic writers such as Brentano, Eichendorff, or Hoffmann often did so by stressing these writers' differences from Novalis, a poet whom they considered romantic in the negative sense of the word (Müller-Seidel 1953, 276; Peter 1980, 17). Such judgments were soon to change radically, however. Both Richard Samuel, who had left England for Australia after the end of World War II as founder of the department of German at the University of Melbourne, and Paul Kluckhohn had been quietly "gathering the ashes" in preparation for a new and expanded version of their 1929 edition until Kluckhohn's death in 1957 caused Samuel to look for new partners. He found them in Heinz Ritter, Gerhard Schulz, and Hans-Joachim Mähl, who were to contribute both individually and collectively to a new and better understanding of *Heinrich von Ofterdingen.*

6: Additions via Editions — 1960-1970

THE APPEARANCE OF a historical-critical edition of the works of Friedrich von Hardenberg may not seem so significant until one recalls that the Tieck and Schlegel version of their friend's writings had a major, and negative, effect on the course of scholarship for at least a century. Indeed, Ewald Wasmuth's four-volume reissue of his 1943 Novalis edition still follows the principle established by Tieck and Schlegel of arranging the "fragments" according to subject matter rather than in chronological order. As late as 1957, for many readers and scholars Novalis was still the timeless mystic whose oracular utterances had little connection to the circumstances of their composition. In his afterword to volume one Wasmuth does express the hope that the manuscripts from the von Hardenberg family archives, which Salman Schocken had acquired through an auction in 1930 and had taken with him into exile from Nazi Germany, might one day be made available for a critical and complete edition (Wasmuth 1953, 561). This wish became possible in May of 1960, shortly after the appearance of volume one of the new Kluckhohn and Samuel edition, when Ernst Beutler, director of the Freies Deutsches Hochstift in Frankfurt am Main, acquired these Novalis manuscripts and granted Richard Samuel permission for their use in what then became the historical-critical edition, whose sixth and final volume is still to appear.

With respect to *Heinrich von Ofterdingen*, the quantity and quality of scholarly publications increased exponentially after the appearance of volumes two and three of the historical-critical edition in 1965 and 1968, which conclusively demonstrated the necessity of regarding the philosophical, scientific, and professional writings of Friedrich von Hardenberg as prerequisites for a full understanding of his poetic works. But by 1961 Heinz Ritter's philological accomplishment of establishing the time period during which Novalis worked on this novel had major implications for its interpretation. In his last published article, Paul Kluckhohn had reported that his earlier dating of the Klingsohr tale from the beginning of 1799 needed to be revised as a result of the recovery of manuscripts outlining plans for this work, whose graphological characteristics indicated a composition no earlier than the summer of 1799 (Kluckhohn 1958, 397). As a result of his even more exacting studies of changes in Hardenberg's handwriting patterns, Ritter proved that these plans for *Heinrich von Ofterdingen* dated from January 1800. This dating not only eliminated the possibility of ascribing the Klingsohr tale to an earlier, allegedly immature period of Novalis's poetic development but also placed the writing of part one of the novel within a time of intense professional activity and flatly contradicted Tieck's depiction of a long, relaxed, and isolated process of poetic creation

(Ritter 1961, 163-70). Although Kluckhohn was too sophisticated a scholar to take Tieck's sentimentalized depiction at face value, it is interesting to note how his own preconceptions of Novalis's image of the poet affected the interpretation of these manuscript findings. Confronted with the sentence "Man kann die Poësie nicht gering genug schätzen" (1: 335), Kluckhohn assumes a writing error on the part of Novalis that turned the intended meaning "One can not estimate poesy highly enough" into its exact opposite (395). Ritter, however, understands this notation as the key word for Klingsohr's remark to Heinrich that poesy is really nothing special nor confined to a single guild of people such as writers but rather the characteristic mode of production of the human spirit (1961, 169; 1: 287; 116).

Ritter's article, though, is not free of speculative elements. While his argument is plausible enough that the absence of notes on the first chapter of the novel and the mining episode in chapter five suggests that these had been written during Novalis's December 1799 stay at the salt production facility in Artern, Ritter goes one step further and ascribes the conception of the entire novel to a visionary moment Novalis must have experienced atop the nearby Kyffhäuser mountain (174-75). Likewise, while arguing against the identification of the figure of Mathilde in the novel with Novalis's first fiancée, Sophie von Kühn, Ritter replaces Sophie with Julie von Charpentier, his second betrothed — a process he further accentuated in his book *Der unbekannte Novalis*, in which Julie's father, not Goethe, becomes the prototype for the poet Klingsohr in *Heinrich von Ofterdingen* (1967, 219-22). Such a search for biographical correspondences with characters in the novel, which has the effect of reducing the already thin plot to a roman à clef, demonstrates how the *Ofterdingen* research of the early 1960s was still in the process of transition from the accumulated mythology of the previous 150 years.

Even Richard Samuel's 1963 interpretation of *Heinrich von Ofterdingen* in Benno von Wiese's two-volume collection of essays on the German novel serves more as a recapitulation of previous scholarship than an indication of directions for future research. After brief opening remarks on the importance of Goethe's *Wilhelm Meister* for the early German Romantics, a report on the genesis of *Heinrich von Ofterdingen*, and an overview of the plot, structure, and style of part one of the novel that returns to an identification of Klingsohr and Mathilde with Goethe and Sophie von Kühn, Samuel provides a discussion of the language of the first part that builds on the work of Walzel and Kayser in its meticulous analysis of the simple phrasing, quietly melodious sentence structure, and prevalence of images of water and fire as signifiers of the sensual and erotic in life and death (279-85). Instead of further discussing connections between the language of the first part and the message it conveys, however, Samuel chooses to follow Küpper's example and engage in a lengthy reconstruction of plans for the second part of the novel that culminates in the contention that the seventh chapter in this part would have been expanded to become a third part of the novel — a speculation that is devoid of philological evidence. Likewise, Samuel's concluding comparisons of *Heinrich von Ofterdingen* with the Bildungsroman tradition, Goethe's *Faust*, and Wolfram von Eschenbach's *Parzival* are so heavily qualified by significant differences that in effect they do little more than attest to the singularity and poetic significance of Novalis's creation without making clear where the specific accomplishment lies.

Herbert Uerlings, with all due respect for Samuel's profound knowledge of Novalis, sees in this essay an example of the relative helplessness with which Novalis scholarship reacted to *Heinrich von Ofterdingen* through at least the middle of the 1960s (1991, 398). But the problem is more than a matter of individual or even collective inadequacies. The German literary canon, after decades of misuse as a proof of cultural superiority, no longer possessed a self-evident meaning, and critics had yet to discover a fresh approach to these works. Seen in this light, Samuel's decision to revise and republish Kluckhohn's 1928 introductory essay rather than to provide a fresh paradigm for the new edition is symptomatic of a prevailing lack of critical orientation among Western Germanists during the early 1960s.

For East German criticism on Novalis and Romanticism, on the other hand, lack of orientation was hardly the problem. Georg Lukács may have fallen from official favor because of his participation in the Hungarian revolt of 1956, but the essential features of his attacks on German Romanticism are evident in Claus Träger's 1961 essay on Novalis and ideological restoration. Träger performs a telling and long-overdue critique of the ideological components in the work of scholars like Obenauer and Kluckhohn, but in his discussion of Novalis's own writings he substitutes polemics for analysis: according to Träger, the political writings of Novalis demonstrate that in essence the realm of the Blue Flower is nothing other than the kingdom of Germano-Prussian reaction (634). As for *Heinrich von Ofterdingen*, Träger varies Novalis's description of *Wilhelm Meisters Lehrjahre* as a *Candide* against poesy by calling his experimental novel a *Candide* against life in that Novalis renounces Goethe's attempt at the humane integration of an average individual into a productive bourgeois society and instead prefers the apotheosis of an exceptional artist freed from all such bonds (654). Träger interprets the criticism of the rationalistic utilitarianism of the Scribe in the Klingsohr tale as a wholesale rejection of reason and Enlightenment and thus finds it all too understandable that Western scholars paid no attention to Fritz Strich's warnings against Romanticism in his 1949 preface to the fourth edition of *Deutsche Klassik und Romantik oder Vollendung und Unendlichkeit* (German Classicism and Romanticism, or Perfection and Infinity, 9) and continue their imperialistic investigations of Novalis under the mantle of an aestheticist disregard of all social and political questions (659-60). For Träger, literary scholarship is an element of the class struggle, and the appropriation of Goethean Classicism as a part of the heritage of the German Democratic Republic also requires an attack against present and past attempts to establish a free people on free German soil. While Träger's later writings on Novalis provide deeper insights into the historical specificity of German Romanticism, this early essay certainly conveys a sense of the Cold War climate in which he wrote it.

Dietrich Löffler's 1963 Leipzig dissertation provides a more differentiated discussion of *Heinrich von Ofterdingen* from an East German Marxist perspective. Hans Mayer, his principal advisor, had already discerned an apparent contradiction between Novalis, the regressive poet, and Friedrich von Hardenberg, the progressive mining specialist (Mayer 1959, 25). Löffler goes one step further by consigning to the realm of legend the image of Hardenberg as a sick, immaterial enthusiast and stressing his desire to reform the world in his immediate vicinity by conscientious work as a mining inspector and civil administrator (Löffler 1963, 52). And while retaining the prevailing East German view of Novalis as a reactionary political theorist, Löffler also finds such tendencies largely absent from *Heinrich von Ofterdingen*, although he does see Hardenberg as assenting to the inhumanity expressed in the Crusaders' song (130-36). Like Gerhard Schulz in his Leipzig dissertation, Löffler interprets the novel's praise of idyllic poverty as a protest against capitalistic acquisitiveness and notes that this is no mere Romantic anticapitalism; various characters also celebrate trade and production (117). This discussion of the social and economic elements of the novel, which Samuel had touched upon only in passing, attains an explicitness not to be surpassed until Ulrich Stadler's work of the late 1970s. In like fashion, Löffler revises Samuel's 1925 discussion of medieval religiosity in the novel by observing that the piety and work ethic of the miner and the hermit are more suggestive of the German Pietism Novalis knew from his own upbringing than the monkish asceticism of the Middle Ages (126-27). But while taking note of the curious blending of the medieval and the modern, Löffler does not reflect upon its possible poetological significance — once again a task for future researchers, and one that Helmut Gold was to explore in his 1990 discussion of mining symbolism in the novel.

For Löffler, the main problems with *Heinrich von Ofterdingen* lie in the formalistic idealization of reality that he regards as its essentially Romantic feature. While he readily admits that there is no one single type of novel, his concluding assessment that *Heinrich von Ofterdingen* lacks all characteristics of the classic bourgeois novel found in *Wilhelm Meister* (240) is decidedly a value judgment. Calling the reconstruction of part two of the novel from the extant notes a senseless undertaking, Löffler nonetheless regards the Klingsohr tale as a prototype of what was to come and finds it possesses neither the entertaining lightness of Wieland's tales nor the epic breadth of eighteenth-century novels

(239-40), nor for that matter any inner connection with the first part of *Heinrich von Ofterdingen* itself (215). Noting that modernist writers increasingly have seen Novalis as their artistic precursor, Löffler explains the novel's initial lack of success and later acclaim as a result of changing sociopolitical circumstances: at a time when the failure of the bourgeoisie appeared only temporary, readers could not understand German Romanticism's rejection of the path offered by Goethe; once the cultural and societal crisis became permanent, bourgeois modernists such as Hermann Broch discovered their affinity with Novalis (240-42). In the light of such theories, it will be interesting to examine the reasons for the renaissance of German Romanticism in East German literature and scholarship of the 1970s.

A counterbalance to both excessive identification and overhasty criticism is the explication of Novalis's poetics of the novel that Gerhard Schulz provided in 1964; Reinhold Grimm gave even more prominence to this article published in the *Jahrbuch des Freien Deutschen Hochstifts* (Yearbook of the Free German Foundation) by reprinting it four years later in his edition of studies on German theories of the novel. Arguing against the still prevalent tendency to regard Novalis's poetological remarks as a kaleidoscopic mixture of unconnected aperçus, Schulz stresses the necessity of following Novalis's thoughts on the novel as these ideas developed between 1797 and 1800 (82). And as a warning against picking out isolated remarks and then stressing their modernity, he observes that unlike most modern authors, for whom outward unconnectedness is usually the expression of inner disunity, Novalis brought entirely different philosophical and scientific presuppositions to bear upon his aesthetic judgments and poetic works (103). In such methodological caution, one can already discern the care that Schulz and Hans-Joachim Mähl were to take in establishing the precise context of Novalis's thoughts in their editorial introductions and commentaries for volumes two and three of the historical-critical edition.

With the exception of Oskar Walzel and Walter Benjamin, earlier critics had tended to regard Friedrich Schlegel as the theoretician of the Jena Romantics and Novalis as the intuitive poet who at most put into practice what his friend had postulated with regard to the novel. Schulz, however, shows how Hardenberg's intensive readings in transcendental philosophy, coupled with his mathematical and scientific studies at the Mining Academy in Freiberg, led to his unique understanding of poetry as the symbolic construction of the transcendental world, the approximate realization of an infinite idea (87). In discussing the notes on variations of figures that Walzel and Bus had shown were so important for Novalis's poetic practice in *Heinrich von Ofterdingen*, Schulz also does not fail to stress that even as Novalis studied and admired this technique in Goethe's *Wilhelm Meister* two years before his work on *Heinrich von Ofterdingen*, he draws from this study the philosophical consequence that all people are variations of a complete individual — a mystical idea that does not correspond to Goethe's morphological investigations of human possibility (91-92). In like fashion, Schulz cautions against transferring to *Heinrich von Ofterdingen* any conceptions of the Bildungsroman drawn from the study of *Wilhelm Meisters Lehrjahre* or seeing in the figure of Klingsohr a veiled depiction of Goethe: Novalis was not interested in depicting Heinrich's personal development or portraying individuals from his own circle of experience, and Klingsohr's words of advice largely correspond to Novalis's poetological concepts; one can at most speak of Klingsohr as the portrait of the Romantic artist that Goethe could have been had he paired his artistic talent and sense for the real with a grasp of the universal (99-101; on the topic of Klingsohr as a portrait of Goethe, see Schlagdenhaufen 1967). As for Novalis's achievements, Schulz absolves him of empty fantasizing and testifies to the deep moral seriousness of his art, but states in conclusion that by postulating poetry as the true reality on which the empirical world should orientate itself, Novalis set goals for art that it is not able to fulfill and that ultimately would lead to its dissolution (109-10). Whether or not this final judgment by Schulz does full justice to Novalis's conception of his novelistic efforts as "*Übergangsfahre* vom Unendlichen zum Endlichen," or years of transition from the infinite to the finite (4: 281), his study stands as an exemplary combination of sympathetic understanding and critical distance often lacking in previous scholarship on Novalis.

In her significant study of the fairy tales and novellas incorporated in Goethe's novels and those of his Romantic contemporaries, which went into its second edition two years after its 1964 publication, Erika Voerster provides an explication of the Romantic theory of the inlaid tale and detailed analyses of its practice by Novalis, Tieck, Friedrich and Dorothea Schlegel, Arnim, and Eichendorff. After discussing the presence of this technique in *Don Quixote*, *Wilhelm Meisters Lehrjahre*, and *Hamlet* as well as the Romantics' interpretations of such plays within plays and stories within stories, Voerster draws attention to the importance of self-reflective thinking for Fichte's philosophy and early Romantic aesthetics. By so doing, she provides a greater context for appreciating the significance of the two tales told by the merchants within *Heinrich von Ofterdingen*, Klingsohr's tale at the end of part one, Heinrich's two dreams, and also the manuscript he encounters in the hermit's cave that appears to contain his life story. With respect to the three increasingly complex tales within the novel, Voerster detects a pattern of ever greater isolation from the Golden Age and ever greater effort on the part of poets to restore this lost harmony, which, however, also becomes increasingly universal and permanent (142-43). In the tale of Atlantis, the second song sung by the youthful poet retells his story, contains an inner reflection on its significance, and has a bearing on Heinrich's later love for nature and Mathilde, thus establishing multiple reflections on the main themes of poetry and love in the novel as a whole (127-29). This principle of poetry reflecting upon itself is repeated in the Klingsohr tale, where the spectacle Ginnistan stages for Eros in the realm of her father represents a story within a story that anticipates both the conclusion of the Klingsohr tale and the planned end of the novel. But the tales of Arion and Atlantis, as well as Heinrich's dreams and the hermit's manuscript, have similarly anticipatory functions. Voerster regards the way Novalis arranged such correspondences as unique in German Romanticism and comparable to Goethe's artistry in *Wilhelm Meister*, although resting on entirely different philosophical, even metaphysical, premises (156-57). Such comparisons with Goethe, once freed from the Bildungsroman paradigm, make possible a greater appreciation of the respective merits of *Wilhelm Meister* and its Romantic cousin.

Voerster's standpoint forms a pleasant contrast to the argument of Oskar Serge Ehrensperger, a student of Emil Staiger whose 1962 dissertation on the epic structure of *Heinrich von Ofterdingen*, published in book form in 1965, repeatedly postulates an intuitive principle of composition on the part of Novalis and also fails to discern any deeper connections between the Atlantis and Klingsohr tales and the main body of the novel. Ehrensperger's decision to disregard the poetological theories of Novalis as irrelevant to his undertaking (1) has the consequence that his view of the novel, like that of so many of the allegedly text-immanent readings from the previous decade, is predetermined by a conception of Novalis as a childlike, pure, religious character with a spiritualized, ethereal relationship to reality (2). Thus it is not surprising that he discerns as the recurring, albeit unconscious, structural principle of the novel a fleeting mention of earthly reality followed by conversations that almost immediately dissolve into the infinite realms of dream and poetry (36). Robert Leroy likewise ascribes the metaphors associating dreams, water, and night with love and poetry to the unconscious poetic process at work (Leroy 1963, 1965, 1968). Such interpretations indicate that the notion of the Romantic artist as inspired genius still prevailed over the increasingly clear evidence of the conscious artistry Novalis employed in the construction of his novel, which in the first part of *Heinrich von Ofterdingen* distinguishes the master artist Klingsohr from Heinrich, his poetic apprentice.

Hans-Joachim Mähl soon put an end to such schematic evaluations of *Heinrich von Ofterdingen* through his magisterial treatment of the idea of the Golden Age in the works of Novalis. Mähl first traces the development of this idea from Hesiod through Greek and Roman antiquity, Judeo-Christian conceptions of the Apocalypse, late medieval legends of the sleeping emperor who would return like a messiah to revive the Holy Roman empire, pastoral poetry from the Renaissance through the eighteenth century, and the philosophical chiliasm of Kant and Fichte. In the second half of his study, he shows how Novalis incorporated the various poetic, religious, political, and philosophical components of this motif in his own work, with *Heinrich von Ofterdingen* as the culmination point. Whereas Ehrensperger asserts a move from the finite to the infinite in this novel, Mähl makes a vastly more detailed and convincing case for a simultaneous poetic transposition in the exact opposite direction. In a close reading of the passage from chapter five in which a moonlit night awakens in Heinrich a sense of the fundamental unity of the world, Mähl demonstrates how the initial perception of outer reality causes Heinrich to delve into the infinity within him but how this in turn leads him to construct the image of a massive cathedral of being uniting past and future in an all-inclusive harmony of earthly creatures. Mähl concludes by calling this passage an example of what Novalis meant by the romanticization of the world through the medium of language (2: 545): the everyday takes on a mysterious hue, the known acquires the dignity of the unknown, and the finite receives an infinite touch; but at the same time the mysterious, unknown, and infinite become visible and comprehensible as well (Mähl 1965, 422).

Responding to Hiebel's contention that the tales told in the first part of *Heinrich von Ofterdingen* have little or nothing to do with its content, Mähl points out that not only are there interconnections between the tales and the outer plot, but there is also an intricate overlay of time references that turn the image of the Golden Age into past memory, future longing, and latent present (408-9). He takes issue with Korff's contention that Novalis had located the Golden Age in a romantic Middle Ages and stresses that Novalis is interested rather in depicting the process whereby the Golden Age can be realized everywhere and at every time (417-18). Referring back to his earlier chapters on the Golden Age as a postulate and a principle of approximation, Mähl reminds his readers that Novalis was aware that his novel was fiction rather than reality, but for him it was the task of the poet to make present what was absent but longed for in an imperfect world. Only through fairy tales could the idea of a kingdom of love and peace become a palpable image that might inspire people to work toward its realization (413-14). At the beginning of his study Mähl felt obliged to explain that the word *utopia* in the subtitle of his work did not refer to the nineteenth century's understanding of this term as chimera or illusion but rather to the long literary tradition of ideal times or realms made present by an imagined realization (2-3). By the end of the 1960s, as student revolts swept the Western world, the topic of utopia became current among literary and political theorists alike and was to remain so in West Germany for at least another decade: it is not surprising that Richard Faber cites extensively from Mähl's work in a study claiming that the rallying cry of the Parisian students in May 1968 — "L'imagination prend le pouvoir" (the imagination takes power) — was an idea that Herbert Marcuse derived explicitly from Novalis (Faber 1970, 11-12). Though Faber's proselytizing tone here is more like Hiebel's approach to literary interpretation than the type of careful scholarship practiced by Mähl, it serves as a sign of how the poetic message of Novalis now seemed more timely than ever.

Before turning to these tumultuous years at the end of the decade, however, we should first consider less dramatic but nonetheless significant outgrowths of a renewed interest in Novalis, namely readers' editions of *Heinrich von Ofterdingen*. In 1964 Palmer Hilty provided the first complete English translation in more than a century. Hilty's introduction relies more on details from Hiebel's work than might have been desirable for purposes of awakening interest in those who read it before the translation itself, and he apologizes in advance for his rendering of the lyric poetry (10); but all in all *Henry von Ofterdingen* emerges as a recognizable image of the original, albeit without the paralipomena to part two that Tieck had woven into his report on the novel's continuation. Wolfgang Frühwald, in his 1965 edition of the novel for the widely used Reclam Universal Library series, provides both Tieck's narration and also the plans for part two, allowing readers not familiar with the historical-critical edition the opportunity to compare the raw notes with Tieck's reworking of them. For part one, Frühwald also restores the punctuation of the first edition of 1802 — a textual advance adopted in the 1977 reissue of volume one of the historical-critical edition. And in addition to a very serviceable bibliography, he supplies an afterword that considers and builds upon the critical literature of the preceding years. Although Frühwald follows Küpper and Samuel in postulating a part three to *Heinrich von Ofterdingen* — Mähl's refutation of this thesis had not yet appeared in print (Mähl 1965, 416) — he devotes more space to a discussion of the importance of mirroring techniques in the novel as we know it, interpreting this as a Romantic variant on the Platonic myth of the cave. Thus the journey to Augsburg is the outer equivalent to the inner journey that Heinrich undertakes, and the antinomies between West and East, Christianity and Islam, male and female, sword and lute, action and contemplation that Heinrich encounters in chapter four of part one are destined to be resolved within and by him in the second part of the novel (Frühwald 1965, 233-37).

To be sure, as of 1968 the Golden Age had arrived neither in earthly terms nor with regard to Novalis editions, where Emil Staiger omitted the Klingsohr tale from his selection of the poems and novels of Novalis on the grounds of its unintelligibility (Staiger 1968, 48). Gerhard Schulz took a less extreme and more philological approach in his Novalis edition of the following year by providing a commentary to the Klingsohr tale (Schulz 1969a, 711-22) that surpasses in exactitude and detail the one supplied by Kluckhohn and Samuel in volume one of the historical-critical edition. Schulz continued his efforts to make the life and thoughts of Novalis accessible to a wider reading audience by writing the volume in the Rowohlt series of illustrated monographs on illustrious artists and thinkers. While the marketing strategists no doubt chose the light blue tint of the cover picture as a subliminal advertisement for the poet of the Blue Flower — whose long, flowing hair could not have been more in fashion in 1969 — also of significance is the fact that this is a reproduction of the only life portrait of the mature Friedrich von Hardenberg rather than of the 1845 drawing by Eduard Eichens that contributed so much to the image of Novalis as a dreamy youth. In his presentation of the life and works of Novalis, Schulz likewise dispenses with the old myths and makes accessible the new information that he and his fellow editors had been so instrumental in bringing to light.

In the chapter on *Heinrich von Ofterdingen*, Schulz puts the polemics against Goethe into perspective and cautions against too hasty a search for biographical elements in the novel, although he does make the revealing point that Heinrich's maternal attachment corresponds to his author's affection for his mother as opposed to his often strained relationship with his father. Alluding to the unmistakable sexual overtones of Heinrich's dream of the Blue Flower and the episode in the Klingsohr tale in which Ginnistan seduces Eros in the guise of his mother, Schulz regards *Heinrich von Ofterdingen* as an attempt to transform and sublimate these erotic impulses, so that Mathilde and Cyane become messengers from the one true mother and the various older males with whom Heinrich comes into contact serve as teachers and substitutes on a higher level for his father (Schulz 1969b, 139-43). Schulz provides a fine interpretation of the syncretistic New Mythology proclaimed by Friedrich Schlegel and attempted by Novalis in both his Klingsohr tale and the image of the Blue Flower that opens the novel, but he does not hesitate to voice his reservations about the efficacy of this attempt: the Blue Flower has petals the color of heaven, while its roots sink into the earth; it combines Thuringian flower sagas with alchemistic mysticism and Indian lotus flower symbolism; but as a symbol of hope for love and peace it does not possess the simple persuasiveness of the Biblical dove (146-48). And yet Schulz concludes his book with a remark that suggests a reason why Novalis, now seen as a writer interested in changing the world for the better, was soon to become an emblem in the youth counterculture of West Germany, with even a rock band named after him: while one may regard with skepticism Novalis's dream of the regeneration of humanity, such a dream is fortunately ineradicable (163).

In *Texts and Contexts*, the second volume of a series on periods in German literature, J. M. Ritchie likewise endeavors to supply English readers with a view of Novalis, *Heinrich von Ofterdingen*, and the Romantic novel that negates the clichés still circulating about the poet of the Blue Flower. Stressing the importance that Friedrich Schlegel placed on the novel when he called Goethe's *Wilhelm Meister* one of the three tendencies of the age along with the French Revolution and Fichte's *Wissenschaftslehre*, Ritchie notes that *Heinrich von Ofterdingen*, ostensibly set in the Middle Ages, "makes constant references forward to Novalis' own post-revolutionary age" (119) and that the French Revolution is at least as important, if not as evident, as the influence of Goethe and Fichte in determining the conception of the novel as the synthesis of war-ring forces. This statement, which would have been inconceivable at the be-ginning of the 1960s, suggests how the paradigms of literary scholarship were in flux by the end of the decade. But Ritchie also reminds his English readers that long before the images of Novalis as "amiable enthusiast, poetic dreamer, simple-minded German mystic or crack-brained rhapsodist" had become cur-rent, Carlyle had likened him to the German Pascal. And so he closes his lucid and insightful explication of *Heinrich von Ofterdingen*, which prepared the way for the renewed interest in Novalis among Anglo-American scholars in the years to come, with the following quote from Carlyle's tribute to Novalis:

> Both are of the purest, most affectionate moral nature; both of a high, fine discursive intellect; both are mathematicians and naturalists, yet occupy themselves chiefly with Religion; nay, the best writings of both are left in the shape of "thoughts," materials of a grand scheme, which each of them, with the views peculiar to his age, had planned, we may say, for the furtherance of Religion, and which neither of them lived to execute. (Carlyle 1829; quoted in Ritchie 1969, 142)

Ritchie's essay stands in the worthy tradition of Carlyle in that it makes com-prehensible to an English-speaking audience the work of a writer whom even students of German literature were more likely to know by a doubtful reputa-tion, and it does so in a fashion calculated to awaken further interest. Imme-diately before the reference to Carlyle, Ritchie draws a parallel between Novalis and a more contemporary German writer, Kafka; suggests that the un-answered questions of *Heinrich von Ofterdingen* lend it a fascination that is also part of its mystique; and argues that "there is a sense in which the fragment is complete as it stands, since the essential message has been successfully con-veyed" (141-42) — a point that even critics like Schulz and Mähl had not yet considered.

The same year that Ritchie's essay appeared, Eckhard Heftrich offered a different assessment of *Heinrich von Ofterdingen*, namely that its second part indicates a depletion of poetic energy that would have boded ill for any further continuation of the novel. By the time Heinrich and Sylvester launch into their conversation on morality and poetry, he says, Heinrich is the mouthpiece of his author that he was in danger of becoming from the beginning of the novel, through whom the miracles of poetry are discussed, not enacted (112-13). This thesis, which resembles Ehrensperger's analysis of the epic structure of *Hein-rich von Ofterdingen*, differs from it in that it is the product of an intensive dis-cussion of the connection between thought and poetry in the poetological theory of Novalis. In a prefatory note, Heftrich explains that this study, on which he worked between 1963 and 1966, was not published until 1969 so that he could refer to the printed version of the third volume of the Novalis edition whose galley proofs he had been using since 1965. Of particular value for his study are Mähl's investigations of Novalis's encounters with neoplatonic and cabalistic thought in the voluminous eighteenth-century compendia of Tiedemann and Sprengel, which Mähl had documented in his 1963 study "Novalis und Plotin" and incorporated into his editorial commentary on the encyclopedic "Allgemeines Brouillon" (General Sketchbook). Like Mähl, Heftrich brings Hardenberg's reflections on writers like Plotinus and Paracelsus in connection with the critique of Kant and Fichte's half-hearted attempts at intellectual experimentation.

What Heftrich does not employ, however, are the commentaries by Gerhard Schulz on Novalis's speculations on science and nature from this same period that are also contained in volume three of the historical-critical edition. Thus Heftrich develops an image of Novalis as Orphic poet that does not take into consideration the fundamental differences between premodern and German Idealistic thinking with regard to the transformation of the earth: Novalis does not need to depict the actions of a new Orpheus in his novel if he can succeed in awakening this poetic capacity within his readers. To a certain extent, Heftrich, like Kluckhohn, limits his analysis by failing to consider the implications of Romantic poetry as *progressive Universalpoesie* (progressive universal poesy) for Friedrich Schlegel and Novalis, who believed that all human beings had an inherently poetic (that is, creative) potential that ideally they could manifest in all aspects of their daily life. Ritchie alludes to this idea when he points out that Novalis describes the activities of the miner Heinrich encounters in such a way that one might assume he were speaking about an artist's work (Ritchie 1969, 130-31). Such a perspective might have helped to unite the individually interesting but curiously disparate chapters of Heftrich's book, such as the initial discussion of the artistic atheism that Novalis thought he recognized in *Wilhelm Meisters Lehrjahre* (21-25) or the worthwhile reading of Novalis's theory of the fairy tale as the self-penetration of chaos (116-28). But as the first critic who consciously attempted to make full use of the scholarly apparatus of the historical-critical edition, Heftrich set a worthy example for future efforts, which were to come to fruition in the next decade of research on *Heinrich von Ofterdingen*.

Compared with Heftrich's ambitious interpretive work, Johannes Mahr's monograph on the path of the poet in *Heinrich von Ofterdingen* seems more like a regression to the unmitigated close-reading approaches of the 1940s and 1950s. Mahr concentrates his attention on the first part, treating it as a self-contained work of art, and pointedly excludes consideration of the beginning to part two, the notes for its continuation, or any of Novalis's earlier writings (1970, 13-21). When one recalls, however, that the main title of Mahr's study, *Übergang zum Endlichen* (Transition to the Finite), is a paraphrase from a letter of Novalis to Caroline Schlegel in which Novalis articulates his goal as a novelist (4: 281) months before he began his work on *Ofterdingen*, it would appear that Mahr has violated his principles even prior to the first sentence of his book. As has so often been the case in Novalis criticism, preexisting assumptions about Novalis and the nature of *Heinrich von Ofterdingen* dictate the interpretive results and thereby make highly suspect the attempt to achieve a "pure" reading of the novel. And while Mahr's methodical chapter-by-chapter approach to the work does have the merit of pointing out shortcomings in earlier interpretations of individual parts of the novel, such as that attempted by Haufe (Mahr 1970, 169), it also lays such stress on Heinrich's development as a poet that in the end the reader is left with an understanding of *Heinrich von Ofterdingen* as a type of Bildungsroman — a contention that Jürgen Jacobs was soon to dispute in his 1972 study of the genre, in which he argues that Heinrich is not and was not intended to be a fully developed character and that it makes better sense to separate *Ofterdingen* entirely from the tradition of the Bildungsroman (142-43).

Mahr's avowed concentration on the text of the novel to the exclusion of all other considerations also leads to some peculiar vagaries of interpretation. In his treatment of Heinrich's dream of the Blue Flower, for instance, Mahr uses the father's dream as the paradigm for judging that of his son (62), thus overlooking other segments, such as Heinrich's immersion in the waters of the cave, which represent a new addition to the traditional motifs from the Kyffhäuser saga contained in the father's dream. Heftrich had interpreted this immersion scene in the tradition of Orphic and early Christian rites of initiation (Heftrich 1969, 84-101), but even this discussion of the provenance of such motifs did not answer the question of the purpose behind their employment. For all their achievements, neither Heftrich nor Mahr's methods unlocked key elements to the novel.

Helmut Schanze's computer-generated index to *Heinrich von Ofterdingen*, published in 1968, is at first sight an even more radical reduction of the novel to its lexical elements than that attempted by Johannes Mahr. But in terms of its potential usefulness for scholars interested in word and motif studies, it represents a precursor to the thematic word index to Novalis published twenty years later in volume five of the historical-critical edition. In addition, the article Schanze published in 1970 on the theory and practical application of such an index documents the conscious artistry of Novalis as to the choice of words, punctuation, and sentence rhythm in a more exacting way than earlier attempts by scholars like Kluckhohn, Samuel, Kayser, and Haufe.

What further distinguishes Schanze's study from the works of these critics and also from Mahr's close reading of *Heinrich von Ofterdingen* is the methodological sophistication and self-reflection he brings to bear on his findings. As Schanze observes, a complete index dissolves the "texture" of a work of literature, but this same process of estrangement also allows a fresh look at its "material" and the contexts within which the author employs it (1970, 21). While earlier commentators had remarked already on the paratactic style of

Heinrich von Ofterdingen, Schanze was able to demonstrate that the most common word in the novel is the coordinating conjunction *und*, which with 2,189 entries far surpasses in frequency even the definite articles *die* and *der* (with 1,503 and 1,285 occurrences respectively) — which, according to statistical analyses, are normally the two most frequently employed words in contemporary German. Such a statistic may at first seem unremarkable, but Schanze also analyzes the relative frequency of this word in the individual chapters of *Heinrich von Ofterdingen*, and here he discerns unmistakable differences between the "narrative style" of certain chapters and the "conversational style" of units such as chapter eight (29-30) — a finding that contradicts Kayser's assertion of a "unified style" throughout the novel. And by including asterisk signs in the index beside all those instances where a word begins with a capital letter, Schanze also draws attention to Novalis's bestowal of poetic quality on this humble connecting word *und* by noting its frequency as the first word in lines of poetry and also in the pronouncements on the nature of poetry in chapter eight, where its relative lack of frequency makes a sentence such as Heinrich's following remark stand out all the more (31-32): "Und eben in dieser Freude, das, was außer der Welt ist, in ihr zu offenbaren, das tun zu können, was eigentlich der ursprüngliche Trieb unsers Daseins ist, liegt der Ursprung der Poesie" (1: 287; 116).

As the above example suggests, Schanze brings more than merely statistical skills to his enterprise. In 1966 he had published a book on the topic of Romanticism and the Enlightenment that emphasized in positive terms the intellectual ties between these two periods in the works of Novalis and Friedrich Schlegel. And his article on Friedrich Schlegel's theory of the novel had appeared in the volume on German theories of the novel edited by Reinhold Grimm that contained Gerhard Schulz's investigation of Novalis's poetics of the novel. Schanze thus was in an excellent position to combine an acute awareness of the latest research on the poetic theories of Novalis and Friedrich Schlegel with a reconsideration of what word and stylistic studies of *Heinrich von Ofterdingen* might have to contribute toward a renewed understanding of the novel.

Schanze's first departure from long-held opinions regarding German Romanticism has to do with the principle of unconscious artistic creation evident as late as 1969 in Heftrich's work (86). Schanze stresses conversely the conscious artistry of authors like Schlegel and Novalis, which connects them with the tradition of rhetoric in poetry and proceeds from the assumption of a deliberate selection and arrangement of words for purposes of achieving a desired effect (1970, 22-23). His master stroke lies in choosing the word *blau*, or blue, as a demonstration of Novalis's highly controlled employment of vocabulary. Ever since Tieck and Heine, the Blue Flower had come to stand for the dreamy flight from reality allegedly synonymous with *Heinrich von Ofterdingen*,

Novalis, and German Romanticism itself. But Schanze identifies another one of Tieck's editorial sins: his transforming a remark in Novalis's notes — "Farbencharakter. Alles blau in meinem Buche. Hinten Farbenspiel — Individualitaet jeder Farbe" (1: 346) — into an assertion that the novel was intended to maintain the same color character and always remind one of the Blue Flower (1: 366; Schanze 24). Even if one counts all the variants of the color blue, such as bluish, dark blue, light blue, light heavenly blue, and blackish blue, the total number of occurrences still only equals the 26 times the words *gold* and *golden* appear in the novel (24-25). But the color blue does appear frequently enough in key passages of the novel, such as Heinrich's two dreams and the Klingsohr tale, to impress the reader with its symbolic import — a striking example of the "poetical economy" that Novalis had emphasized in the course of his critique of *Wilhelm Meisters Lehrjahre*. By the time Schanze points out that the German word for *day* appears twice as frequently in *Heinrich von Ofterdingen* as that for *night* and that the vocabulary of the novel contains a larger number of philosophical terms and abstractions (28-29), it becomes clear that it is not so much the text of this novel that has determined its interpretations as the expectations raised and reechoed by generations of critics. Published at a time when literary theorists like Hans Robert Jauss had made current the term *Erwartungshorizont*, or horizon of expectations, to describe the way readers first react to a particular piece of literature, Schanze's study made it clear there were quite a few horizons that still needed to be expanded before the peculiar combination of chaos and order he saw as characteristic of *Heinrich von Ofterdingen*'s poetic structures might become manifest to more readers. It is to such interpretations during the 1970s that we now turn.

7: New Colors for the Blue Flower — 1971-1980

B Y THE END of the 1960s, the major work on Novalis editions had been completed. In 1975 Richard Samuel published volume four of the historical-critical edition, which provided the text and commentary to Friedrich von Hardenberg's diaries, letters, and correspondence to and about him, a fair amount of which material had been previously unavailable. As much as these documents helped to further demystify the image of Novalis and confirm the more sober portrait painted by scholars such as Gerhard Schulz, they had no major impact on interpretations of *Heinrich von Ofterdingen* written during the 1970s. As Hannelore Link observed in the preface to her 1971 study of abstraction and poetry in the work of Novalis — a dissertation written under the direction of Walter Müller-Seidel — one of the central weaknesses of Novalis research from the beginning had been its excessive emphasis on what she called "biographism" (7). As a corrective both to such an approach and to the tendency to paraphrase the text rather than interpret it, Link proposed to direct her attention to formal aspects of Novalis's writings in the hope of disclosing more a method of thinking than a particular content. Some fifty years previously, of course, Oskar Walzel had stressed formal aspects of *Heinrich von Ofterdingen*, and with great benefits to subsequent research on the novel. But Link's approach reflected a continuation of the more recent methodological sophistication demonstrated by Helmut Schanze in that it made explicit use of theoretical insights derived from the Russian formalists of the 1920s that the conservative German critics of that decade neither knew of nor would have acknowledged if they had. In this regard, her study serves as paradigmatic for the new directions in Novalis scholarship during the 1970s, in which insights derived from critical methodologies such as reception history, interdisciplinary studies, semiotics, neo-Marxism, and poststructuralism would help bring about some radically new approaches to *Heinrich von Ofterdingen* and provide new color to overworked critical fields.

Link begins her study with some general remarks on the ambivalent meaning of the term *abstraction* in that it implies both a negative movement away from a certain matter and a positive heightening of that which is abstracted. With specific regard to poetry, abstraction departs from the normal conventions of language and representational thinking, but at the same time this "semantic displacement" — as Viktor Šklovskij calls it — becomes a key component of literary creativity (14). From the standpoint of the reader, meanwhile, such an abstraction from accustomed patterns not only disappoints prior expectations but also challenges an active approach to the text at hand that goes beyond a focus on the content of the work — precisely what traditional critical approaches to Romanticism had neglected or overlooked (16).

In his own characterization of the process of romanticizing the world, Novalis had spoken of the necessity of giving the commonplace, normal, and familiar a heightened sense, a mysterious aspect, and the majesty of the unknown (2: 545) — a procedure he later attempted in his dream of the Blue Flower. It is therefore no surprise that Link begins her interpretation of *Heinrich von Ofterdingen*, which she considers the author's most thorough attempt to restructure the relationship between poetry and normal reality, with a discussion of this dream sequence; only now it is the critic, not the author, who hopes to impart fresh vigor to seemingly overworked terrain. Link recognizes in *Heinrich von Ofterdingen* a form of reception aesthetics (141) that has begun as early as the first sentences of the novel, where Heinrich recalls the tale of the Blue Flower the mysterious stranger has just told him (154). And whereas Mahr had used the dream of the elder Ofterdingen as the prototype for that of the son, Link points out that the father's rationalistic interpretation of his dream's significance is contradicted by a statement in the dream itself that in the flower before his eyes he has seen the wonder of the world (1: 202; 22); indeed, the retelling of this dream repeats images his son had experienced and thereby heightens their degree of reality (141). In other words, it is not the experience of a dream but rather its communication within a social context that helps it come to life. Employing the verb suffix —*ieren* so beloved by Schlegel and Novalis, Link stresses that it is the process of poeticizing the world that occupies a central role in part one of *Heinrich von Ofterdingen*. In this respect she provides an illustration of what Schlegel meant by an "esoteric" interpretation of this novel when he discussed it in his journal *Europa* in 1803. Her remarks, however, contain infinitely more detailed analysis than that provided by Schlegel, as well as productive use of the best insights of her most recent predecessors — such as Striedter's concept of the figures in *Heinrich von Ofterdingen* as being pre- and postfigurations of one another, or Voerster's study of the interplay among the various sections of the novel.

Also different from Schlegel's remarks are Link's observations on the fundamental problems connected with Novalis's esoteric approach to literature. It is not so much that this method of transforming the world runs the risk of ignoring earthly reality or becoming absorbed in its self-enclosed artistic creation, as earlier critics had alleged; in the second chapter of her work Link documents the care with which Novalis uses his reflections on the process of abstraction in his notebooks and fragments to achieve a productive tension between the twin poles of everyday reality and its poetic transformation. Instead she sees Novalis's weakness lying in his unbounded trust that the delicate balancing act between reality and poetry that he had achieved in his life and reflections was immediately capable of being cultivated in others (179-80).

Whereas the rallying cry of protestors at the 1968 Congress of Germanists in West Berlin had been "Macht die Blaue Blume rot," Richard Faber had argued that, with respect to the utopian intentions of works such as the *Hymnen an die Nacht*, the Blue Flower was already red (Faber 1970, 11) in the sense that it exemplified a type of revolutionary Romanticism in the spirit of Marcuse, Bloch, and Benjamin. Link, on the other hand, cautions that present-day readers should not expect of Novalis any more than the attempt to achieve change by inspiring inner transformations in his readers that in turn affect their responses to a nonutopian reality; it is in this dynamics of reflection that she sees his poetic work's greatest present justification (181). By avoiding a modish championing of Novalis that disregards fundamental differences between the end of the eighteenth century and our own age, Link achieved one of the most significant breakthroughs in contemporary Novalis scholarship.

Throughout her study Link repeatedly cautions that its isolation of the process of abstraction represents a single, albeit important facet in the writings of Novalis, which then needs to be integrated into a consideration of his work as a whole. In her discussion of Novalis's reflections on philosophy and science, she draws particular attention to his literary dialogues and their emphasis on the value of hypotheses and experiments, although she understands the frequent recourse to scientific phenomena in both his theoretical and his more narrowly poetic writings as sources for analogies rather than as ontological verification of his speculations (70). Other researchers, however, had been turning their attention to the content of Novalis's work in natural philosophy. In the process, they established that Novalis's studies in mining, chemistry, physics, mathematics, medicine, and optics not only had a deep impact upon his theoretical writings and his poetic imagery but also provided him with the conviction that he had discovered patterns linking nature and humanity in one harmonious whole. Once one understands this principle of Novalis's thinking, it becomes much clearer why he believed his poetic writings could serve as the basis for altering the way human beings look at and behave toward the world around them.

In the study entitled "Another Glance at Novalis' 'Blue Flower,'" Géza von Molnár considers not only whence Novalis may have derived his imagery, as had scholars like Hecker and Hiebel, but also what he made of it. Molnár interprets the near-equal attention to gold and blue in *Heinrich von Ofterdingen*, which Schanze had documented, as a productive employment of Goethe's contention that blue and yellow were the only true colors (1973, 276-77). In his 1970 dissertation, *Novalis' Fichte Studies: The Foundations of his Aesthetics*, Molnár had already traced the relationship between polar opposition and basic unity that Novalis derived from his study of Fichte's dialectical philosophy and made a recurring pattern in his own reflections; it is not surprising, he argues, that Novalis should have been so interested in making use of Goethe's optical experiments for his own poetic purposes — not just in the dialectic between light and dark in the *Hymnen an die Nacht,* but also in the color symbolism within *Heinrich von Ofterdingen*:

> Yellow signifies unity with the accent on the perspective of light, and that is exactly the function of gold in the fifth chapter, where that symbol predominates.... Blue, on the other hand, connotes unity from the perspective of night, since it is the color that the dark surface assumes when it radiates towards a light one. (283-84; see also Molnár 1986, 444-49, for an expanded discussion of these points)

In the same year that Molnár's study appeared, Walter Wetzels interpreted the Klingsohr tale and its employment of terms and procedures from late-eighteenth-century ideas about electricity and galvanism as Novalis's attempt to achieve a "science fiction" incorporating the latest discoveries in chemistry and physics in a story of universal redemption. A century before Wetzels's article, Haym had pointed out the presence in the Klingsohr tale of images derived from galvanist theory, but for him these ideas were little more than pseudoscience and hence hardly worthy of any extended treatment. In contrast to Haym, however, Wetzels — whose dissertation had dealt with Johann Wilhelm Ritter, the Romantic physicist and close friend of Novalis who had discovered the existence of ultraviolet rays in the course of his experiments — stresses that at the time he wrote the Klingsohr tale, Novalis shared his ideas on galvanism with respected natural scientists such as Ritter and Alexander von Humboldt, and that he took care to depict the various resuscitation of characters in his tale in a way that accorded with standard experimental procedure. Only when we recognize the factual details of these poetic experiments does their symbolic import become more significant, as for example when the kiss Eros gives to Freya completes the electromagnetic circuit and awakens this Sleeping Beauty in a unique wedding of love and science (1973, 173-75).

In the following year Elisabeth Stopp took a closer look at another much maligned aspect of *Heinrich von Ofterdingen,* namely the beginning of part two, which as late as 1969 Eckhard Heftrich had regarded as romanticized kitsch and which in 1970 Johannes Mahr mentioned in passing as still in need of a comprehensive interpretation (247). Stopp signals by her title's reference to Friedrich Schlegel's words in 1803 regarding the "transition from novel to mythology" in *Heinrich von Ofterdingen* that she regards the opening chapter of part two as a successful realization of the poetological goals shared by Novalis and Schlegel: "the miraculous irrupts into the real world, the phenomena of nature and of the human mind are transfigured in the light of the imagination and at the same time subjected to philosophical inquiry in a more consistent way than was the case in Part I" (1974, 320). On the one hand, she argues, Heinrich's vision of Mathilde and his dialogue with Cyane evoke motifs in the novel that hitherto had been consigned to the realm of dreams and fairy tale; in addition, the philosophical dialogue with the physician and naturalist Sylvester

permits an explicit interweaving of science and poetry. In conjunction with
Charles Barrack's more conceptually orientated discussion of the concept of
conscience in *Heinrich von Ofterdingen* (1971) as demonstrated in the dialogue
between Heinrich and Sylvester, Stopp's formal analysis of the beginning to
part two of the novel makes a convincing case for the argument that, regardless
of whether or not Novalis would have been able to realize his ambitious plans
for *Heinrich von Ofterdingen*, his final weeks of work as an artist demonstrate
an increasing ability to expand the form of the novel (For a discussion of
Heinrich von Ofterdingen in comparison with the endings of other German
Romantic novels, see Schuller 1974, especially 69-110).

The year 1975 saw the appearance of the most ambitious attempt to date
to discuss the poetry of Novalis in the context of its author's reflections on
philosophy and the sciences. In a voluminous study, Johannes Hegener traces
Novalis's attempt at a Romantic encyclopedia of knowledge for the advance-
ment of humankind that deliberately combines scientific disciplines and modes
of thought in its individual entries. Pointing to recent Anglo-American discussions on the necessity of reconciling the Two Cultures (the sciences and the
humanities), Hegener sees in the work of Novalis a particular relevance for the
present in that here one finds an individual trained in the most advanced
thinking of his day who nevertheless employed poetry as the medium for integrating individual discoveries and disciplines into a coherent and satisfying
whole (1975, 15-16).

In a lengthy chapter on the Klingsohr tale, Hegener reflects on the relationship between the universe as macrocosm and humanity as microcosm, citing many of Novalis's notebook entries as documentation of the author's
familiarity with this ancient topos. One problem with Hegener's approach,
however, is precisely his extensive quoting from the notebooks and fragments
to the detriment of both their explication and that of the Klingsohr tale. Hegener's discussion of the characters in this story as parts of one huge cosmic
person (142) is stimulating, but the ensuing pages of his interpretation provide
little more than hints as to how this being is depicted as separated at the beginning of the tale but reunited into a world family at its conclusion (163). The
problem is compounded in the second section of the chapter, which begins
with a promising account of the character Fabel's role in progressing from the
infancy of poetry in the Orient to her mastery of scientific processes by the end
of the tale (165-68), but which continues with ever briefer and more general
comments on progressions within the tale from many religions to one religion,
from sickness to health, from immorality to morality, and from dead regions to
live ones (169-75). Had Hegener made more use of recent research on Novalis
in his work, he might have focused his remarks better; the section on the
transitions between colors and shadows to a new, enduring light in *Heinrich
von Ofterdingen* (217-32), for example, would have benefited immensely from
a productive use of Géza von Molnár's study on Novalis and Goethe's color

theories. Nonetheless, Hegener deserves credit for his attempt to view Novalis's thoughts on poetry, philosophy and the sciences in a holistic way.

A contrary and in many ways more satisfying approach to the Klingsohr
tale is Karl Grob's investigation of the blind spots of texts and language, which
he augments with reflections on the temporal nature of allegory derived from
Walter Benjamin and Paul de Man: whereas time stands still in the symbol as
defined by Goethe, Baroque and Romantic allegory strive to depict a temporal
process (1976, 131-32). For this reason, Grob views the presence of Eros and
Freya — characters in the Klingsohr tale whose mythological names refer to
the Greek and Nordic gods of love — as indications that Novalis was interested in a depiction of the history of the modifications of love from polarity to
unity (134). In setting forth this idea, he achieves an excellent complement to
Hegener's discussion of this tale that gains by its intensive rather than extensive approach to its subject matter.

In addition, Grob is the first Novalis scholar, to my knowledge, who makes
use of Jacques Derrida's poststructuralistic approach to textual interpretation.
In his detailed discussion of Novalis's very early Fichte studies revolving
around a theory of the sign, Grob correctly notes that Novalis begins his work
with a critique of Fichte's failure to reflect on the fact that the presentation of a
philosophy of identity necessarily involves its deconstruction (108): "Wir ver-
lassen das *Identische* um es darzustellen" (2: 104). In the case of Novalis, Grob
argues, the depiction of a kingdom of eternal peace at the end of the Klingsohr
tale with the help of Fabel represents a deconstruction of the symbol as the
unity of subject and object, because the figure of Fabel itself constitutes a reflection on the constructed, textual nature of this synthesis (165-66). Grob
concludes his study with an observation on Novalis's understanding of the fairy
tale that anticipates Alice Kuzniar's notion of "delayed endings" as characteristic of Novalis's approach to depictions of the Parousia, or Second Coming: if
the character of Fabel were reconciliation itself, as criticism hopes to find in
her, she would have ceased singing long ago; but she continues to sing (170).

Grob's attention to deconstructivist aspects of Novalis's thought, for all the
praise accorded it by Herbert Uerlings in his discussion of Novalis's theory and
practice of the fairy tale (1991, 391-96, 508-12), may have appeared in print
somewhat before its time; it accorded ill with patterns of ideology criticism
then prevailing in West German literary scholarship, which used its own interpretation of Marxism as a solid base from which to criticize all opposing
positions. Typical for the mid-1970s in this regard is Roland Heine's book
Transzendentalpoesie, which recognizes the emancipatory impulses of Friedrich
Schlegel and Novalis's concept of a self-reflexive literature informed by
thought patterns from German Idealism but also sees in the Blue Flower an
attempted construction of a higher world via a symbol that makes the real
world increasingly indefinite (1975, 152). Heine's study is thus a critique not
only of Novalis but also of Richard Faber's attempt to "paint the Blue Flower

red" in a kind of revolutionary Romanticism (7). It also attempts to refute
Hannelore Link's thesis that *Heinrich von Ofterdingen* is a novel reflects upon
its own limits; rather, Heine sees this achieved in E. T. A. Hoffmann's *Der
goldne Topf* (147).

Ever since Heinrich Heine praised E. T. A. Hoffmann at the expense of
Novalis in *Die romantische Schule*, Hoffmann has enjoyed special treatment by
leftist critics of German Romanticism. As Klaus Peter has observed, for a long
time the only full-length book on a German Romantic author published in the
German Democratic Republic had been Hans-Georg Werner's 1962 dissertation on Hoffmann, at a time when Claus Träger's diatribes against Novalis
were still ringing throughout East German scholarship (1980a, 23-25). But by
the mid-1970s, both the societal climate and the intellectual atmosphere in
East Germany were changing rapidly; in the period of relative artistic freedom
that saw the publication of such works as Ulrich Plenzdorf's *Die neuen Leiden
des jungen W.* (The New Sufferings of Young W; 1973) — a modern-day adap-
tation of Goethe's *Werther* that suggests that the youthful alienation from society that characterized Goethe's protagonist is also present in contemporary
East Germany — critics such as Träger began to dismantle the unconditional
championing of Goethe at the expense of the Romantics that had to that point
been a matter of official state policy. In an essay published in 1975 that deals
with the origins and standpoints of German Romanticism, Träger emphasizes
the utopian ideals of unalienated labor and political freedom found in the
writings of the early Romantics (308); even if the word *utopian* here still has
the connotation of non-Marxist and hence *unscientific*, Träger concedes that
with respect to such ideals, writers like Novalis and the young Friedrich
Schlegel were more radical than their more "realistic" contemporaries Goethe
and Hegel, who were more willing to make compromises with the existing
powers (329-31). Träger's essay ends with the suggestion that it is now time
for East German society to appropriate parts of its cultural heritage that it has
previously not understood and appreciated. In the 1978 volume of the East
German literary history dealing with German literature between 1789 and
1830, the section on Novalis ends with a remarkably sympathetic explication of
the poetics of the fairy tale in *Heinrich von Ofterdingen*. Hans-Dietrich Dahnke
— whose earlier stout defense of the Lukácsian antithesis of German Classicism and Romanticism Träger had criticized in his 1975 essay as undialectical
(see Peter 1980, 28) — now praises the poetic intensity, logic, and talent Novalis displays in his attempt to transform the sphere of normal life (Dahnke
1978, 437), although he notes that later German bourgeois literature was not
able to make productive use of Novalis's utopian message.

A crisis in literary reception of utopian messages, however, also was taking
place in East German society of the late 1970s. With the 1976 expulsion of
Wolf Biermann, the dissident Marxist songwriter, and the ensuing crackdown

on any gesture of solidarity with Biermann, there came an abrupt end to the attempt to allow an official forum for the type of individual expression now symbolized by German Romantic poets and artists. It is no coincidence that the East German writer Christa Wolf uses the meeting of Heinrich von Kleist and Caroline von Günderode — two Romantic writers who later committed suicide — in her story *Kein Ort. Nirgends* (No Place on Earth, 1979) as a sign of her own sense of desolation and isolation in an East Germany increasingly under the control of its state security apparatus. With respect to Novalis scholarship, for the time being, at least, socially oriented criticism freed from the clichés of the past developed in the west of Germany rather than the east.

In 1976 Hans-Joachim Beck had taken a new approach to comparisons between *Heinrich von Ofterdingen* and *Wilhelm Meisters Lehrjahre* by viewing them in light of the socioeconomic positions of their respective authors. Both novels begin with the conflict between the "poetry of the heart" and the "prose of conditions" that Hegel had deemed constitutive of the modern novel (56). But Beck argues that while Goethe's solution to this conflict in the novel is the mercantilistically ordered world represented by the Society of the Tower, as a compromise between feudal and middle-class elements, Novalis operates from a model similar to the economic liberalism advocated by Adam Smith and the political dynamism unleashed by the French Revolution (134-36). These concluding remarks in Beck's book are little more than speculative suggestions, especially compared with Ulrich Stadler's fullydeveloped arguments only a few years later on Novalis and his poetics of economics, but they do open the way to the possibility that the allegedly dreamy Novalis might actually have understood his novel as a nonmimetic, mythologized presentation of socioeconomic forces at work in his age. Beck thus took a big step beyond conventional Marxist aesthetics in interpreting literature as a reflection on social conditions rather than a simple reflection of them (123).

The following year Helmut Pfotenhauer took a similarly sophisticated approach to a consideration of the supposed modernity of Novalis. Rather than engaging in another search for correspondences between the Romantic poet's theories and the later practice of the French Symbolist poets, Pfotenhauer asks whether the seeming omnipotence of Heinrich von Ofterdingen as poetic subject might not itself be a symptom of that deficiency of the individual as an integrating center of reality that was to become a major theme in nineteenth and twentieth-century novels (1977, 112-13). Turning to the same Hegelian concept of the conflict between the individual and society that Beck had employed, Pfotenhauer discusses the conversation between father and son in chapter one of *Heinrich von Ofterdingen* and observes how quickly they come to general agreement, especially when one compares this scene with Wilhelm Meister's much more painful and extended differences with his father (115). Novalis seems to be casting his work not as a novel but as a mythical fairy tale (119-21; see also Rogers 1977 for an interpretation of the tale of Atlantis in

Ofterdingen as the literary equivalent of Novalis's critique of *Wilhelm Meister*). Pfotenhauer also understands the phenomenon of war and strife in the novel as the means for eliminating whatever elements do not easily accede to poetic transformation. Alluding to correspondences between passages in Novalis and Freud's discoveries of the depths of the psyche, Pfotenhauer sees in Novalis's work the glorification of the drive toward undifferentiated satisfaction in death that lies below the thin layer of human culture (122) and provides as examples what he identifies as motifs of incest and cannibalism in the Klingsohr tale (124). Pfotenhauer overshoots the mark in such instances, at least in this reader's opinion, but he has the virtue of presenting his criticisms in energetic and straightforward fashion. And his postulated connection between Freud and Novalis, here only one facet of a multilevel critique of *Heinrich von Ofterdingen*, will become a main focus of Kenneth Calhoon's 1992 monograph entitled *Fatherland*, albeit with very different results.

Pfotenhauer's interest in the precarious nature of the supposedly autonomous poetic subject in *Heinrich von Ofterdingen* is shared by Friedrich Kittler in an essay on the Romantic invention of sexuality that he presented at a 1977 interdisciplinary conference on Romanticism in Germany and later had published as part of a special volume of the *Deutsche Vierteljahrsschrift für Literaturwissenschaft und Geistesgeschichte*. In Kittler's discussion of sexuality, however, it is not Freud but rather the theories of Michel Foucault and Jacques Lacan that serve as reference points. For Kittler, sexuality has not become a theme in Romantic literature because of its suppression in the waking world of the middleclass; instead it is a cultural coding and socialization technique in the service of those institutions of power and knowledge that have also produced the notion of the autonomous human "subject" (1978, 107-8). Kittler interprets the sexualized family in the Klingsohr tale not as an expression of hidden tensions in Novalis's own family, as had Gerhard Schulz, but rather as an explicit reflection on changing patterns in familial organization whereby even in aristocratic and prosperous middle-class families the mother assumes the nurturing role hitherto assigned to the wet nurse. The shifts in appearance between Ginnistan and the mother of Eros in the tale, their couplings with the father, and Ginnistan's sexual initiation of Eros all partake in the matrilinear dynamics of deficiency and desire discussed by Lacan (104-5). By the end of the eighteenth century, Kittler argues, literature has become a hermeneutics of family ties, which makes possible (and tautological) its later psychoanalytic interpretation (112).

Kittler's short article — together with the discussion of E. T. A. Hoffmann, Freud, and Lacan published by Klaus Peter as the final essay in his 1980 collection of essays on German Romanticism since 1945 — serves as the prelude to a series of intriguing publications discussed in greater detail in the chapter on scholarship dealing with *Heinrich von Ofterdingen* during the 1980s.

Kittler draws deserved attention to the figure of the mother in the Klingsohr tale, whose ashes — dissolved and then drunk in an act that Kittler inexplicably refers to as a baptismal ritual (105), though the connection with the Christian ceremony of the Eucharist seems a more appropriate comparison — serve to make her invisibly present to all who receive her (1: 312; 144). His reference to the ideology of motherly love propagated in the pedagogy of the Enlightenment allows interesting connections between matrilinear orality and the multiple pairings and love whispers at the end of the tale, which he understands as the production of an omnipresent Mother that has displaced the symbolic Father (105). But the stress that Kittler places on the mother's orality, as opposed to the tyranny of the Scribe, also leads him to postulate the elimination of this latter character as the only figure whose place in the final tableau the fairy tale forgets to mention (105).

That Novalis "forgets" to mention the Scribe in his fairy tale's conclusion is, to put it mildly, debatable: Perseus, who turns to stone the figures of the Fates and the sphinx, which then serve as the fundaments for the marriage bed of Eros and Freya (1: 309, 315; 142, 148), also presents Eros with a set of marble chess pieces that he identifies as the remains of the enemies of Eros and that Sophie calls a reminder of war and the former dark times (1: 314; 147). It seems reasonable to assume that these figures are the remnants of the Scribe and his followers, whom Fabel had enticed into the same mad tarantella as the Fates (1: 308; 139), particularly as Novalis refers to "petrifying and petrified reason" in his suggestions to Friedrich Schlegel on how to understand his fairy tale (4: 333). It might appear unfair and carping criticism to lay such stress on this one interpretive oversight on Kittler's part were it not for the fact that both Kittler and Jens Schreiber later stress this "forgetfulness" as a cornerstone of their arguments to overturn past practices in German literary criticism.

Kittler's iconoclastic approach to literary interpretation does differ radically from the close readings Christel Gallant and Gordan Birrell provide in their respective studies *Der Raum in Novalis' dichterischem Werk* (Space in the Poetic Work of Novalis, 1978) and *The Boundless Present: Space and Time in the Literary Fairy Tales of Novalis and Tieck* (1979). Birrell remarks in his introduction that "for many people, the idea of interpreting fairy tales evokes uncomfortable memories of Freudian analysts going to work on 'Little Red Riding Hood' and *Alice in Wonderland*, finding meanings which no one had guessed, or wanted to guess, and singling out only those elements in the tales which seemed to substantiate their own theses" (1979, 3). One can only wonder what Birrell might have said about Kittler's article had it appeared in print before his own book went to press. He likewise makes it clear that his approach to the analysis of the function of time and space in the fairy tales of Novalis and Tieck "has little in common with the highly formalized techniques of French structuralism" (5).

But neither should the unwary reader make the mistake of equating Birrell's position with an anachronistic return to the work-immanent approaches of the 1940s and 1950s, which all too often substituted paraphrase for interpretation. Like Christel Gallant in her equally subtle treatment of space in Novalis's poetic work, Birrell proceeds inductively — from individual structural elements of the fairy tales of two Romantic authors through the themes they underscore to general conclusions about diverging directions within German Romanticism. And like Gallant he makes it clear that the superficial reproaches against the alleged formlessness of Novalis and German Romanticism could hardly be farther from the truth.

Gallant begins her analysis of *Heinrich von Ofterdingen* with a reference to Ehrensperger's distinctions between the levels of narrated reality, the many conversations in the novel, and what Ehrensperger terms the absolute realm of the dreams and fairy tales (1978, 33). But she quickly moves beyond what Ehrensperger had to offer by demonstrating that Novalis achieves the sense of unity his novel evokes through a structuring of space that interconnects not only these three levels but also the various types of spaces she distinguishes within the second part of her study: landscapes, the human habitat, housing, physical matter, mountains and seas, the cosmos, and the afterlife. Noting that the dominant forms of spatial organization in Novalis's work are the paths that characters follow (118), she points out that there often is a back-and-forth motion associated with their movement, as in the polar division between palace and country house in the tale of Atlantis (131) or in Fabel's movement between the various realms of the Klingsohr tale (135). Only after establishing such patterns, which culminate in Cyane's answer when Heinrich asks where they are going — "Immer nach Hause" (Home, all the time; 1: 325; 159) — does Gallant observe that Hans-Joachim Mähl has determined that a similar dynamics of motion is characteristic of Novalis's early Fichte studies (138-39). Continuing in the paths traced by Jurij Striedter and Hannelore Link, Gallant identifies the "prefiguration" of many formal aspects of Novalis's narrative work in his philosophical writings. In fact, she concludes her study with the demonstration that the individual points of narrative constitute the midpoints of concentric circles and all-inclusive spheres of cosmic harmony. As she observes, Novalis has made use of geometrical figures — the point, the line, the circle, and the sphere — as constitutive elements of his poetic universe (171-73). In other words, it is simply not the case that Novalis was uninterested in the spatial organization of his tales. If one compares *Heinrich von Ofterdingen* with even a novel like Goethe's *Wilhelm Meisters Lehrjahre* by applying the standards of "realism" common to later nineteenth-century German and European novels as normative standards, Novalis's work is bound to appear woefully lacking; judged from the perspective of its author's own dictum that the novel should be a sensuous realization of an idea (2: 570; Gallant 173), *Heinrich von Ofterdingen* is remarkably successful.

Working independently from Gallant, Gordan Birrell not only confirms many of her findings but also provides consideration of the further dimension of time within these tales. Whereas Gallant concludes her study by discussing the connections between Novalis's philosophical speculations and his artistic production, Birrell notes at the beginning of the chapter "Self-Appropriation and the Long Journey Home: Space in the *Märchen* of Novalis" that Novalis was not only familiar with Kant's understanding of time and space as fundamental modes of human perception but also considered conventional notions of space and time to be "merely symptoms of mental weakness or insufficient elasticity of thought" (1979, 8). Accordingly, in Birrell's view, the spatial separation between characters or between people and places in the fairy tales of Novalis signals a state of alienation in mankind and nature alike, while the narrative progression of these tales portrays the resolution of this estrangement into the "Traum einer unendlichen, unabsehlichen Gegenwart" (1: 87), or dream of a boundless present — a quote from *Die Lehrlinge zu Sais*, Novalis's other unfinished novel, that is the source of the title of Birrell's book. As Birrell remarks about the conclusion of the Klingsohr tale, while "the final unified tableau represents not only the resolution of all philosophical or conceptual tension, but the annihilation of articulated space itself," Novalis also employs "the image of concentric circles" to indicate a new plentitude and harmony transcending the former divisions existing within the tale (30). Birrell thus makes clear why it is not surprising that Novalis would have regarded the fairy tale as the canon of poetry, for in this genre he had the freedom to depict the emancipation from predetermined patterns of perception toward which his novel *Heinrich von Ofterdingen* ultimately progresses.(For further discussions of the fairy tales of Novalis within the context and tradition of the German and European *Kunstmärchen*, or artistic fairy tale, see Schumacher 1977 and Apel 1978.)

In the chapter "Waiting for Fabel: Time in the *Märchen* of Novalis," Birrell proceeds a critical step beyond Gallant's account in discussing the problematic side of Fabel's effortless linkage of what otherwise would have remained paralyzed and incomplete realms. Here too he provides reference to the philosophical presuppositions that underlie Novalis's literary works: "Fundamental to Novalis's optimism is the belief that any such interaction between two formerly distinct zones must inevitably bring both of them closer to a state of unity, and that the forces of cohesion are ultimately more powerful than those of disjunction" (69; 3: 341). But while this concept of "nature as existing on the very threshold of perfection" (77) may predetermine the happy endings of all of Novalis's fairy tales, the recurring impasses that Fabel needs to overcome in the heavens, on earth, and under the earth also suggest "the approaching crisis of

Romantic progressivity" (85) made explicit in the literary fairy tales of Ludwig Tieck. Such a reading of the Klingsohr tale lends support to Pfotenhauer's thesis that the "modernity" of *Heinrich von Ofterdingen* may actually lie in its involuntary betrayal of what Birrell calls "the ultimate tenuousness of Novalis's optimism" (85). While one would need to balance this assessment against Karl Grob's interpretation of the conclusion of the Klingsohr tale, which interprets Fabel's final song as a necessary reminder of the provisional and artistic nature of the work, in many respects Birrell has provided a persuasive critique of the limits of Romanticism.

Another close reading of Novalis that resulted in significant new understanding is David Scrase's article "The Movable Feast: The Role and Relevance of the *Fest* Motif in Novalis' *Heinrich von Ofterdingen*." Whereas nineteenth-century critics such as Julian Schmidt had understood the scene depicting the feast Heinrich experiences in Augsburg as a fleeting sign of undeveloped realism in the novel, Scrase demonstrates that in this banquet Novalis combines pagan and Christian elements also found in the love feasts occurring in the Atlantis and Klingsohr tales in chapters three and nine: "The unquestionable relevance of universal love as a means to a restoration of lost harmony and the role of the poet in this process are matched by the importance of the *Fest* as the most fitting vehicle for such events" (1979, 30). He refers in particular to the conjoining of food, intoxication, and physical-spiritual love in the so-called *Abendmahlshymne*, or communion hymn, of Novalis (1: 166-68) that also appears in the motif of the feast throughout *Ofterdingen*. And once Scrase analyzes images in the Klingsohr tale that Pfotenhauer had understood as cannibalistic and interprets them in the context of a reworking of German Baroque and Pietistic poetry on the Eucharist, the sacrificial death and consumption of the Mother become examples of "a myth mythologized" (33).

The notion of a combination of Christian and pagan images in Novalis's poetry of Novalis is illustrated again in the article by Robert Leroy and Eckhard Pastor on Heinrich's dream of the Blue Flower, which they interpret as the initiation of the Romantic poet. For them, this dream's occurrence on Midsummer Night represents a conjoining of folk traditions with the baptismal imagery associated with the Christian feast day of John the Baptist (1979, 38, 44-45). In a close reading of this dream they distinguish three levels that lead up to the vision of the Blue Flower as a discovery of the latent analogy between spirit and matter in the world as a whole (49-50). By the time Heinrich begins his journey into the world at the beginning of chapter two, Novalis has acquainted his readers with the Romantic cosmos his hero contains within him (54). And when Leroy and Pastor identify Heinrich's father as a type of Enlightenment figure (40), they allude to a conflict between the Enlightenment and a nascent Romanticism that Novalis intends to resolve through a redemption of the father's repressed yearnings.

The combinatory nature of the poetic principles found in *Heinrich von Ofterdingen* is the main focus of John Neubauer's book *Symbolismus und symbolische Logik* (1978). This study has not received the attention it deserves, at least not within Novalis scholarship — perhaps because the poet's name is not mentioned within the title. Yet even a cursory glance at the book's table of contents would suffice to show that Neubauer turns again and again to Novalis as a seminal figure in the history of combinatory analysis, which he traces from its mystical-mathematical roots in Pythagoreanism through the work of Leibniz to its ultimate applications in the writings of twentieth-century authors such as Kafka and Valéry. Fortunately for readers of English, Neubauer incorporates central insights of his chapter "*Heinrich von Ofterdingen* und der moderne Roman" (147-61) into the treatment of this novel in his book on Novalis for the Twayne World Author Series. When discussing Novalis's *Wilhelm Meister*-critique, for example, Neubauer observes that "the notes for *Ofterdingen* clearly demonstrate that he developed his compositional ideas from those combinatorial and serial principles in mathematics which he believed to be the structural basis of Goethe's *Meister*" (1980, 129). In his earlier book, Neubauer took pains to emphasize that Oskar Walzel had already discussed the importance of Novalis's employment of variations and *Bouts-rimé* as a compositional technique, but he added that Walzel had not seen these techniques as part of a longstanding combinatory tradition whose philosophical implications Novalis recognized and shared (1978, 140-46). For his English and American readers, Neubauer remarks that this variational principle was "an artistic mirror of a Leibnizian universe" and provides the translation of a passage from Novalis that I was to use three years later in my opening discussion of "The Myth of Death and Resurrection in *Heinrich von Ofterdingen*":

> All men are variations of a single complete individual, i.e., of a marriage.... If a simple variation such as Natalie and the beautiful soul already awakens such deep pleasure, how infinite must the pleasure be of somebody who registers the whole in its powerful symphony? (2: 564; Neubauer 1980, 129; Mahoney 1983, 53)

Like J. M. Ritchie a decade before, Neubauer draws attention to aspects of *Heinrich von Ofterdingen* that may remind today's readers of Kafka's narrative style, such as the almost total coincidence of the narrator's perspective with that of the passive protagonists. He points out, though, that Novalis and Kafka employ similar techniques for very different artistic purposes: "Neither author integrates or complements the protagonist's perceptions. But while Kafka aims at a sense of confusion, alienation, and disorientation, Novalis aims to sharpen the readers' sensitivity to intimations from another world which remain imperceptible amidst the humdrum of everyday" (135). In the remaining sections of his chapter on *Heinrich von Ofterdingen*, Neubauer provides a useful overview of the function of the novel's lyrical, narrative, and dialogic components;

sketches the outlines of the planned "Fulfillment" to part one's "Expectation"; and provides a brief resume of critical responses. Neubauer concludes this chapter by observing, "Because of its abstractness and incompleteness, *Ofterdingen* will never attract a large readership, but it will probably continue to elicit admiration from a small band of apprentices and initiates" (Neubauer 1980, 152). One can only hope that through his lucid and stimulating remarks Neubauer may help increase this circle of initiates among English and American readers.

In rereading the published version of my dissertation, *Die Poetisierung der Natur bei Novalis* (The Poeticizing of Nature by Novalis, 1980), I recognize in it the convergence of some key strands of Novalis research during the 1970s: an interest in Friedrich von Hardenberg's scientific training and its impact on the imagery of his poetic works; a transcendence of the outmoded dichotomy between the Enlightenment and Romanticism postulated for more than a century and a half by supporters and critics of the German Romantics alike; an attempt to ascertain the contemporary relevance of Novalis's writings; and, finally, a critique of the limits of his poetics and philosophy based on an analysis of their presuppositions and consequences. On the first point, my study traces the development of the metaphors of fluidity in Novalis's writings from their origins in late eighteenth-century theories of chemistry and natural philosophy, particularly with regard to the notions of absolute dissolution and chemical permeation, to their appearance in works like *Die Lehrlinge zu Sais* or Heinrich's dream of the Blue Flower (48-60). Second, I explain how it happened that a poet like Novalis would have attempted to integrate such theories and speculations into his writings. The scientific breakthroughs of the seventeenth and eighteenth centuries not only led to the conviction that human beings were now in a position to triumph over natural forces rather than be dominated by them; their objectification of nature also brought about the conditions for the emotional identification with nature that became increasingly prominent in the course of the eighteenth century, as poets and philosophers attempted to recover that harmony with nature they perceived as having been lost through an excessive development of man's cognitive faculties (10-11). In other words, Romanticism is not the opposite of Enlightenment thinking but rather an outgrowth from it — a thesis that my doctoral advisor Klaus Peter advanced this same year in his groundbreaking work *Stadien der Aufklärung* (Stages of Enlightenment, 1980b) with regard to Enlightenment and Romantic concepts of politics, morality, and literature.

As for the contemporary relevance of Novalis's writings, my study paints the Blue Flower green, so to speak, in that it emphasizes the ecological awareness contained in Novalis's transformation of the Fichtean notion of nature as "non-Ego" in favor of the "I and Thou" relationship that reappears over and over in Heinrich's loving interplay with his natural environment, such as when, in the second part of the novel, flowers, trees, nocturnal breezes and the evening star comfort him after the death of his beloved Mathilde (68). As did Hegener and Neubauer, I emphasize the fact that Novalis came to such views not in spite of the most advanced philosophy, mathematics, and science of his day but with the help of insights gained from his detailed work in these areas. For Novalis, the "poeticizing" of nature did not involve a sickly-sweet sentimentalizing but rather the creative construction of a new vision of the world based on what he believed to be principles implicit in nature itself. On this topic, my thesis converges with that first advanced by Richard Faber on utopian aspects of the writings of Novalis. It reappears in a 1979 volume Faber coedited, in which Wolfgang Kloppmann's "materialistic" reading of the central, fifth chapter of *Heinrich von Ofterdingen* treats the miner's work as a model of what Karl Marx would later term unalienated labor.

Unlike Kloppmann and Faber, however, I do not conclude my study with an evocation of Novalis as a precursor of unorthodox Marxists such as Benjamin, Bloch, and Marcuse but rather attempt a critique of shortcomings in his poeticizing and romanticizing of nature. According to the logic of Novalis's own philosophy of nature and the plot of his fairy tales, which deal with the overcoming of progressively greater tensions and the achievement of correspondingly greater states of harmony, the initial conflict between Heinrich and his father should require an extensive development before its resolution; instead, the father not only quickly recalls his own dream of the Blue Flower but also is revealed never to have acted as a negative force on his son's development even prior to Heinrich's dream. Areas within Novalis's own life where he encountered significant difficulties and obstacles — love, relations with his father, his experiences in the salt works in Saxony — receive so untroubled a depiction in *Heinrich von Ofterdingen* that in many ways the plot of the novel is more a fairy tale than the poetic inserts themselves (74-75). Rather than regarding this as a result of artistic inability or logical inadequacy on the part of Novalis, I understand it as symptomatic of the central dilemma of German Idealism's triadic philosophy of history — the question of how to proceed from a highly developed but fragmented state of being to the posited renewal of the Golden Age. Nor is this aporia confined to the world around 1800; I observe that the confidence of Novalis and his contemporaries that they would be able to transform the world according to their utopian visions takes on a melancholy hue seen in the context of the environmental ravages in capitalistic and socialistic countries alike (13). One of my major goals in writing my doctoral dissertation had been to use Novalis as a sort of case study for analyzing the failure of the "cultural revolution" as I had witnessed and experienced it in the wake of the student protests of the 1960s. Just as East and West German writers during the 1970s turned to images of poets from the time of Goethe and the German Romantics in their disquisitions on social and personal stasis

— I think here not only of Plenzdorf's *Neue Leiden des jungen W.* and Wolf's *Kein Ort. Nirgends,* but also of Peter Schneider's *Lenz* (1973) and Peter Härtling's *Hölderlin* (1976) — so too post-1968 scholarship on Novalis provides its own sort of simultaneous reflection on two eras of emancipatory hopes, social realities, and largely thwarted expectations.

For example, Ulrich Stadler's book *Die theuren Dinge: Studien zu Bunyan, Jung-Stilling und Novalis* (The Dear Things: Studies of Bunyan, Jung-Stilling and Novalis, 1980) offers not only an analysis of the interplay between economics and literature but also a call for the reform of the world, both couched in key Marxian terms such as alienation, reification, and commodity fetishism. At the 1977 symposium on German Romanticism, Stadler had distinguished himself with a presentation on Novalis's philosophy of money, in which he pointed out that an aversion to gold as commodity exists parallel with Novalis's call for the introduction of paper currency such as the assignats used during the French Revolution, whose progressive inflation led to their loss of worth (1978). In *Die theuren Dinge,* Stadler portrays *Heinrich von Ofterdingen* as the grandiose but ultimately unsuccessful attempt to give back to commodities their dignity as objects (239-40). Whereas the merchants in this novel understand their journey to Augsburg as means toward the end of selling their wares, for Heinrich this journey becomes a wonderful instrument linking him with the world in much the same harmonious way as do the treasures of the poet Arion or the underground discoveries of the miner (144-45).

As I did in my study, Stadler sees Novalis's technical training and experience as providing a concrete application for the dialectic between ego and non-ego in Fichte's philosophy, with correspondingly more emphasis on the mediating force (155-56). But he also develops another idea as central to Novalis's attempt to overcome the chief dilemma of German Idealism: the conviction that the existence of evil is the precondition for the victory of good. Mankind's alienation will transform itself into its opposite through the "schaffende Betrachtung" (1: 101), or productive contemplation, that Novalis sees as the essence of poetry and that for him grows out of the consciousness of an inadequate world. In his extensive interpretation of chapter four of *Heinrich von Ofterdingen,* Stadler demonstrates how the avaricious crusaders unwittingly acquaint Heinrich, through Zulima, with the lute, lyric poetry, the wonders of the Orient, and the longing for true art as opposed to their drunken songs of conquest and possession (205-24). But Stadler also considers an unrealizable desire on the part of Novalis the notion that Heinrich would have become a hero as well as a poet in the second part of the novel. In his comparison of *Heinrich von Ofterdingen* with the allegorical voyages to Jerusalem described in John Bunyan's *Pilgrim's Progress* and Jung-Stilling's *Das Heimweh* (Homesickness, 1794-97), Stadler contends that Heinrich is a much more passive hero than those of the other two novels, because otherwise he too will degrade himself and the objects around him into mere means to an end. And thus the idealistic work of art — very much against the original intent of No-valis — ultimately becomes an aesthetic substitute for an alienated world rather than a model for its transformation; it is the call for such a transformation, not its artistic representation, that Stadler regards as an unfulfilled challenge of Romanticism (240-41).

If one follows the argument put forward by William Arctander O'Brien in "Twilight in Atlantis" — a comparison of the theory and practice of poetry in *Heinrich von Ofterdingen* with the statements attributed to Socrates in Plato's dialogues — poetry has for Novalis a subversive quality that removes it equally from unqualified praise or censure. While the description of poetry offered by Klingsohr and the merchants seems on the surface to refute Socrates's rejection of poetry and poets as useless, unreliable, and even downright dangerous, the actual tales they tell or songs they sing have a profoundly destabilizing effect on their listeners: "The function of signs in the Atlantis story underlies the benefit *and* dangers of the poets to the state. The poets' ability to manipulate and invest signs with meaning — and for Novalis even kings are signs — is both necessary and dangerous for the foundation of regimes" (1980, 1318). O'Brien argues that while the plot line of this former story may seem mild in tone, in that the seduction of the princess ultimately leads to the production of the long-sought heir to the throne, the Klingsohr tale deals with revolutions in the heavens and on earth in a decidedly more violent way through the incin-eration of the Mother:

> In both cases the renewal is figured by Novalis as the violation of a feminine source that enables its continued presence, but, where the Atlantis story con-ceals its violation in a romantic cave (we should perhaps remember that ac-cording to the *Critias* Poseidon built Atlantis as a hideaway for his beloved), "Klingsohr's Fairy Tale" thrusts the violation and its role in the process of re-newal almost brutally into view. (1323)

Whether or not one accepts O'Brien's contention that in the Klingsohr tale Novalis deliberately reworks images of the sun and of the cave from Plato's *Re-public* as a way of reminding his readers that even the "sun" of Socrates is itself a representation or fiction (1324), one must acknowledge his skill in making clear the conscious artistry of this poet's work. It is therefore not surprising that in his footnotes O'Brien lists Neubauer and Grob as scholars who have honed his critical sensibilities (1330-31). And his reference to the matriarchal lineage for poetic and political legitimacy in *Heinrich von Ofterdingen* (1316-17) reveals an aspect of the novel that was to receive increasing attention in the following decade, when feministic and deconstructionist approaches to literary theory became the new major critical paradigms.

8: (De)Constructive Criticism — 1981-1991

B Y THE YEAR 1980, studies of *Heinrich von Ofterdingen* had attained a height of sophistication that overshadowed even the significant accomplishments of the 1960s. As we approach the present, the number and quality of editions and publications continue to climb at a dizzying pace, making it increasingly difficult to trace lines of critical development, as our vantage point grows less distant from the objects of our survey. The title for this chapter suggests a possibility for ordering the profusion of research during the 1980s and early 1990s. In addition to those studies and critiques of *Heinrich von Ofterdingen* that built upon the achievements of their predecessors in examining the historical and intellectual roots of this novel, there were also interpretations that called into question not only the earlier findings but also their logocentric premises. In the latter half of the 1980s there developed a more pronounced tendency to see in Novalis and *Heinrich von Ofterdingen* important perspectives related not only to literature, but also to ecological and feminist redefinitions of social practice. Research on *Heinrich von Ofterdingen* can therefore be placed in the matrices of debates that characterized the sharp rise of interest in literary theory on both sides of the Atlantic during the 1980s. (For a stimulating and concise overview of major movements in literary theory, see Eagleton 1983.)

Ulrich Stadler's chapter on *Heinrich von Ofterdingen* in a 1981 collection of new interpretations of novels and stories of German Romanticism may serve as a good starting point for this survey, because Stadler not only draws upon main ideas from his study on *Die theuren Dinge* but also provides some references to directions in earlier research. Although many of the interpretations contained in this volume, which was edited by Paul Michael Lützeler, begin by tracing the critical, literary, and popular reception of the work in question, Stadler refrains from more than a sketch of such developments, saying — as I have mentioned in the introduction to my own study — that this is not the place to provide a definitive, detailed reception history of *Heinrich von Ofterdingen*. Instead, he advances a hypothesis as to why Novalis and his Blue Flower have become synonymous with German Romanticism while *Heinrich von Ofterdingen* has remained comparatively unread. He speculates that this novel's difficulty lies not in its vocabulary or level of abstraction but rather in its postulation of the world-redeeming quality of poetry and its incorporation of the reader into this mission: whoever refuses to heed the call is likely to react with estrangement and incomprehension to the novel as a whole (142-43).

In the part of his essay devoted to literary interpretation, Stadler traces the influence of Hardenberg's readings of the philosophers Hemsterhuis and Fichte in determining the option for the transformatory powers of the poetic imagination — a method that Friedrich Strack was soon to employ in detail within his book on Novalis. Stadler stresses as literary antecedents not only Goethe's *Märchen* and *Wilhelm Meisters Lehrjahre* but also *Dschinnistan* — the collection of fairy tales published by Christoph Martin Wieland between 1786 and 1789 that provided the story for Mozart's *Magic Flute*. (For correspondences between this opera and the Klingsohr tale by Novalis, see Kaiser 1980; see Zagari 1982 for a discussion of the theatrical and operatic nature of key vignettes in the Klingsohr tale.) Stadler points out that the device of using several characters to create a composite individual is a frequent feature in *Dschinnistan* (148) as well as *Heinrich von Ofterdingen*, and that in many instances there are even striking similarities in vocabulary between passages in Wieland's tales and Novalis's novel. Stadler also accentuates differences between the two authors, however; whereas Wieland emphasizes the difference between the products of our imagination and their substrate in reality, Novalis aims to abolish the qualitative difference between the two realms; thus it is not surprising that in his poetic program for the second part of *Heinrich von Ofterdingen* he should have the character of Astralis state that the world becomes dream and the dream becomes world (1: 319; 152; Stadler 1981, 149).

Stadler also notes the greater emphasis placed on the feminine element in the Klingsohr tale than in Goethe's *Märchen* and the transformation of the characters and the world itself through the power of love, which in Goethe's tale forms and fashions (*bildet*) but does not rule at the end of the story, as it does in Novalis's answer to this work (149). According to Stadler, similar principles determine Novalis's critique of *Wilhelm Meisters Lehrjahre*: the members of the Society of the Tower remain attached to the principles of material acquisition and protection of property that for Novalis can never serve as the basis for a secure existence, as both *Heinrich von Ofterdingen* and *Glauben und Liebe* repeatedly emphasize (153-56; see Phelan 1983-84 for a further discussion of gold as a symbol and commodity in *Heinrich von Ofterdingen*). Stadler provides a sociological explanation of why a young noble such as Friedrich von Hardenberg would criticize the acquisitiveness of society rather than identify himself with its principles; Hardenberg is an early example of those intellectuals in late-eighteenth-century Germany who hoped to establish an aristocracy of *Bildung*, or cultivation, that would compete against the powers of the statusquo without calling for a bloody revolution such as had occurred in France. While Stadler seriously doubts the practicability of the message of *Heinrich von Ofterdingen* as exemplified in its portrayals of poet-redeemers, he remarks that this novel is likely to exercise a fascination as long as there exists a *Bildungsschicht*, or cultivated layer of society, that likewise is willing neither to revolt violently nor to accept the existing power structures (157).

J. J. White's study "Novalis's *Heinrich von Ofterdingen* and the Aesthetics of 'Offenbarung'" concentrates on a somewhat different aspect of this novel's attempts to transform tradition without making an open break with it; whereas writers like Lessing, Fichte, and Niethammer questioned the importance of biblical revelation for an Age of Enlightenment, Novalis was searching for the ideal medium for future revelations, and for him such a medium proved to be poetry (1981-82, 94-96). White discusses four specific episodes in *Heinrich von Ofterdingen* that exemplify a creative use of the pattern of revelation: the conversation between Heinrich and his father regarding the significance of the son's dream, Heinrich's vision of the transfigured Mathilde at the beginning of "Die Erfüllung," the ensuing conversation on morality and poetry between Heinrich and Sylvester, and the revelation of a new millennium at the conclusion of the Klingsohr tale. White notes that while Novalis does not dismiss the Bible as an example of revelation, by the time the manuscript to *Heinrich von Ofterdingen* breaks off, the Bible has become an example and no more; and the logic of the story suggests that Heinrich himself is destined to become a type of poet-messiah that make a Christian savior unnecessary (115-16).

In "The Myth of Death and Resurrection in *Heinrich von Ofterdingen*," produced independently of White's work, I come to similar conclusions about Novalis's free adaptations of Christian beliefs, particularly as they relate to the content and structure of his principal novel. Quoting from a fall 1798 notebook entry in which Novalis states that every person's life should be and will be a Bible, which he designates as the highest task of writing (3: 321), I note that *Heinrich von Ofterdingen* begins with a vision of paradise whose fulfillment is the goal of the remaining action — a pattern that Novalis regarded as the organizational principle of the Bible (Mahoney 1983, 56). But with the help of Stadler's observations on the importance of the feminine element in *Ofterdingen*, I contend that Novalis — in a transformation of the figure of Mignon from Goethe's *Wilhelm Meisters Lehrjahre* that simultaneously builds upon narrative patterns from the latter poet's *Märchen* — employs the characters of Zulima, Mathilde, and Cyane as key mediators in the process of bringing the dream of the Blue Flower to earthly fulfillment:

> The spirit of love and poetry is not to remain a lifeless ornament, as was Mignon's fate in Book VIII of the *Lehrjahre*. Instead, Ofterdingen's encounters with the Mignon figures of Zulima, Mathilde and Cyane gradually open his eyes to a realm uniting death and life, past and present and the poetic beliefs of the most diverse peoples. (54. For a further discussion of the theme of death in *Wilhelm Meister* and *Ofterdingen*, see Hauer 1985.)

In this contribution to the longstanding debate on whether or not Novalis believed in reincarnation and subsequently depicted this belief in the configurations of persons within his novel, I argue that his creative interpretation of the Fichtean notion of *Ich* brought him to understand self-identity as a bond of love uniting individuals with one another and with the world. In such a view, eternity pertains not to the temporal form of personality but rather to the love that permeates it (60-62). It is in this light that I interpret the otherwise cryptic allusion to a "Dreyeiniges Mädchen" (1: 342), or triune maiden, in Novalis's plans for the continuation of *Heinrich von Ofterdingen*: this reference pertains both to the trio of Zulima, Mathilde, and Cyane and to Novalis's underlying belief in the potential divinity of humanity in female as well as male form. Such notions that were to lead feminist critics like Marilyn Chapin Massey to cast a sympathetic eye on *Ofterdingen*, and the Klingsohr tale in particular, as "the revelation of the religion of the goddess" (1985, 114).

In a later article, "Stages in Enlightenment: Lessing's *Nathan der Weise* and Novalis's *Heinrich von Ofterdingen*," I follow the lead of Klaus Peter in interpreting German Romanticism not as a reactionary antithesis of the Enlightenment but rather as the outgrowth of tensions in late-eighteenth-century thought; here I focus on "Nathan's Ring Parable, a symbol of the eventual obsolescence of revealed religion, as envisioned by Lessing, and the Klingsohr-Märchen, as the keystone of Novalis's attempts to create a new Bible through literature" (1987, 200-1). But, as the reception history of the Klingsohr tale also makes clear, instead of writing a bible readily understandable by its readers, Novalis ended up producing at best a cult book for a small circle of initiates. I conclude by observing that this New Mythology of the Early Romantics in Germany, "intended to counteract the fragmentation of Western civilization at the beginning of the nineteenth century, served more as a reflection of this state than as a correction of it" (213).

While most Novalis scholars of the 1960s and 1970s had stressed the progressive aspects of Novalis's attempted merger of the Pietistic Christianity of his childhood with the most advanced philosophical and artistic thought patterns of late-eighteenth-century Germany, Stadler and I questioned Novalis's effectiveness. Friedrich Strack's *Im Schatten der Neugier: Christliche Tradition und kritische Philosophie im Werk Friedrichs von Hardenberg* went so far as to ask whether the actual result was not an unfortunate and even dangerous symbiosis, of which the work of Novalis represents a particularly flagrant but by no means unique example (1982, 7). The reference to the "Shadow of Curiosity" in Strack's title alludes to the negative consequences of modern subjectivity's emancipation from the constraints imposed upon it by orthodox Christian religiosity; according to Strack this has had the effect of making subjectivity into its own god, whose productive imagination then develops technical or practical models for the transformation of the world without regard to any moral principles. Strack begins his book with an interpretation of Heinrich's conversation with his father that independently confirms White's thesis that the elder Ofterdingen is echoing words by Lessing and Fichte on the anachronistic nature of biblical revelation, only to have his son demonstrate by his dream that the miraculous and magical are still very much a part of earthly existence. In an extensive discussion of this dream, Strack calls it the key to the entire novel, indeed to the entire philosophy and poetics of its author (51-52), in the sense that Novalis here employs structures drawn from the Pietistic notion of inner rebirth, but for purposes of depicting the freeing of the self through its own devices (74-75; see also Saul 1985/86 for a comparison with baptismal scenes in other eighteenth-century German novels such as Goethe's *Werther*). Strack contends that it is an all too human god that appears in Novalis's poetic work, a god whose chief love is not for suffering humanity but rather for his own creative powers (219). But Strack also sees in the anxieties unleashed both by the death of Novalis's fiancée Sophie von Kühn and by the awareness of his own frail and threatened health a psychological explanation for the poetic attempt to turn the human creature into a divine creator (268).

While Strack's premises differ radically from Lacanian literary theorists, it is significant that he too ultimately sees *Mangel* (deficiency, 281) as the prime impulse for the writings of Novalis. The question remains, of course, as to what end Novalis fashioned his poetic visions: are they signs of the power-mad technocrat dispelling fears of his own mortality by Faustian projects, as Strack would have it, or rather the prescriptions of the poet, as "transcendental physician" (2: 535), undertaken in the hope of healing the world's ills? The formulation of this question suggests my own preferences as to its answer, but Strack deserves credit for drawing attention to the incipient hubris in Early Romantic aesthetics that caused Henrik Steffens, a fellow student of Novalis at the Mining Academy of Freiberg, to describe this movement in retrospect as an "intellectual tower of Babel" laid low by its overweening pride and the mutual incomprehension of its own adherents (see Schulz 1969b, 163).

Like Stadler, Strack had first advanced his theses in an exploratory essay in the 1978 volume *Romantik in Deutschland* before further developing his ideas on the "divine" art of Romanticism. Friedrich Kittler followed this same pattern by publishing in the 1980s a series of studies that had their genesis in his 1978 essay on the Romantic invention of sexuality discussed in the previous chapter. In "Die Irrwege des Eros und die 'absolute Familie'" Kittler provides a detailed analysis of the Klingsohr tale in *Heinrich von Ofterdingen*: while the wandering Eros ascends to heaven and revives the disintegrated nuclear family there through his union with Freya, Fabel descends into the underworld and transforms the sterile realm of the Fates though the magic of art. In either case, according to Kittler, the subsystems of Heaven and Hades are stabilized through members of the complex earthly family, whose own instability is produced through the doubling of the mother in the figure of Ginnistan and the resulting adulterous and incestuous chains of attraction linking father, mother, Ginnistan, and Eros (1981, 424-28; for a Freudian reading of figure doubling in *Heinrich von Ofterdingen*, see Delphendahl 1982). Kittler provides a novel interpretation for the conclusion of the spectacle that Ginnistan stages for Eros and that leads to his seduction: the vision of Eros in plantlike union with a young maiden is the literary equivalent of the mirror stage of individual development, as described by Jacques Lacan, in which the infant child imagines an ideal of unity and perfection resulting from its first awareness of incompleteness and helplessness (430). It is worth noting that Strack chooses this same scene, which he claims is Novalis's deliberate modification of a vision from Jakob Böhme detailing the love of the virgin Sophia (Wisdom) in the flower of Christ, as an example of the marginal presence of Christian ideas in a nominally Christian iconography (1982, 241-42; for a further discussion of Novalis and Böhme see Paschek 1976). But whereas Strack criticizes the hybrid and hubristic character of Novalis's literary-philosophical imaginings, Kittler aims to correct the pretenses of German Idealism from an entirely different direction; for him the allegedly autonomous poetic subject is in fact an object that erases deficiency in an imaginary fashion (1981, 430). The explication of this psychosocial process — only hinted at in the second half of Kittler's interpretation of the Klingsohr tale (456-57), which largely focuses on the enmity between the Mother and the Scribe and the latter's alleged "disappearance" from the text, as critiqued in the previous chapter — receives a fuller treatment both in Jens Schreiber's *Das Symptom des Schreibens: Roman und absolutes Buch in der Romantik* (The Symptom of Writing: Novel and Absolute Book in Romanticism, 1983) and Kittler's own book-length study entitled *Aufschreibesysteme 1800/1900* (1985), translated into English in 1990 as *Discourse Networks 1800/1900.*

In *Das Symptom des Schreibens* Schreiber explains both the "reading fever" of the late eighteenth century and the corresponding dramatic increase in the number of novels written in Germany as symptoms of the unfulfillable desire for the Other, in the Lacanian sense of the term, which resulted from the newly emerging dynamics of the bourgeois nuclear family and which finds exemplary manifestation in the dream of the Blue Flower (192-203). At the same time, he contends, another eighteenth-century phenomenon developed, namely "university discourse," which reacted (and still reacts) to this repressed desire by first denying it and then absorbing it into archives and regulated discussions (2). Schreiber constructs his work, a revised version of his dissertation, as an attack against traditional approaches to literary interpretation and an uncovering of the true meaning of Romantic love as portrayed in novels such as *Heinrich von Ofterdingen.*

Schreiber is successful in detailing the tension between the Enlightenment's encyclopedic efforts and the philosophical systems of German Idealism, on the one hand, and on the other, the Early Romantic attempt at the creation of a New Bible of poetry, although the account of scholarly work given earlier in this chapter should make it clear that his findings are not as unprecedented or as revolutionary as he often claims them to be. He convincingly indicates that, for Novalis, poetry and especially the fairy tale were media for ascending to the highest of revelations. Through a comparison of Goethe's and Novalis's conceptions of the novel and the fairy tale, Schreiber shows how in Romanticism that which Goethe considered impossible was supposed to become not only possible — Goethe's definition of the fairy tale — but real, which for Goethe was the dominion of the novel alone (166-67). He maintains that the Klingsohr tale is a piece of writing that paradoxically proclaims the end of writing in that the Scribe disappears from view by its finish (168) — a notion derived from Kittler that Schreiber repeats at greater length at the close of his interpretation of *Heinrich von Ofterdingen* (240-50) without offering any further proof for this assertion. Equally symptomatic of Schreiber's method of argumentation is a quote from the German translation of Jacques Derrida's *Of Grammatology* regarding the horizon of absolute knowledge in the dissolution of writing in logos, which Schreiber then uses as support for his conclusion that every novel about revelation as the end of writing only repeats the impossibility of revelation (168). Despite his criticism of the logocentric mode of Western thinking, in essence Schreiber adapts an interpretative practice characteristic of theological thinking in the broadest sense of the term: whereas for many German literary critics of the 1970s an argument was not complete without a reference to Marx or one of his followers, for Schreiber writers like Derrida and Lacan have become the authority figures whose mere citation serves as the proof of a position. Schreiber leaves unexplored the question as to whether Novalis's conception of language — so very different from that held by Derrida and Lacan — might not have some value on its own, in the sense that the poetic structures of his tales are designed to break through the closed circles that both Schreiber and Kittler claim to see as characteristic of writing systems. As we shall see, not only Karl Grob but also Alice Kuzniar and Géza von Molnár have demonstrated that it is possible to make use of stimulating insights derived from French poststructuralism and still do justice to the "delayed endings" that Kuzniar finds in the writings of Novalis and the aesthetic and moral freedom that Molnár locates in them.

Schreiber's study, for all its strictures against "university discourse" and its unflattering references to "critical epigones" of Romanticism such as Stadler and Grob (227-28), is likely to prove impenetrable reading for all but the most resolute practitioners of this same discourse. Friedrich Kittler's 1985 book *Aufschreibesysteme 1800/1900*, on the other hand, is a work that may enthrall some scholars and infuriate others, but its wide-ranging discussion of a variety of periods, authors, and works as well as its ingenious incorporation of details from a variety of disciplines make it of interest also to an broader reading public; It is thus not surprising that Stanford University Press has issued an English translation under the title *Discourse Networks 1800/1900*, to which the ensuing page numbers and quotes will refer. In addition to Kittler's thorough background in German literature around 1800 and the intimate knowledge of the theories of Derrida, Lacan, and Foucault evident in his earlier work, he here extends his field of investigation to the time period that was not only the heyday of literary modernism but also the epoch that produced the forerunners of poststructuralism: Nietzsche, Freud, and Saussure. Kittler's aims are not those of traditional intellectual history, however. As the German title of his book indicates, his principal interests are not authors, but rather "inscription systems." And as David Wellbery rightly observes in the conclusion of his preface to the English translation, one major difference distinguishes Kittler's work from Walter Benjamin's arguments in the essay "The Work of Art in the Age of Mechanical Reproduction": "Like Benjamin, Kittler sees the modernist intervention as a break or rupture, but he refuses to invest this transformation with the historico-philosophical meaning of 'emancipation'" (Wellbery 1990, xxxii). In other words, one discourse network may supplant the other, but this is of little or no comfort to the human bodies who remain inscribed within them.

In the first chapter of his work, entitled "The Mother's Mouth," Kittler ex-amines in detail the transformation in late-eighteenth-century primary educa-tion of German children to which both he and Schreiber had so often alluded. In the decades immediately prior to 1800, Kittler maintains, mothers began teaching their children (and themselves) to read, using primers that, unlike earlier readers with their strings of Biblical names and their theological dis-course, featured monosyllables whose combination and augmentation led from meaning to meaning, as *a* leads to *ach* and then to *sprach*. Mothers' and chil-dren's reading experiences were designed as to be sealed with bonds of affec-tion, memory, and pleasure, reinforced by the illustrated engravings in the primers, which depicted happy children and mothers in the primal act of reading (47-51). Women were no longer seen as subordinate to fathers but rather as complements and shapers of men, whose *Bildung*, or cultivated for-mation, gave them a special status in the civil service, the writing profession, and the university in the years around 1800. But Kittler also argues that while women in their plurality were encouraged to become readers, as representatives of the Mother they neither spoke nor wrote themselves but rather enabled (male) authors to write (67).

In the succeeding chapter, on "Language Channels," Kittler establishes astonishing and often convincing parallels between these simple reading primers and the canonic texts of German Romanticism. With regard to the highly audiovisual sensuality of German Romantic prose, he supplies a fasci-nating interpretation of the scene in *Heinrich von Ofterdingen* in which the protagonist encounters a mysterious and unreadable manuscript. Like engrav-ings in the primers that depict and hence reinforce the act of reading, the il-lustrated Provençal manuscript provides young Heinrich a glimpse into the poetic destiny that awaits him; he reads his own life into the figures he sees represented in the manuscript. "In the hermit's cave," Kittler observes, "the feedback between the book and its consumer transforms the book's identity and makes the consumer into a producer" (120). Commenting on the lack of individuality in Heinrich's character, which critics have often cited as a major weakness of the novel, Kittler judges it to be a conscious stratagem on the part of Novalis to allow the male reader to project himself into the novel in the same way that Heinrich and the young readers of primers do with the books at their disposal. Kittler makes another stimulating point: unlike traditional biblical stories, which called for the imitation of exemplary lives, the hermit's manuscript provides only tantalizing suggestions and an incomplete ending; this corresponds perfectly to the aesthetic intent of Novalis, for whom life "is not a novel given to us, but one made by us" (2: 563; Kittler 121-22).

Kittler spells out this process in more detail in the article "*Heinrich von Ofterdingen* als Nachrichtenfluß" (*Heinrich von Ofterdingen* as Information Flow, 1986), which he wrote for the second, expanded collection of essays on Novalis edited by Gerhard Schulz. To those critics who complain about the relative paucity of action in this novel compared with the large numbers of conversations, Kittler counters that here conversations do not replace action ("Handlung"), they are action (508). *Heinrich von Ofterdingen*, Kittler argues, does not take place in the Middle Ages of its plot, but rather in the present of its discourse, which aims at the creation of a new caste of educated civil servants as a social control mechanism more effective than the theologians of old (499-500; for a reading of *Heinrich von Ofterdingen* as a prototypical historical novel, see Saul 1984, 151-84). Just as these civil servants were expected to be able to synthesize the most disparate of data, while the new philosophy of university education, as developed by figures such as Fichte, stressed the interpretative work of the seminar above the traditional verbatim copying of lectures, so too is the main purpose of Heinrich's travels from Eisenach to Augsburg no mere acquisition of experience but rather its transformation through discourse; the Romantic data processing of *Heinrich von Ofterdingen* calls for RAMs, not ROMs — not "Read Only Memories" but rather "Random Access Memories." With respect to the Scribe, Kittler here offers an interpretation that seems to me more convincing than his earlier stress on this figure as writer: Sophie, or wisdom, in the Klingsohr tale valorizes Fabel's scribbling over the Scribe's labored treatises, not because of the former's orality, for here she writes with the Scribe's own pen (1: 295-96; 126), but because Fabel writes freely and not reproductively (496-97).

The fact that these female figures serve as virtual incorporations of wisdom and narrative poetry might have given Kittler pause to reconsider his earlier theses that women neither speak nor write themselves but only enable male authors to do so. But both in *Discourse Networks* and in Kittler's essay on *Heinrich von Ofterdingen* as information flow one continues to find statements such as this:

> Because Mathilda, who is the novel's allegory of speechless Love, cannot even express her speechlessness, her father speaks up for her. And because Love makes men speak, Heinrich, the novel's allegory of Poetry, translates Mathilda's speechless love and so becomes a poet. (Kittler 1990, 73)

Kittler's remarks refer to a statement by Klingsohr that love is mute and only poetry can give it voice (1: 288; 116). What Kittler fails to mention, however, is that, following this statement by Klingsohr, both Heinrich and Mathilde launch into an extended love duet in which speeches and kisses flow freely and it is often difficult to tell precisely who is speaking at any moment. One may interpret this scene, of course, in various ways. In my view, it is precisely at this point that Astralis, the female spirit of poetry, is born anew through the love union of Heinrich and Mathilde (1: 318; 152; Mahoney 1980, 63-65). Gail Newman, whose 1985 dissertation deals with women and the poet in *Heinrich von Ofterdingen*, understands this dialogue between Heinrich and Mathilde as a narcissistic amalgamation of Mathilde's self into Heinrich's personality "since she is at base merely a projection of the man who loves her" (1989, 66); Jens Schreiber discusses the scene in his Lacanian reading of *Heinrich von Ofterdingen*, in which love is merely a four-letter word for "desire" (Schreiber 209-10). But it will not do to quote selectively or misleadingly for the sake of making one's point, and Kittler has the tendency to do so all too frequently, such as when he conflates the real exclusion of women from German university discourse in the years around 1800 with their alleged exclusion from poetic discourse in the second part of *Ofterdingen* (1986, 501-3), though it is Cyane — Heinrich's sister in spirit and in many ways a Fabel-like character — who leads him to Sylvester for the final set of conversations in the novel (1: 324-25; 158-59).

    Given Kittler's deep affinity for Foucault's thinking, it is not surprising that he refuses to accept such transcendental poetics at their face value but rather understands them as the product of a gendered "discourse network" (Cyane is left to prepare dinner while Heinrich and Sylvester, whom he interprets as the equivalent of a philosophy professor à la Fichte, do all the talking). But it is questionable whether women inside and outside this novel were as silent as Kittler here makes them out to be. Without wishing to idealize the situation of female authors at the beginning of the nineteenth century, I would caution the reader not to forget that women such as Bettina Brentano, Sophie Mereau, Caroline Schlegel, and Rahel Varnhagen participated in the discourse network that developed during the German Romantic period and that novels such as Friedrich Schlegel's *Lucinde* and Novalis's *Ofterdingen* are the products of intense discussion within these circles on the need for a new vision of interpersonal and intersexual relations. Feminist critics such as Lynda E. Boose have suggested that the often pessimistic conclusions of American New Historians regarding the possibility of successful subversive resistance to dominant institutions may be a by-product of their post-new-left background *and* their all too frequent elision of women's voices from their analyses (1987, 738-42). Similar criticisms could be leveled against the Foucauldian premises of Kittler's *Discourse Networks*; his stress on the unreality of the autonomous human subject and the inescapability of Western society's inscription systems indicates how far he has removed himself not only from the relative optimism of Novalis and his contemporaries but also from the hopes of cultural revolutionaries during the 1960s.

One direction in German literary scholarship, though, in which emancipatory urges have increased in recent years is the area of women's studies. After an initial critique of eighteenth-century male visions of *imaginierte Weiblichkeit*, or imagined femininity (Bovenschen 1979, Becker-Cantarino 1979), and their constrictive effects on female self-understanding, feminist scholars of the 1980s pursued two separate but not unrelated strategies. In addition to turning their main attention to German female readers and novelists in the decades around 1800, they investigated the extent to which German Romantics such as E. T. A. Hoffmann and Novalis might be said to have written in the same diffuse, fluid way heralded by poststructuralist feminists such as Hélène Cixous, Luce Irigaray, and Julia Kristeva. A most fascinating book in this latter direction is Marilyn Chapin Massey's *Feminine Soul: The Fate of an Ideal*. Massey analyses the near deification of women by German writers and pedagogues such as Pestalozzi, Novalis, and Friedrich Fröbel — both in the light of the claims by some contemporary feminists regarding women's ostensibly innate creative qualities and with respect to counterarguments by other feminists that such a belief merely replicates a mechanism of oppression that fashioned women during the eighteenth and nineteenth centuries into ineffectual domestic angels while the men stormed out into the wide world they claimed as their own domain. Massey admits that the notion of a feminine soul was used as a device of ideological oppression, but she also advances the argument that its initial formulation by writers like Pestalozzi and Novalis, in its reversal of orthodox Christianity's traditional image of the deficient female soul in need of male supervision and its emphasis on the nurturing, cooperative nature of human beings, is more liberating than the critiques of religion (and femininity) launched by thinkers such as Marx and Freud: "To engender true freedom, to take the opiate of religion away, Novalis sought to create a new religion, a religion of the mother-lover. *Heinrich von Ofterdingen* is its poetic manifesto" (1985, 100). In her view, it is not this novel by Novalis but rather his friends' later attempts to "finish" it in interpretations and reworkings like Schleiermacher's *Weihnachtsfeier* (Christmas Eve, 1806) — that clergyman's contribution to German moral renewal in the wake of Prussia's defeat by Napoleon in 1806 — that served to domesticate and suppress the vision of the female god, particularly as portrayed in the Klingsohr tale:

The order of this new world, which Fable and Eros go out to establish throughout the kingdom, is one of fluid forms held above destructive chaos. It is one in which war is confined to a chess game, a game kept only as a reminder of a troubled time in the frozen kingdom. Above all, it is one of satisfied desire. Now Eros, shedding his armor, recognizes Freya as his true lover and, in a mirror reversal of his mother-lover's awakening of the king, arouses the princess from a deep sleep with a kiss. (123)

At times Massey gets entangled in the complex narrative of the Klingsohr tale, as when she incorrectly understands the father of Eros to be identical with Arcturus, the king of the frozen kingdom and the husband of Sophie. But Massey more than compensates for such interpretative lapses in her analyses of the images of the feminine soul in this novel, which she complements with a discussion of Novalis's scientific speculations on the primeval fluidity of creation and then links with key ideas of Luce Irigaray on female sexuality and woman's language (128-33). She also contrasts the philosopher Fichte's understanding of language, which for him is only a tool for communicating an innate and utterly rational universal law, with the sensuous dreams and images that Heinrich finds in the innermost reaches of his feminine soul:

As confused and crazy as the dreams of the blue flower may be, they at least free the imagination and engender the pleasure that seeks to transform society in cooperation with an infinitely creative material life force. This is a pleasure that seeks, not control over nature, but the potential to produce bodies that can be endlessly responsive to each other. (135)

In the conclusion to her work, Massey stresses that contemporary feminists must do more than simply recover such articulated but effectively suppressed products of male imagination; now it is *they* who must do the imagining, and in a way that brings religion and gender in opposition to the male-dominated culture of death and nuclear destruction she sees predominating throughout contemporary Western civilization. But the images she cites by writers like Cixous and Irigaray certainly resonate with those she has identified in the Klingsohr tale (184-85), and they remind us that notions of masculinity and femininity are themselves cultural constructs that are constantly in flu. If literature can enable males and females alike to imagine new ways of relating to themselves and the world, it can play a material role in helping to bring such products of their imagination ever closer to earthly fulfillment, as Novalis hoped it might.

Massey does, however, overdetermine the interpretative possibilities in *Heinrich von Ofterdingen* in what she understands and critiques as Heinrich's return home at the conclusion of the novel as we know it (126-27); while aware of the fact that Novalis has left us with "a fragmented, open-ended piece," she overlooks the answer Cyane gives to Heinrich when he asks her where they are going: "Immer nach Hause" (1: 325; 159). Alice Kuzniar uses these words — perhaps the most famous and oft-quoted lines in *Heinrich von Ofterdingen* — as a key support for the central argument of her study *Delayed Endings: Nonclosure in Novalis and Hölderlin*:

> Reversing teleological expectations, Novalis answers the question of where we are going: always homeward ([*Werke* 1978] 1: 373). Indeed, progressive movement towards a telos is deceptive; only seemingly (*scheinbar*) do we move forward ([*Werke* 1978] 2: 60, no. 129). But the child's famous response in the second, unfinished part of *Heinrich von Ofterdingen* not only undermines teleological direction but also perpetuates the inversion: the emphasis on the reply should be placed on the adverb *always* — "Immer nach Hause." (Kuzniar 1987, 82-83)

Kuzniar argues that German writers like Hölderlin and Novalis — in their dissatisfaction with the bloody, inconclusive outcome of the French Revolution — developed notions of temporality and nonclosure that differ both from Christian eschatology, with its emphasis on the parousia, or Second Coming, and from its secularized and politicized variants in Enlightenment and Marxian thought but correspond closely with a key poststructuralist concern: "What does it mean to lose the belief in endings and ultimacies?" (2). For this reason, Kuzniar attempts not so much a deconstructive reading of Hölderlin and Novalis as an explication of narrative, semantic, and thematic patterns that indicate a profound affinity with contemporary critical sensibilities (11). She understands these two writers' search for delayed endings as symptomatic of a new and skeptical concept of time whereby the concept of "the end of all things" no longer possesses the regulatory character it still had for philosophers of history like Kant and Condorcet: "In different ways, Hölderlin and Novalis now, as we shall see, *sustainedly* delay the parousia. They turn their historical inheritance of apocalyptic aporiae into the very logic that drives their writing" (71).

In her chapter on Novalis (72-132), Kuzniar begins with a critique of scholars such as Mähl, Mahr, Heftrich, and Faber, whose attempts to find in Novalis "a substitute for or a translation of Christian salvation history" (74) have led in her view to serious misreadings of the poetic texts themselves, because these critics overlook Novalis's continuous deferral of finality. In her interpretation of *Heinrich von Ofterdingen*, she emphasizes the temporal gaps and discontinuities between the chapters as well as those between the main plot and the narrative inserts: "Seen separately and in themselves, the fairy tales function as tokens of progressivity. However, as digressions halting the narrative, they act as relapses. Ideally, the narrative would link together the various inserts. But do the tales stand consecutively and causally *nacheinander* instead of contiguously *nebeneinander*?" (109).

Kuzniar opts for contiguity, the second of the above alternatives, but she fails to consider not only that the temporal gaps in the narrative gradually decrease in the course of "Die Erwartung" — chapters six through nine, for example, all take place within twenty-four hours of one another — but that scholars like Erika Voerster and Hannelore Link have already provided convincing evidence of intertextual linkage between the fairy tales and the main plot. Nor does she do full justice to those sections of the novel that serve as commentary and interpretation of the work as a whole, as when the hermit characterizes the incomplete, incomprehensible manuscript discovered by Heinrich as the story of the marvelous fortunes of a poet, in which poetry is presented and praised in its manifold relations (1: 265; 91). Kuzniar argues that even if Novalis had finished *Heinrich von Ofterdingen*, the novel still would have remained a fragment in the sense that this episode in the hermit's cave puts readers in the same relation to Heinrich as Heinrich was to the manuscript:

> We see ourselves as Heinrich, browsing eclectically through the hermit's library "mit unendlicher Lust" [with infinite pleasure], reading "zu wiederholten Malen" [over and over again], all the while wishing nothing more longingly than to be able to read the book and to grasp it completely. (132. See also Kuzniar 1988, 83-84.)

That *Heinrich von Ofterdingen* can have such a mesmerizing effect on the reader is no doubt true. But whether it is designed to keep one enthralled in the solitary confines of one's study is another matter. The fact that Novalis constantly interrupts dreams, tales, and private readings as a necessary prerequisite for Heinrich's ongoing search for the Blue Flower has implications that *Delayed Endings* does not fully address, but these receive extensive coverage in the other major study on Novalis published in 1987, namely Géza von Molnár's book *Romantic Vision, Ethical Context: Novalis and Artistic Autonomy*.

Like Kuzniar, Molnár wants to win a contemporary audience for Novalis. But while Kuzniar's study draws freely and creatively upon ideas of Derrida and those European and American critics indebted to him, Molnár directs his arguments against those tendencies in poststructuralism that turn everything into text and language. He sees rather in the theoretical writings and poetic practice of Novalis a conception of language as the point of mediation between self and world. The title of his book succinctly alludes to the central contention of his argument: Novalis may have opted for art rather than moral philosophy as his preferred medium of expression, but his "Romantic vision" remains linked to ethical concerns: "The affirmation of Fichte's moralism makes it obvious that Novalis's poetics do not then, nor at any other time, proclaim art as an absolute or nonreferential endeavor; art originates with reference to the characteristically human capacity for free moral agency and addresses itself to it" (1987, 93).

Molnár interprets *Heinrich von Ofterdingen* as an artistic presentation of the ideas Novalis developed from the time of his studies with Schiller at the University of Jena through the formulation of his unique contribution to German Idealism in the months after the death of Sophie von Kühn in 1797: "The topic is the inner change the individual must undergo in order to perceive self and world in a relationship that is not frozen into a state of permanent opposition" (99). What Novalis found lacking in Fichte's philosophy as early as 1796 — namely love, whose receptivity serves as a counterbalance to pure activity — now serves as the driving force in the opening scene of the novel in Heinrich's longing for the Blue Flower. Molnár observes that it is only at the end of the first part of the novel, after Heinrich has met Mathilde, his beloved, that the poet Klingsohr fashions the consciously created dream world of the fairy tale: "Heinrich's dream is an entirely personal experience, and yet it is potentially everyone's. Klingsohr realizes this potential, and in order to do so his tale contains no persons at all but only a group of allegorical figures that represent the self's various faculties and features" (117; see also Blackall 1983, 126-27, for a concise discussion of the events and characters in this tale).

In his interpretation of the scene in which Ginnistan seduces Eros, Molnár provides an answer to critics who hold that *Heinrich von Ofterdingen* and literature in general represent a never-ending replication of desire in search of an unattainable goal: Eros loses sight of Freya, whom Molnár understands as the "peace that ends all longing" (119), at that moment when he mistakes the dream world of Ginnistan for reality. Conversely, he regains his orientation after imbibing the water commingled with the ashes of his mother: "Giving up that object means giving up that one blue flower so that all may be blue" (120). Both in this chapter, "Dreams and Fairy Tales" (100-20), and in the succeeding ones on *Heinrich von Ofterdingen* — "The Journey" (121-47) and "Journey's End" (148-60) — Molnár deftly combines detailed analyses with an explication of the novel as a whole.

Molnár articulates the goal of Heinrich's poetic journey once more in his final remarks in the chapter "Novalis in Contemporary Context" (193-202), where he identifies as the ultimate concern of Novalis the formation of a human community via the medium of language: "The 'house of language,' so it turns out, is not the hermetic edifice for which it is currently still hailed and decried. Neither exclusive palace nor confining cell, it stands wide open to the world on which it rests and is host to the spirit that unites its inhabitants. Nearly two centuries ago, Novalis had already referred to that house with his concept of *Poesie*" (201-02). In his preface to this volume in the series Theory and History of Literature, Jochen Schulte-Sasse gives precedence to Novalis's theory and practice of language not only over deconstructionism but also over Jürgen Habermas's attempts to renew transcendental philosophy as practiced by Fichte (Schulte-Sasse 1987, xv-xxv). In other words, both Molnár and Schulte-Sasse regard the study of this supposedly ethereal Romantic poet as a possibility for orientation amid the aesthetic and sociophilosophical debates of our time. And the high theoretical level on which both of them argue should serve to induce interest and respect in those readers for whom Novalis and *Heinrich von Ofterdingen* hitherto have been no more than names.

Romantic Vision, Ethical Context may represent the pinnacle achievement of Novalis scholarship during the 1980s, but it is surrounded by many other worthy efforts, for this decade witnessed not only the studies already discussed but also a wide variety of useful editions of Novalis's works. Hanser in Munich followed its two-volume set *Werke, Tagebücher und Briefe* (1978), edited by Hans-Joachim Mähl and Richard Samuel — whose commentary volume by Hans Jürgen Balmes provides better and more extensive notes to *Heinrich von Ofterdingen* (Balmes 1987, 134-91) than the historical-critical edition itself — with a one-volume condensation that was in its third edition by 1984. In 1983 Hans-Dietrich Dahnke praised the humanistic concerns of Novalis in a one-volume edition of his writings, including *Heinrich von Ofterdingen*, for the East German series Bibliothek deutscher Klassiker; by 1985 this volume was in its third edition, while in 1989 there appeared a second, revised version of the volume on Novalis edited by Claus Träger and Heidi Ruddigkeit for Reclam Verlag in Leipzig. In 1987 Reclam Verlag in Stuttgart issued a revised edition of *Heinrich von Ofterdingen* for which Wolfgang Frühwald supplied an updated bibliography and afterword that reflect the advances in Novalis scholarship since the original edition in 1965. In addition, Ursula Ritzenhoff edited a 1988 book on *Heinrich von Ofterdingen* for the Reclam series Erläuterungen und Dokumente that provides not only an extensive commentary on individual words, motifs, and episodes (5-134) but also documents relating to the writing of the novel and to its reception in the nineteenth and twentieth centuries (135-221). In that same year the fifth, supplementary volume to the historical-critical Novalis edition appeared; its chief features are the name, place, and subject indices — the latter of which takes up almost half of the volume (5: 419-819) and permits for the first time the comparison of words and motifs from *Ofterdingen* with the entire range of Novalis's works, notes, and letters. With publications in the 1980s of translations of *Heinrich von Ofterdingen* into Italian, Rumanian, Bulgarian, Japanese, and Hungarian (see Uerlings 1991, 634-35), it became possible to speak of this novel as a recognized component of world literature.

In the stimulating afterword to his 1982 edition of *Heinrich von Ofterdingen*, Jochen Hörisch indicates how this novel presents models of subjectivity and intersubjectivity that not only were revolutionary for their day but still speak to contemporary concerns. He sees in it a revision of the Kantian model of self-reflection that shifted the emphasis from "I think" to the following four modes of self-definition: I possess, I desire, I am finite, and I interpret (227). Making use of Stadler's economic approach and Kittler's psychoanalytic one to *Ofterdingen*, Hörisch argues that the Atlantis tale provides a model for being reconciled with one's self by loving others, while in the Klingsohr tale the re-nunciation of the mother provides access to the love feast and *Kußgeflüster* (whisper of kisses; 1: 315; 148) that characterize its conclusion (231, 236). Hörisch also brings Novalis's affirmation of death, which for so long has irri-tated critics, in conjunction with Heidegger's analysis of time as the constitu-ent of human existence (237-38). Finally, he argues that as a work of poetry *Heinrich von Ofterdingen* makes evident that its depictions of economic ex-change, love, and time are interpretive models to be accepted, rejected, or modified; they are not immutable laws of order, and neither are the social practices to which they serve as a response (241). In short, Hörisch sees in this German Romantic novel a critique of Enlightenment positions but by no means a glorification of irrationalism or anti-intellectualism — which is the conclusion that Hermann Kurzke later reaches in his monograph (1988, 98-100). Considering Hörisch's spirited advocacy of *Heinrich von Ofterdingen*, which develops ideas from his doctoral dissertation, *Die fröhliche Wissenschaft der Poesie* (The Gay Science of Poesy, 1976), it is not surprising that in 1987 he coedited with Ernst Behler the proceedings of a conference exploring the timeliness of Early Romanticism. This book includes the presentations of Willy Michel, Ulrich Stadler, Hans-Georg Pott, Manfred Frank, Friedrich Kittler, Jochen Fried, and Helmut Schanze on key ideas in the works of No-valis and how they relate to issues under debate in contemporary literary the-ory.

Idealismus und Aufklärung: Kontinuität und Kritik der Aufklärung in Philo-sophie und Poesie um 1800 (Idealism and Enlightenment: Continuity and Criticism of the Enlightenment in Philosophy and Poetry Around 1800) is a 1988 collection of the presentations given at an international interdisciplinary conference. Addressing the prevailing tendency on both sides of the Atlantic to criticize instrumental reason for having liberated society from the rule of kings and priests at the end of the eighteenth century only to have developed subse-quently into an even more tyrannical and destructive force worldwide, these presentations on Idealism and Enlightenment investigate the extent to which German thinkers around 1800 had attempted to provide correctives to what they viewed as distortions of Enlightenment's liberating goals. In an essay en-titled "Aufklärung via Mythologie" (Enlightenment via Mythology), coeditor Christoph Jamme explores the connections between late-eighteenth-century attempts to gain technical control over nature and the efforts of Hölderlin, Schelling, and the young Hegel to combat the reification of nature (and hu-manity) through a New Mythology that would incorporate the latest develop-ments in science and philosophy but also preserve the subjectivity of nature. He regards this concept, which the Early Romantics also espoused, as being of more than merely historical interest; it provides a model for current calls for an ecological ethics and a holistic understanding of the world (55-58). Immediately following this essay, Hartmut Böhme examines a specific example of this mythology in the "beautiful mining" depicted by Novalis in chapter five of *Heinrich von Ofterdingen*, where Heinrich learns that human history ultimately is an integral part of the universal history of nature (Böhme 1988, 59-79; see also Burwick 1986, 102-38, and Esselborn 1987 for further detailed investigations of the scientific components of Novalis's New Mythology, particularly with regard to the Klingsohr tale).

In a monograph on mining motifs in the literature of German Romanticism that draws upon ideas first articulated by Hartmut Böhme, Helmut Gold investigates why German writers between 1790 and 1840 depicted mining to a far greater extent than writers in other European countries. He observes that, although individual German states such as Saxony had by this time taken the administration of mining under their control, capitalistic methods of production did not begin to appear until after 1830. Around 1800, mining for precious metals was still regarded as an art, and the skilled workers possessed a pride and self-esteem dating back to their high status in medieval German society. It was in this unique historical situation, Gold argues, that Novalis presented his portrayal of the miner in *Heinrich von Ofterdingen* as a composite of old and new ideas: the miner is "modern" in that he shows no fear of the cave allegedly inhabited by dragons and other fierce monsters, but "traditional" in his attitude to work, religion, and nature, which he depicts as a living and loving being in the two songs he sings (1990, 87-88). Gold points out, though, that not all such depictions of mining in German Romanticism are so positive. E. T. A. Hoffmann's story *Die Bergwerke zu Falun* (The Mines at Falun, 1819) — like Tieck's *Der Runenberg* (The Rune Mountain, 1802) a direct response to *Heinrich von Ofterdingen*— depicts a feminized, seductive, but also dangerous nature that eventually brings about the death of the main protagonist. Tieck's late novella *Der Alte vom Berge* (1828) provides a decidedly unromantic view of contemporary mining conditions in Germany, where the title figure, "the old man of the mountain," is no longer a miner but rather the mine's owner, whose handsome profits cannot assuage a decidedly pessimistic attitude toward life. Gold concludes by noting that the motif of mining as a form of simultaneous criticism and utopian thinking was possible only for the Early Romantics; by 1850 a romanticized view of mining had become ideological kitsch (203). Nonetheless, Gold observes that contemporary calls for communicative discourse with nature, ecofeminism, and "soft technology" decidedly stand in the tradition of the models first proposed in German Romanticism, in which a descent into the depths of the earth first became a metaphor for exploring unexamined aspects of nature, history, economics, and the human psyche. But he also cites Theodor Adorno's warnings about the danger of an ontological understanding of "depth": if we dig below the surface in the hope of finding something already existing in us or in the objects around us, we are bound to be disappointed; true depth lies in the dynamics between these two poles (232-33).

Gail Newman investigates precisely such a procedure in her article "Poetic Process as Intermediate Area in Novalis's *Heinrich von Ofterdingen*." Drawing upon the observations of the British psychoanalyst D. W. Winnicott on the creative games young children play when investigating the borders of self and other, Newman regards the image of the Blue Flower and the novel it initiates as models of the process of hovering between subject and object that Novalis developed from his studies of Fichtean philosophy. "Heinrich's relationship to the stories he finds and constructs through creative interpretation," she notes, "is rife with paradox: he must find an essence of himself in the stories if they are to have any effect on him at all, yet only if they remain strange can they exert the power to dissolve familiar boundaries and push him beyond himself" (1990, 27). The gap between sign and referent, in other words, serves as the productive moment in language, not only for Heinrich, but also for those of us who read his story. And while this creative interplay between self and world may characterize the work of the artist, Newman argues that it is also found in the labor of the miner and in the mediating activity of the merchants in the novel. She concludes her article therefore with the statement of the poet Klingsohr that poesy is the characteristic mode of activity of the human spirit (32; for a further discussion of the profession of the poet in *Heinrich von Ofterdingen*, see Moisan 1988).

As a fitting conclusion to this chapter, I turn to a piece of scholarship that has been of invaluable help to me in my own research, namely Herbert Uerlings's *Friedrich von Hardenberg, genannt Novalis: Werk und Forschung* (Friedrich von Hardenberg, Named Novalis: Work and Scholarship, 1991). In this magisterial study, Uerlings investigates the theoretical, political, and poetic works of Novalis and evaluates all relevant criticism since the initial publication of the *Schriften* in 1802. Being aware of the distortions visited upon Novalis's works by overly enthusiastic devotees as well as hostile critics, Uerlings does not write another proclamation of the "modernity" of Novalis but instead explores the implications and limits of what he calls Novalis's narrative construction of immanent transcendence (14, 230). He maintains that Novalis did not intend his political, philosophical, and poetic writings to represent reality as it currently exists or is ordained to become but rather as what Novalis hoped to see approximated in life through its depiction in art (609-13). Referring to recent studies on narrativity in historiography and literature by scholars such as Hayden White and Reinhart Koselleck, Uerlings makes evident the remarkable theoretical sophistication embedded in Novalis's seemingly naive writings, but he adds his own critique of a writer whose utopian goals he deeply admires: it is not that Novalis placed too high a value on art or saw it as a replacement for an unsatisfactory reality but rather that he overestimated his abilities and those of his contemporaries to make use of the tensions between utopian ideal and existing reality. Like Ulrich Stadler, Uerlings understands the work of Novalis as the product of a specific set of historical circumstances, at a time when many other German intellectuals and artists of his generation had a faith in *Bildung* that we no longer share today. Uerlings also notes, however, that in this scheme of narrative construction Novalis not only expects disappointments but uses them as an impetus for renewed efforts: the "delayed endings" analyzed by Kuzniar are an integral part of Romanticism as unending progression (622-25). The epilogue to Uerlings's study is entitled "Konstruktion oder Dekonstruktion?" (615), but Uerlings makes it clear where his own critical preferences lie — namely in a utopian thinking that does not claim to possess the certitude of salvation history but that still hopes to promote changes for the better (625). With regard to *Heinrich von Ofterdingen*, which he gives the lengthiest treatment by far (398-519), Uerlings takes a thematic rather than a chronological approach, with special attention to the following areas: the dream of the Blue Flower, the form and poetics of the novel as a whole, comparisons between *Wilhelm Meister* and *Ofterdingen*, the concept of reality presented in this novel, new directions in discourse theory, and a lengthy section on the Klingsohr tale that is subdivided into nine categories. When one considers that Uerlings surveys not only the extensive literature on this one novel but also that on the entire oeuvre of Novalis, the magnitude of his achievement becomes even more impressive.

9: A Very Good Year — 1992

THE YEAR 1992 proved to be a notable one for Novalis scholarship in many respects. On May 2 the newly founded International Novalis Society celebrated the 220th birthday of the poet by convening at his birthplace in Schloß Oberwiederstedt, Sachsen-Anhalt. The sheer existence of this building was cause enough for celebration. In 1945 East German authorities had converted this residence of the von Hardenberg family from what they considered a relict of feudalism into a home for the elderly but had not provided funds for adequate maintenance; by 1981 its increasingly desolate condition made it no longer suitable for human habitation and it was abandoned to the elements. Scheduled for demolition in the fall of 1987, the building was saved only by a local citizens' initiative, which after much effort persuaded East German state officials to employ the money set aside for the demolition of a cultural landmark for its preservation instead. Above all, though, it was more than fifteen thousand hours of voluntary weekend work by local youths and other involved citizens that enabled four rooms, including the site of Novalis's birth, to be opened to the public on May 2, 1989. With the fall of the Berlin Wall and the subsequent reunification of East and West Germany, new public and private funds became available, helping to turn what had been an abandoned ruin into a cultural and social center for young and old alike as well as the headquarters for the International Novalis Society. One might regard this regeneration of the birthplace of Novalis as symbolic of the ongoing interest in a writer who oftentimes has been regarded as outmoded, only to be rediscovered and reclaimed by a new generation of readers and critics.

At the inauguration of the International Novalis Society, Florian Roder delivered another birthday present by donating a copy of his new study of the life and works of Friedrich von Hardenberg to the society's envisioned research library on Early Romanticism. As late as 1991, Herbert Uerlings had regarded a comprehensive and reliable biography as one of the major needs in Novalis scholarship (9). In its charter, the International Novalis Society declared its intention to make the significance of Novalis and Early Romanticism better known. Roder's *Novalis: Die Verwandlung des Menschen. Leben und Werk Friedrich von Hardenbergs* (1992) addresses both of these tasks by being accessible to general readers while incorporating the latest research into its account of Novalis's life and works. In his justification of the massive study — over 950 pages in length — on an individual who did not reach the age of thirty and whose philosophical reflections and poetic works remained largely incomplete or unpublished at his death, Roder contends that the works of Novalis contain the seeds of possibilities for a transformation of ourselves and the world that require careful elaboration and attention (547). While drawing on the mystical, anthroposophical categories of thought developed by Rudolf Steiner earlier in this century, Roder also examines the inner consistency of the "paradise of ideas" (3: 446) that Novalis called for and created in his writings. Throughout his study, Roder elucidates Novalis's conception of the alchemy of poetry as a means of effecting the transformation of humankind highlighted in his book's title (396-99), but he also documents how Novalis wrote his poetical works in conjunction with his studies in the sciences and his practical experience as a mining engineer and civil servant. In many respects, Roder and Uerlings have written studies that complement each another admirably. Whereas Uerlings stresses the more secularly utopian aspects of Novalis, Roder concentrates on the esoteric Christian roots of his thinking — such as the concept of Sophia, or divine wisdom — which have not received the same amount of attention in recent decades because of their overemphasis in the years before 1960. As a result, he succeeds in drawing our notice to aspects of Novalis's work and convictions that many contemporary readers are unlikely to share and enables us to reconsider them from a sympathetic but by no means blindly enthusiastic perspective.

Since Roder organizes his study with the help of the terms *Erwartung*, *Erweckung*, and *Erfüllung* (Expectation, Awakening, and Fulfillment), it is fitting that he devotes an extensive chapter to *Heinrich von Ofterdingen*, which he understands as a novel of initiation (649-802). Continuing in the paths charted by Hannelore Link and Elisabeth Stopp, Roder elucidates the esoteric aspects of this novel to which Friedrich Schlegel had referred in 1803, but with the help of insights of scholars such as Walzel (the variation of figures), Schulz (mining motives), and Molnár (Goethe's color theory and the Blue Flower). Roder's special contribution to Novalis scholarship lies in his discussion of the poetic interplay of such images and motifs. He interprets the miner's second song about the castle and its hidden king (1: 248-50; 74-75), for example, as analogous to the Klingsohr tale in that here too Novalis portrays the individual faculties of the soul that need to be brought together in perfect harmony; gold serves as the symbol for wisdom contained in the human soul that longs to become manifest — this is the true philosopher's stone (667-71). Just as the youth's poem in the Atlantis tale transforms the talisman of the princess into a living symbol of mutual love, so we as readers become initiated into the same process as we strive to interpret the mysterious messages in such poems (686-87). Roder makes no pretense of unraveling all the mysteries of *Heinrich von Ofterdingen*, nor does he want to undertake such an impossible task, but he does express hope that his interpretation will encourage his readers to contemplate the unending riches contained in this work (783-84).

Like Roder, Kenneth Calhoon has written a study stressing areas where Novalis's thoughts can continue to stimulate new directions for his readers, but in *Fatherland: Novalis, Freud, and the Discipline of Romance* (1992) we encounter a postmodern, psychoanalytic approach to literature — not in the sense that Calhoon is interested in providing a Freudian analysis of *Heinrich von Ofterdingen* but rather in that he sees Freud's work as part of the post-Enlightenment discourse that Romanticism helped articulate. The "Romance" in his title is the quest for a fatherland where the continued presence of the maternal and feminine would be possible. In his first chapter, "The Politics of Infanticide: Goethe's 'Erlkönig,'" Calhoon investigates a patriarchal structure in which strength of mind and arm preclude erotic tenderness and parental discipline takes upon itself the same arbitrary authority it tries to normalize in nature. If the arguments of Max Horkheimer and Theodor Adorno color the discussion of Freud, Goethe, and Novalis here, the second chapter, "The Political Novalis," identifies Herbert Marcuse as the thinker who brought to the fore the political aspects of psychoanalysis that Freud assiduously avoided but that Calhoon sees as present in Novalis's writings. The title of the next chapter, "The Philosophical Unconsciousness," is much more than a witty reference to Fredric Jameson's neo-Marxian use of Freud in *The Political Unconscious* (1981), for Calhoon here argues persuasively that *Heinrich von Ofterdingen* makes manifest key needs and motivations of post-Kantian philosophy such as autonomy and self-referentiality. The fourth chapter, "The Stones Speak! The Romantic Archaeology of the Psyche," highlights a key element in Novalis's aesthetics countervailing the narcissistic search for an undifferentiated peace that can be found only in death: a capacity for "sustained *difference*" (113, Calhoon's emphasis) that enables young Heinrich to forsake the carousing, marauding Crusaders, who drown everything foreign in an alcoholic stupor, in favor of the Saracen maiden Zulima. And the succeeding chapter, "Allegories of Plot," contrasts the seamless surveillance of the Society of the Tower in Goethe's *Wilhelm Meisters Lehrjahre* — which Calhoon, following Franco Moretti's 1987 study, interprets as a Bildungsroman that "represents a disavowal of the French Revolution, or at least a denial of the irreversibility of its effects" (131) — with the breaks of continuity in *Heinrich von Ofterdingen*, an unfinished novel whose revolutionary, grotesque form is contingent on the shattering of the past and which grows out of ruins and the remembrance of loss.

Throughout his study, Calhoon draws both upon works of European Romanticism and upon leading contemporary literary theorists to buttress and amplify his arguments. In the final chapter, "'Kubla Khan' and the Oriental Hallucination," he employs Coleridge's poem, with its marginalized fecund female (as opposed to the Khan's creation by decree) as counterpart both to the catastrophe unleashed by the procreation of a child in Kleist's *Das Erdbeben in Chili* (The Earthquake in Chile, 1807) and to the resolution of crisis in the Atlantis tale in *Ofterdingen*, where an actual conception in the wilderness heals

social divisions and ensures the survival of the kingdom. Both in the conclusion to this chapter and in the ensuing epilogue, Calhoon uses the magic wand
of analogy so beloved by Novalis (3: 518) and draws comparisons between
Heinrich von Ofterdingen and the protofascistic literature treated in Klaus
Theweleit's *Männerphantasien* (Male Fantasies, 1980), which abhorred the
fluidity and sexual arousal in which young Heinrich revels. Calhoon does so,
however, not for the purpose of establishing a link between Romanticism and
National Socialism but rather to suggest that Theweleit's critique partakes of
arguments whose images are commonplaces of German Romanticism. "By revealing the brutality of war as a regressive deformation of eros," he notes,
"Klingsohr's tale allegorizes what Chapter Four of *Ofterdingen* makes clear and
what Zulima herself explains; that is, there is something instinctual about
military aggression" (158). Nor does Calhoon fail to discuss Heinrich's encounter with Zulima in the context of Edward Said's interpretation of Orien-
talism as the product of a Western, colonizing imagination (153-54). In short,
Fatherland is likely to open up new vistas to English-language readers conversant in contemporary literary theory but for whom poetic texts in German
Romanticism are terra incognita.

In *Private Lives in the Public Sphere: The German Bildungsroman as
Metafiction* (1992), Todd Kontje provides a similar service for readers who may
be familiar with the term *Bildungsroman*, but not with the novels that Dilthey
had employed when defining this genre or with the interpretative and ideological ballast it has since acquired in German literary scholarship. In his introductory chapter, Kontje not only informs his readers about recent debates
on the usefulness of the designation *Bildungsroman* but also provides them
with his own fresh understanding of novels such as *Wilhelm Meisters Lehrjahre*
and *Heinrich von Ofterdingen*. Referring to those same divisions in the reading
public that I have discussed in the first chapter of this study, Kontje observes in
the period around 1800 "the attempt on the part of a few individuals to establish a new literary canon by applying old intensive patterns of reading to a se-
lect body of secular texts. In the process, however, these authors drove a wedge
between high and low culture that threatened to alienate the public from the
very literature originally intended for its enlightenment" (4-5). Kontje understands the novels of Goethe and the German Romantics as "metafictions" in
that they are texts that consciously reflect upon the new, problematic patterns
of relationship between fiction and reality, author and reading public, that they
helped constitute (11). And while Kontje points out the differences between
today's postmodernism and these products of a "patriarchal and provincial national culture," he observes that these latter works foreshadow the debates on
the relationship between art and life that have become increasingly prevalent in
our own century (10-11; for further examples of new understandings of the

term *Bildungsroman,* see Hardin 1991; for a more traditional reassessment of the term, see Jacobs and Krause 1989).

With specific regard to *Heinrich von Ofterdingen,* Kontje applauds Géza von Molnár's understanding of the function of poetry for Novalis as a focal point for human communication, but he notes that abstract references to an "unlimited community of communicants" (Molnár 1987, 201), which Molnár derives from the theories of Jürgen Habermas and Karl-Otto Apel, do not do justice to the actual conditions under which Novalis lived and wrote. Novalis was not dependent on writing in order to make a living and hence did not let market conditions affect the content of his publications, which he directed primarily to his friends and closest literary associates — although his declared intention to have *Heinrich von Ofterdingen* appear with the same publisher and in the same format as *Wilhelm Meisters Lehrjahre* did signal his growing interest in the dynamics of the literary world of his day (Kontje, 98-101). Surveying Novalis's published and unpublished reflections on the nature of language and the contemporary literary scene, Kontje discerns a fluctuation and tension between notions of nonreferential play — such as Alice Kuzniar emphasizes in *Delayed Endings* — and efforts to help create a new reality through the medium of literature. Hence he interprets Heinrich's encounter with the illuminated manuscript in the hermit's cave, his initial dream of the Blue Flower, and even the inserted tales as containing an inherent multivalence that explains how Kuzniar and Molnár could arrive at such fine but mutually contradictory interpretations. He notes in conclusion:

> Novalis's combination of nostalgic longing for mystical presence with a utopian desire for absolute difference does not represent a very practical response to the transformation of the public sphere, but it is a response nevertheless. Whether conceived as a limited canon of texts promising total coherence, or as an alternative model of infinite textual circulation, Novalis's literary utopias define contemporary deficiencies in the institution of literature while suggesting possibilities for its productive transformation. (121)

In his monograph on *Frühromantik* (Early Romanticism, 1992) which like Kontje's study aspires to locate the poetic efforts of Novalis, Friedrich Schlegel, Wackenroder, and Tieck in a precise literary-historical context, Lothar Pikulik sees as the chief characteristic of Novalis's work the attempt to counteract the demystified character of the modern, technical world. He stresses how Novalis, drawing upon the insights of Kant and Fichte on the relationship between subjective apperception of the world and its carryover into human reality, wrote *Heinrich von Ofterdingen* to present an alternate model of how the world could and should be. Just as Heinrich is constantly on the threshold of new vistas in a Middle Ages of a highly symbolic nature, so too Novalis intends to involve his readers in a similar process of inner and outer transformation. Even if the manuscript in the hermit's cave suggests that there was no reality other than that portrayed in it (230), Novalis was well aware that what he offered in *Heinrich von Ofterdingen* was a symbol not to be confused with what it symbolized; for poetry to transform the world, there had to be willing and understanding readers. For Pikulik, *Heinrich von Ofterdingen* is not so much a metaphysical message as it is a type of experiment, a poetic search similar to what its main character enacts (238-40).

A similar understanding of *Heinrich von Ofterdingen* as a poetic experiment characterizes the approach Gerhard Schulz takes in his contribution to a 1992 volume of interpretations of nineteenth-century German novels. Schulz emphasizes that *Ofterdingen* is no example of philosophy or religion in the guise of literature, as admirers and detractors alike have often maintained. He chooses the dialogue between Heinrich and Mathilde in chapter eight as an example of how Novalis employs simple but highly abstract language and narrative patterns, not to convey a specific message, but rather to achieve a type of hypnotic, suggestive effect upon his readers (130-31). And while Schulz stresses the metaphysical components of Novalis's thinking, he also draws attention to the images of love and death in this novel, such as the dream sequence in which Heinrich first loses Mathilde and then is reunited with her. Such scenes, Schulz argues, are the most original and affecting moments in *Heinrich von Ofterdingen*; even though Novalis did not live long enough to complete his planned apotheosis of poetry, he has left behind an attempt to touch upon the limits of human powers and powerlessness with the help of language and creative fantasy (136-38).

In my 1992 article "Human History as Natural History in *Die Lehrlinge zu Sais* and *Heinrich von Ofterdingen*" I begin with a quote by Anton Kaes that raises to a general principle what Schulz identifies as a prime characteristic of the poetic works of Novalis:

> All cultural production has a social dimension: it articulates what a society lacks and desires. It delivers in the make-believe world of fiction what cannot be had or said in reality. In order to reactivate this social dimension of a literary text, one must reconstruct the question(s) that the work answers and addresses. The classical works of German literature in particular need to be understood once again as answers to questions that have their basis in the material as well as the ideological world. (Kaes 1989, 215)

To this insight I add the reminder that "the questions we ask are themselves triggered by areas in the text that address, challenge, or otherwise activate our own present concerns and our goals for the future" (1). As we have seen in the course of the reception history of *Ofterdingen*, what particular critics have to say often also throws a revealing light on them and their particular historical situation. I understand my investigation of Novalis's model of a mutually enriching interaction between humanity and nature as indicative not only of his dissatisfaction with conditions in the Europe of his day but also of our present awareness that humans could easily become the sources of global destruction if we fail to change our ways. But while the Klingsohr tale may end in a marriage of heaven and earth in which the throne from which Eros and Freya are to reign turns into a wedding bed, its apocalyptic overtones are not likely to appeal to present-day readers, for whom universal conflagration is no longer a mere metaphor but a distinct possibility. I likewise suggest that current readers of *Ofterdingen* are likely to look askance at Novalis's feminization of nature; the "lord of the earth" perspective of the miner (1: 247; 72) hardly qualifies him as the prototype of an ecofeminist (10). But ultimately, I conclude, it is the ability of texts like *Heinrich von Ofterdingen* to provoke such skeptical responses and to encourage the articulation of our own hopes and dreams that helps preserve their freshness:

> Today we may lack the certainty that we are in fact going "Immer nach Hause" (1: 325; 159) or else choose, as does Alice Kuzniar, to place the stress on "Immer" rather than "Nach Hause" [1987, 83]. But Novalis can still serve as a welcome companion as we search for a realization of the ecological insight that the earth is indeed our οἶκος, is indeed our home, and it remains for us to continue the writing of texts that Novalis left unended in more ways than one. (11)

In "Hearing Woman's Voices in *Heinrich von Ofterdingen*," Alice Kuzniar demonstrates once again how much there is to retrieve from this novel if only we as interpreters pay sufficient heed to what previous commentators have overlooked or, rather, overheard: "Heinrich draws on female qualities when it becomes clear that women command the poetic voice to which he aspires" (1992, 1197). In contrast to Kittler and Newman in their readings of *Heinrich von Ofterdingen*, Kuzniar observes that female figures like Heinrich's mother, Zulima, and Mathilde do not serve as a mirror for Heinrich; rather he strives to attain what they already possess in plentitude. For this reason, it is not so much male *Bildung* as female metamorphosis that constitutes Heinrich's ideal goal.

In the Klingsohr tale, Kuzniar notes, Sophie's vessel of water not only tests the Scribe's writing and serves as the source of figural language but also transmits the feminine: "In miming the Christian rite of Communion, this ceremony confers on women the privilege traditionally assigned to the male eucharistic body and its priests. By drinking of the mother, everyone, including each male figure, is transformed or transfigured, now endowed with the capacity to give birth eternally" (1200). Likewise, the waters in Heinrich's second dream betoken not his death but his resurrection, and it is Mathilde's voice that brings him to himself, though he is unable to repeat the word she whispers into his mouth. Heinrich must first learn to hear before he can sing; only after he recognizes his dead beloved's voice at the beginning to part two does he first break into song: "This sequence of events suggests that it is not the poet's language that resurrects the beloved: she must appear first" (1201). Finally, Kuzniar observes that the notes for the conclusion of *Heinrich von Ofterdingen* contain references to the dissolution of a poet into song and to Heinrich's multiple metamorphoses, which suggests that Novalis does not adhere to absolute gender oppositions; males may also partake of the protean mutability chiefly ascribed to the female figures in his novel (1202). "Not surprisingly," she concludes, "this transsexualism is repressed into the textual unconscious, where it has to be gingerly unearthed" (1203-4). But through an interpreter as accomplished as Kuzniar, aspects of *Heinrich von Ofterdingen* that only Marilyn Chapin Massey had hitherto begun to explore have now been brought to the surface. In a year already distinguished by the founding of the International Novalis Society and the appearance of so many other fine books and articles dealing with Novalis, "Hearing Woman's Voice in *Heinrich von Ofterdingen*" serves as one more indication that this novel has finally begun to attain the refined form evoked by its author, who called the true reader "the extended author":

> And if the reader were to revise the book according to his [or her] idea, then a second reader would purify it even more, and so — due to the fact that the processed substance comes repeatedly into freshly active containers — the material finally becomes an essential component or unit of efficacious spirit [*Geist*]. (2: 470)

Epilogue: On the Fulfillment of Expectations

IN THE KLINGSOHR tale, the ninth and concluding chapter of the first part of *Heinrich von Ofterdingen*, after the individual characters partake of the transfiguring draught offered them by Sophie, the text states that expectations have been fulfilled and exceeded (1: 312; 144). But while this tale provides at least some idea as to how the novel might have ended, Novalis lived only long enough to begin writing part two, the planned "Fulfillment" of the "Expectation" of part one. A review of the reception history of *Ofterdingen* likewise might serve to guard present-day readers and critics of Novalis against the overly confident assumption that we finally have discovered the magic elixir of comprehension that had eluded previous generations. In 1929 — the year in which Paul Kluckhohn and Richard Samuel published their first edition of Novalis's writings — it appeared as though a great new renaissance in studies on Novalis and German Romanticism were underway. In retrospect, in the scholarship on *Ofterdingen* written during the 1920s we can detect the buildup of forces that were soon to find their destructive outlet in Nazism; it was not until the 1960s, in the wake of the revised, historical-critical edition, that Novalis research finally began to emerge from the critical backwater into which it had settled. And future evaluators may not prove to be as sanguine in evaluating what at the moment appears to be an increasing growth in the quantity and quality of scholarship on *Heinrich von Ofterdingen*.

Such cautionary words notwithstanding, I would argue that there is no denying the impressive gains of the past three decades and the achievements of the year 1992. Interested readers now have access to vastly improved editions and textual apparatus to *Heinrich von Ofterdingen*. In the critical literature, reductionist reliance on Novalis's biography has become a thing of the past, and more careful attention to the wording and structure of the text has enabled scholars employing a variety of critical methodologies to explore new ways of access to a work that to many nineteenth-century critics appeared more a mystic jumble than a coherent, well-crafted work of art. Not least, the foundation of an International Novalis Society makes explicit the coincidence between the growth of a worldwide exchange of ideas and the rise of quality in Novalis scholarship. During both the first half of the nineteenth century and the decades immediately before the First World War, foreign critics like Carlyle and Lichtenberger — unencumbered by the ideological ballast attached to the term *Romanticism* in German-speaking countries — had led the way in offering innovative viewpoints on Novalis and *Heinrich von Ofterdingen*, even if their suggestions left little or no immediate trace in prevailing patterns of criticism in Germany. Such findings indicate how vital it is that scholars and nations alike pay careful heed to voices from outside their immediate ken. Just as during the past three decades German readers and scholars have needed to relearn what Romanticism might be in order to discover some of the treasures contained in *Ofterdingen*, so too we can all benefit from the type of sympathetic, understanding dialogue between individuals and cultures that Novalis illustrates throughout his novel.

There is likely to be no lack of future innovative studies of *Heinrich von Ofterdingen*. With regard to two main areas of recent *Ofterdingen* criticism — the literary-historical context in which Novalis wrote his novel and those aspects of this work that touch upon present-day concerns or directions of thought — the year 1993 witnessed further advances. At the 1993 meeting of the International Novalis Society, Herbert Uerlings delivered a talk titled "Novalis in Freiberg" — scheduled for publication in 1994 in a volume on Romanticism in Dresden edited by Walter Schmitz — and provided further evidence of the importance of Novalis's mining and scientific studies for his poetic works, including *Heinrich von Ofterdingen*. The concluding chapter of volume one of Manfred Engel's *Der Roman der Goethezeit* (The Novel of the Age of Goethe, 1993) focuses on the coincidence of unity and difference in *Heinrich von Ofterdingen* as a recurring pattern throughout both this novel and the "transcendental stories" of authors like Hölderlin and Friedrich Schlegel — an idea that deserves consideration in conjunction with Todd Kontje's approach to *Ofterdingen* from the previous year. And in her article "Romantic Chaos: The Dynamic Paradigm in Novalis's *Heinrich von Ofterdingen* and Contemporary Science," Joyce Walker makes use of key ideas in contemporary chaos theory in illuminating Novalis's critique of the Newtonian model of an orderly, predictable universe and suggesting that the narrative structure of his novel allows for limitless, aperiodic flow and process as an outgrowth of its initial conditions — an observation that one could apply to future directions in Novalis research as well.

With respect to the reception history of *Heinrich von Ofterdingen*, work still needs to be done on Hispanic and Eastern European criticism as well as on the state of Novalis scholarship in Japan — the latter being the subject of a talk by Nobuo Ikeda scheduled for the 1994 symposium of the International Novalis Society in Oberwiederstedt. Although it lies outside the focus of this study, which has dealt with literary criticism in the strict sense of the term, an investigation of the popular and literary reception of *Heinrich von Ofterdingen* could prove a fascinating topic in that such a study most likely would traverse the extremes of kitsch and literary modernism that developed out of literary Romanticism in the course of the nineteenth century. A final point to ponder is whether *Heinrich von Ofterdingen* is a literary work that requires such extensive commentary to be of interest to a contemporary audience that the critical labor might be more profitably expended elsewhere, or whether it is more a matter of removing encrusted prejudices and prior expectations and enabling the attentive reader to rediscover the delights of a major work of European Romanticism. But perhaps this is a question that readers of this study can best answer for themselves.

Bibliography

Editions containing Heinrich von Ofterdingen

1802. *Heinrich von Ofterdingen: Ein nachgelassener Roman von Novalis.* Berlin: Buchhandlung der Realschule.

1802. *Novalis Schriften,* ed. Friedrich Schlegel and Ludwig Tieck. 2 vols. Berlin: Buchhandlung der Realschule; 2nd ed. 1805; 3rd ed. 1815; 4th ed., Berlin: Reimer, 1826; 5th ed., Berlin: Reimer 1837; vol. 3, ed. Ludwig Tieck and Eduard von Bülow. Berlin: Reimer, 1846.

1837. *Novalis Schriften,* ed. Friedrich Schlegel and Ludwig Tieck; reprint of the 1826 ed. Stuttgart: Hausman.

1837. *Novalis Schriften,* ed. Friedrich Schlegel and Ludwig Tieck; reprint of the 1826 ed. Paris: Locquin.

1842. *Henry of Ofterdingen,* [probable] trans. F. S. Stallknecht. Cambridge, Mass.: Owen; 2nd ed. New York: Moore 1853.

1876. *Heinrich von Ofterdingen,* ed. Julian Schmidt. Bibliothek der Deutschen Nationalliteratur des achtzehnten und neunzehnten Jahrhunderts. Vol. 38. Leipzig: Brockhaus.

1891. *Novalis (Friedrich von Hardenberg): His Life, Thoughts, and Works,* ed. M. J. Hope. Chicago: McClurg.

1898. *Sämtliche Werke,* ed. Carl Meissner and Bruno Wille. 3 vols. Florence and Leipzig: Diederichs; supplementary vol. 1901, ed. Bruno Wille.

1901. *Schriften: Kritische Neuausgabe auf Grund des handschriftlichen Nachlasses,* ed. Ernst Heilborn. 3 vols. Berlin: Reimer.

1903. *Heinrich von Ofterdingen,* ed. Wilhelm Bölsche. Leipzig: Hesse & Becker.

1907. *Schriften,* ed. Jacob Minor. 4 vols. Jena: Diederichs.

1908. *Henri d'Ofterdingen,* trans. Georges Polti and Paul Morisse. Paris: Société du Mercure de France.

1914. *Enrico di Ofterdingen,* trans. R. Pisaneschi. Lanciano: Carabba.

1929. *Novalis: Schriften. Nach den Handschriften ergänzte und neugeordnete Ausgabe,* ed. Paul Kluckhohn and Richard Samuel. Leipzig: Bibliographisches Institut.

1942. *Novalis, Friedrich von Hardenberg: Scelta,* trans. G[iovan] A[ngelo] Alfero and Vincenzo Errante. Milan: Aldo Garzanti.

1942. *Novalis: Henri D'Ofterdingen,* trans. Marcel Camus. Paris: Aubier (bilingual edition).

1943. *Novalis: Briefe und Werke,* ed. Ewald Wasmuth. Berlin: Schneider.

1953-57. *Novalis: Werke, Briefe, Dokumente*, ed. Ewald Wasmuth. Heidelberg: Schneider.

1960- . *Schriften: Die Werke Friedrich von Hardenbergs*, ed. Paul Kluckhohn, Richard Samuel, Hans-Joachim Mähl, Heinz Ritter, and Gerhard Schulz. 4 vols. plus supplementary vols. Stuttgart: Kohlhammer.

Includes:

Vol. 1: *Das dichterische Werk* (The Poetic Works; 1960), ed. Paul Kluckhohn and Richard Samuel, with the help of Heinz Ritter and Gerhard Schulz; revised ed., 1977.

Vol. 2: *Das philosophische Werk I* (The Philosophical Works I, 1965), ed. Richard Samuel, in conjunction with Hans-Joachim Mähl and Gerhard Schulz; revised ed., 1981.

Vol. 3: *Das philosophische Werk II* (The Philosophical Works II, 1968), ed. Richard Samuel, in conjunction with Hans-Joachim Mähl and Gerhard Schulz; revised ed., 1983.

Vol. 4: *Tagebücher, Briefwechsel, Zeitgenössische Zeugnisse* (Diaries, Correspondence, Contemporary Documents, 1975), ed. Richard Samuel, in conjunction with Hans-Joachim Mähl and Gerhard Schulz.

Vol. 5. *Materialien und Register* (Materials and Index, 1988), ed. Hans-Joachim Mähl and Richard Samuel.

1964. *Novalis: Henry von Ofterdingen*, trans. Palmer Hilty. New York: Ungar; paperback reprint 1990, Prospect Heights, Ill.: Waveland.

1965. *Novalis: Heinrich von Ofterdingen*, ed. Wolfgang Frühwald. Stuttgart: Reclam; revised ed. 1987.

1968. *Novalis: Gedichte, Romane*, ed. Emil Staiger. Zurich: Manesse; 3rd ed. 1988.

1969. *Novalis: Werke*, ed. Gerhard Schulz. Munich: Beck; 3rd paperbound ed. 1987.

1975. *Dichtungen und Prosa*, ed. Claus Träger and Heidi Ruddigkeit. Leipzig: Reclam; revised ed. 1989.

1978-87. *Werke, Tagebücher und Briefe Friedrich von Hardenbergs*, ed. Hans-Joachim Mähl and Richard Samuel. 3 vols. Munich: Hanser.

1981. *Werke in einem Band*, ed. Hans-Joachim Mähl and Richard Samuel. Munich and Vienna: Hanser; 3rd ed. 1984.

1982. *Heinrich von Ofterdingen*, ed. Jochen Hörisch. Frankfurt am Main: Insel; 6th ed. 1993.

1983. *Werke in einem Band*, ed. Hans-Dietrich Dahnke. Berlin and Weimar: Aufbau; 3rd ed. 1985.

Works Consulted

Anon. 1803. Review of *Novalis Schriften*. *Neue Allgemeine Deutsche Bibliothek* 90: 49-56. Cited in Novalis, *Werke* 1978, 3: 155-56.

Delbrück, Johann Friedrich. 1803. Review of *Heinrich von Ofterdingen*. *Allgemeine Literatur-Zeitung* 258: col. 574-75. Cited in Novalis, *Werke* 1978, 3: 156-57.

Schlegel, Friedrich. 1803. "Literatur." *Europa* 1: 41-63. Cited in Novalis, *Werke* 1978, 3: 153-54.

Müller, Adam. 1807. *Vorlesungen über die deutsche Wissenschaft und Literatur*. In Müller, *Kritische, ästhetische und philosophische Schriften*, ed. Walter Schroeder and Werner Siebert. Vol. 1. Neuwied and Berlin: Luchterhand, 1967.

Schlegel, Friedrich. 1815. *Geschichte der alten und neuen Literatur*. In *Kritische Friedrich-Schlegel-Ausgabe*, ed. Ernst Behler et al. Vol. 6. Paderborn: Schöningh, 1961.

Tieck, Ludwig. 1815. Introduction to the 3rd ed. of *Novalis Schriften*, x-xxxiii. In Novalis, *Schriften* 4: 551-60.

Koberstein, August. 1827. *Grundriss der Geschichte der Deutschen Nationalliteratur*. Leipzig: Vogel; 5th ed., revised, 1873, ed. Karl Bartsch.

Eckstein, Baron de. 1828. "OEuvres de Novalis (Frédéric, baron de Hardenberg)." *Le Catholique* 10, 129-44.

Menzel, Wolfgang. 1828. *Die deutsche Literatur*. Stuttgart: Franck. Rpt. Hildesheim: Gerstenberg, 1981.

Carlyle, Thomas. 1829. "Novalis." *Foreign Review*, No. 7. In Carlyle, *Critical and Miscellaneous Essays*. Philadelphia: Hart, 1845, 167-87.

Hegel, Georg Wilhelm Friedrich. 1835. *Vorlesungen über die Aesthetik*. In Hegel, *Sämtliche Werke*. Jubiläumsausgabe, ed. Hermann Glockner. Vol. 12. Stuttgart: Bad Cannstatt: Frommann, 1964.

Heine, Heinrich. 1836. *Die Romantische Schule*. In Heine, *The Romantic School And Other Essays*, ed. Jost Hermand and Robert C. Holub, trans. Helen Mustard et al. New York: Continuum: 1985, 1-127.

Menzel, Wolfgang. 1836. *Die deutsche Literatur*, 2nd ed., revised. Stuttgart: Franck.

Ruge, Arnold and Theodor Echtermeyer. 1839. "Novalis." *Hallische Jahrbücher für deutsche Wissenschaft und Kunst*: 2136-52. In Schulz 1986, 1-19.

Laube, Heinrich. 1840. *Geschichte der deutschen Literatur*. Vol. 3. Stuttgart: Hallberger.

Mundt, Theodor. 1842. *Geschichte der Literatur der Gegenwart*. Berlin: Simion.

Gervinus, Georg Gottfried. 1843. *Geschichte der Deutschen Dichtung*. Vol. 5. Leipzig: Engelmann; 5th ed., revised, 1874, ed. Karl Bartsch.

Hedge, Frederic H. 1847. *Prose Writers of Germany*. Philadelphia: Porter & Coates; 2nd ed., revised, 1870.

Prutz, Robert. 1847. *Vorlesungen über die deutsche Literatur der Gegenwart*. Leipzig: Mayer.

Taillandier, Saint-René. 1847. "Novalis." *Académie des sciences et lettres de Montpellier: Mémoires de la section des lettres* 1, 1-39.

Hettner, Hermann. 1850. *Die romantische Schule in ihrem Zusammenhang mit Göthe und Schiller.* Braunschweig: Vieweg.

Schmidt, Julian. 1853. *Geschichte der Deutschen Literatur im neunzehnten Jahrhundert.* Vol. 1. Leipzig: Herbig; 3rd ed., revised, 1856.

Eichendorff, Joseph von. 1857. *Geschichte der poetischen Literatur Deutschlands.* In Eichendorff, *Sämtliche Werke*, ed. Hermann Kunisch. Vol. 9. Regensburg: Habbel, 1970.

Goedeke, Karl. 1859. *Grundriß zur Geschichte der deutschen Dichtung aus den Quellen.* Dresden: Ehlermann; 2nd ed., revised, ed. Edmund Goetze, 1898, 6: 48-51.

Dilthey, Wilhelm. 1865. "Novalis." *Preussische Jahrbücher* 15, 596-650. In Dilthey, *Das Erlebnis und die Dichtung: Lessing, Goethe, Novalis, Hölderlin.* Leipzig and Berlin: Teubner, 1906; 10th ed. 1929, 268–348.

———. 1868. "Novalis." *Westermanns Monatshefte* 25, 272–80.

———. 1870. *Leben Schleiermachers.* In Dilthey, *Gesammelte Schriften*, ed. Martin Redeker. Vol. 13, No. 1. Göttingen: Vandenhoeck & Ruprecht, 1970.

Haym, Rudolf. 1870. *Die romantische Schule: Ein Beitrag zur Geschichte des deutschen Geistes.* Berlin: Gaertner. Section on *Heinrich von Ofterdingen* in *Interpretationen*, ed. Jost Schillemeit. Frankfurt am Main: Fischer, 1966, 3: 118-35.

Brandes, Georg. 1873. *Die romantische Schule in Deutschland* (vol. 2 of *Die Hauptströmungen der Literatur des neunzehnten Jahrhunderts: Vorlesungen gehalten an der Kopenhagener Universität*), trans. Adolf Strodtmann. Berlin: Duncker.

[Hardenberg, Sophie von.] 1873. *Friedrich von Hardenberg (genannt Novalis). Eine Nachlese aus den Quellen des Familienarchivs: Herausgegeben von einem Mitglied der Familie.* Gotha: Perthes; 2nd ed., revised, 1883.

Schmidt, Julian. 1876. Introduction to *Heinrich von Ofterdingen.* Bibliothek der Deutschen Nationalliteratur des achtzehnten und neunzehnten Jahrhunderts. Vol. 38. Leipzig: Brockhaus, i–xxiii.

Schubart, A. 1887. *Novalis' Leben, Dichten und Denken: Auf Grund neuerer Publikationen im Zusammenhang dargestellt.* Gütersloh: Bertelsmann.

Boyesen, Hjalmar Hjorth. 1892. "Novalis and the Blue Flower." *Essays on German Literature.* New York: Scribner's, 307-31.

Bing, Just. 1893. *Novalis (Friedrich von Hardenberg): Eine biographische Charakteristik.* Hamburg and Leipzig: Voss.

Donner, Joakim O. E. 1893. *Der Einfluß Wilhelm Meisters auf dem Roman der Romantiker.* Helsing: Frenckell.

Francke, Kuno. 1895. *Social Forces in German Literature: A Study in the History of Civilization.* New York: Holt; 2nd ed. 1897.

Maeterlinck, Maurice. 1895. Introduction to *Les Disciples à Sais et les Fragments de Novalis.* Brussels: Lacomblez; 2nd ed. 1909; 3rd ed. 1914, v-lvii.

Busse, Carl. 1898. *Novalis' Lyrik.* Oppeln: Maske.

Bölsche, Wilhelm. 1899. "Novalis und das neue Jahrhundert." *Deutsche Rundschau* 101, 188-92.

Huch, Ricarda. 1899. *Blüthezeit der Romantik.* Leipzig: Haessel.

Heilborn, Ernst. 1901. *Novalis, der Romantiker.* Berlin: Reimer.

Bölsche, Wilhelm. 1903. Introduction to *Heinrich von Ofterdingen.* Leipzig: Hesse & Becker, 1-9.

Blei, Franz. 1904. *Novalis.* Berlin: Bard, Marquardt & Co.

Spenlé, Jean Éduord. 1904. *Novalis: Essai sur l'Idéalisme romantique en Allemagne.* Paris: Hachette.

Albert, Henri. 1908. Introduction to *Novalis: Henri d'Ofterdingen.* Paris: Société du Mercure de France, v-xvi.

Bartels, Adolf. 1909. *Geschichte der Deutschen Literatur.* Vol. 1 Leipzig: Avenarius.

Moeller van den Bruck, Arthur. 1910. *Die Deutschen: Unsere Menschengeschichte.* Minden in Westfalen: Bruns; 2nd ed., revised, 3: 164-194.

Strich, Fritz. 1910. *Die Mythologie in der deutschen Literatur von Klopstock bis Wagner.* 2 vols. Halle: Niemeyer. Rpt. Berne and Munich: Francke, 1970.

Farinelli, Arturo. 1911. *Il romanticismo in Germania: Lezioni introduttive.* Bari: Laterza.

Gloege, Georg. 1911. *Novalis' "Heinrich von Ofterdingen" als Ausdruck seiner Persönlichkeit: Eine ästhetisch-psychologische Stiluntersuchung.* Leipzig: Avenarius.

Lukács, Georg. 1911. "Zur romantischen Lebensphilosophie: Novalis." *Die Seele und die Formen, Essays.* Berlin: Fleischel, 93-117. In Schulz 1986, 20-35.

Haussmann, J. F. 1911-12. "German Estimates of Novalis from 1800 to 1850." *Modern Philology* 9, 399-415.

Lichtenberger, Henri. 1912. *Novalis.* Paris: Bloud.

Riesenfeld, Paul. 1912. *Heinrich von Ofterdingen in der deutschen Literatur.* Berlin: Mayer & Müller.

Haussmann, J. F. 1913. "Die deutsche Kritik über Novalis von 1850–1900." *Journal of English and Germanic Philology* 12, 211-44.

Wundt, Max. 1913. *Goethes "Wilhelm Meister" und die Entwicklung des modernen Lebensideals.* Berlin and Leipzig: Göschen.

Woltereck, Käte. 1914. *Goethes Einfluß auf Heinrich von Ofterdingen.* Weida in Th.: Thomas & Hubert.

Alfero, Giovan Angelo. 1916. *Novalis e il suo "Heinrich von Ofterdingen."* Torino: Fratelli Bocca.

Lukács, Georg. 1916. "Die Theorie des Romans: Ein geschichtsphilosophischer Versuch über die Formen der großen Epik." *Zeitschrift für Ästhetik und Allgemeine Kunstwissenschaft* 2, 225-71 and 390-431. Rpt. Neuwied and Berlin: Luchterhand, 1971.

Scheidweiler, Paula. 1916. *Der Roman der deutschen Romantik.* Berlin and Leipzig: Teubner.

Bartels, Adolf, 1919. *Geschichte der deutschen Literatur.* Hamburg, Braunschweig, and Berlin: Westermann; 7th and 8th ed.

Benjamin, Walter. 1919. "Der Begriff der Kunstkritik in der deutschen Romantik." In Benjamin, *Gesammelte Schriften.* Frankfurt am Main: Suhrkamp, 1974, 1: 7-122.

Walzel, Oskar. 1919. "Die Formkunst von Hardenbergs *Heinrich von Ofterdingen.*" *Germanisch-romanische Monatsschrift* 7, 403-44 and 465-79. In Schulz 1986, 36-95.

Feilchenfeld, Walter. 1922. *Der Einfluß Jacob Böhmes auf Novalis.* Berlin: Matthiesen. Rpt. Nendeln/Liechtenstein: Kraus 1967.

Kluckhohn, Paul. 1922. *Die Auffassung der Liebe in der Literatur des 18. Jahrhunderts und in der deutschen Romantik.* Halle: Niemeyer; 3rd ed., Tübingen: Niemeyer, 1966.

Marcuse, Herbert. 1922. "Der deutsche Künstlerroman." Diss. University of Freiburg. In Marcuse, *Schriften.* Frankfurt am Main: Suhrkamp, 1978, 1: 7-344.

Strich, Fritz. 1922. *Deutsche Klassik und Romantik; oder Vollendung und Unendlichkeit.* Munich: Meyer & Jessen; 4th edition Berne: Francke, 1949.

Hesse, Hermann. 1925. Afterword to *Novalis: Dokumente seines Lebens und Sterbens.* Berlin: S. Fischer, 160-64. Rpt. Frankfurt am Main: Insel, 1976.

Kluckhohn, Paul. 1925. "Die romantische Staatsauffassung bei Novalis." *Persönlichkeit und Gemeinschaft: Studien zur Staatsauffassung der deutschen Romantik.* Halle: Niemeyer, 47-57. In Schulz 1986, 98-105.

Obenauer, Karl Justus. 1925. *Hölderlin/Novalis.* Jena: Diederichs.

Samuel, Richard. 1925. *Die poetische Staats- und Geschichtsauffassung Friedrich von Hardenbergs (Novalis): Studien zur romantischen Geschichtsphilosophie.* Frankfurt am Main: Diesterweg.

Bäumler, Alfred. 1926. Introduction to *Der Mythus von Orient und Occident: Eine Metaphysik der alten Welt aus den Werken von J. J. Bachofen,* ed. Manfred Schroeter. Munich: Beck, esp. clxvi-clxxxv.

Mann, Thomas. 1926. *Pariser Rechenschaft.* In Mann, *Gesammelte Werke.* Frankfurt am Main: S. Fischer, 1960, 11: 9-97.

Petersen, Julius. 1926. *Die Wesensbestimmung der deutschen Romantik: Eine Einführung in die moderne Literaturwissenschaft.* Leipzig: Quelle & Meyer.

Kommerell, Max, 1928. *Der Dichter als Führer in der deutschen Klassik: Klopstock, Herder, Goethe, Schiller, Jean Paul, Hölderlin.* Frankfurt am Main: Klostermann.

Kluckhohn, Paul. 1929. "Friedrich von Hardenbergs Entwicklung und Dichtung." Introduction to *Novalis: Schriften.* Leipzig: Bibliographisches Institut, 1: 9-80. In Novalis, *Schriften* 1: 1-67.

Romantik-Forschungen. 1929. Buchreihe des Deutschen Vierteljahrschrifts, No. 16. Halle: Niemeyer.

Includes:

Hamburger, Käte, 1929. "Novalis und die Mathematik," 113-84.

May, Kurt. 1929. "Weltbild und innere Form der Klassik und Romantik im *Wilhelm Meister* und *Heinrich von Ofterdingen,*" 185-204. In May, *Form und Bedeutung: Interpretationen deutscher Dichtung des 18. und 19. Jahrhunderts.* Stuttgart: Klett, 1957, 161-77.

Samuel, Richard. 1929. "Der berufliche Werdegang Friedrich von Hardenbergs," 83-112.

Wiese, Benno von. 1929. "Novalis und die romantischen Konvertiten," 205-42.

Hecker, Jutta. 1931. *Das Symbol der Blauen Blume im Zusammenhang mit der Blumensymbolik der Romantik.* Jena: Frommann.

Hamburger, Käte. 1932. *Thomas Mann und die Romantik: Eine problemgeschichtliche Studie.* Berlin: Junker und Dünnhaupt.

Diez, Max. 1933. "Metapher und Märchengestalt: Novalis und das allegorische Märchen." *PMLA* 48, 488-507. In Schulz 1986, 131-59.

Petersen, Julius. 1934. "Die Sehnsucht nach dem Dritten Reich in deutscher Sage und Dichtung." *Dichtung und Volkstum [Euphorion]* 35, 18-40 and 145-82.

Pongs, Hermann. 1934. "Krieg als Volksschicksal im deutschen Schrifttum." *Dichtung und Volkstum [Euphorion]* 35, 40-86 and 182-219.

Kluckhohn, Paul. 1936. "Berufungsbewußtsein und Gemeinschaftsdienst des deutschen Dichters im Wandel der Zeiten." *Deutsche Vierteljahrsschrift für Literaturwissenschaft und Geistesgeschichte* 14, 1-30.

Bartels, Adolf. 1937. *Geschichte der deutschen Literatur.* Braunschweig, Berlin, Leipzig, and Hamburg: Westermann; 16th ed.

Wiese, Benno von. 1937. "Forschungsbericht zur Romantik." *Dichtung und Volkstum [Euphorion]* 38, 65-85.

Nadler, Josef. 1938. *Literaturgeschichte des Deutschen Volkes: Dichtung und Schrifttum der deutschen Stämme und Landschaften.* Berlin: Propyläen; 4th ed., revised.

Busse, Gisela von. 1938. "Auch eine Geschichte des deutschen Volkes: Betrachtungen zu Josef Nadlers Literaturgeschichte." *Deutsche Vierteljahrsschrift für Literaturwissenschaft und Geistesgeschichte* 16, 258-92.

Korff, Hermann August. 1940. *Geist der Goethezeit, III. Teil. Romantik: Frühromantik.* Leipzig: Weber; 2nd, licensed edition, Leipzig: Hirzel, 1949.

Minnigerode, Irmtrud von. 1941. *Die Christusanschauung des Novalis.* Berlin: Junker und Dünnhaupt.

Reble, Albert. 1941. "Märchen und Wirklichkeit bei Novalis." *Deutsche Vierteljahrsschrift für Literaturwissenschaft und Geistesgeschichte* 19, 70-110.

Alfero, Giovan Angelo. 1942. Introduction to *Novalis, Friedrich von Hardenberg: Scelta*. Milan: Aldo Garzanti, ix-xx.

Bonsels, Waldemar. 1942. Introduction to *Der Hüter der Schwelle: Von Weisheit und Liebe in der Geisteswelt des Novalis*. Munich: Münchner Buchverlag, 7-23.

Camus, Marcel. 1942. Introduction and Notes to *Novalis: Henri D'Ofterdingen*. Paris: Aubier, 5-56 and 425-49.

Kommerell, Max, 1942. "Novalis: *Hymnen an die Nacht*." *Auslegungen deutscher Gedichte*, ed. Heinz Otto Bürger. Halle: Niemeyer, 212-36. In Schulz 1986, 174-202.

Lukács, Georg. 1945. "Die Romantik als Wendung in der deutschen Literatur." *Fortschritt und Reaktion*. Berlin: Aufbau. In Peter 1980a, 40-52.

Barth, Karl. 1947. *Die protestantische Theologie im 19. Jahrhundert: Ihre Vorgeschichte und ihre Geschichte*. Zurich: Evangelischer Verlag.

Bus, Antonius Johannes Maria. 1947. *Der Mythus der Musik in Novalis' Heinrich von Ofterdingen*. Alkmaar: Coster & Zoon.

Steinbüchel, Theodor, ed. 1948. *Romantik: Ein Zyklus Tübinger Vorlesungen*. Tübingen and Stuttgart: Leins.

Includes:

Kluckhohn, Paul. 1948. "Voraussetzungen und Verlauf der romantischen Dichtung" and "Romantische Dichtung," 11-26 and 27-41.

Köberle, August. 1948. "Die Romantik als religiöse Bewegung," 65-85.

Kayser, Wolfgang. 1948. *Das sprachliche Kunstwerk*. Berne: Francke.

Borcherdt, Hans Heinrich. 1949. *Der Roman der Goethezeit*. Urach and Stuttgart: Port.

Nivelle, Armand. 1950. "Der symbolische Gehalt des *Heinrich von Ofterdingen*." *Revue des langues vivantes* 16, 404-27.

Rehm, Walter. 1950. *Orpheus: Der Dichter und die Toten. Selbstdeutung und Totenkult bei Novalis, Hölderlin, Rilke*. Düsseldorf, Schwann.

Hiebel, Friedrich. 1951. *Novalis, Der Dichter der Blauen Blume*. Berne: Francke; 2nd ed., revised, 1972 under the title *Novalis: Deutscher Dichter, Europäischer Denker, Christlicher Seher*.

Schmid, Heinz Dieter. 1951. "Friedrich von Hardenberg (Novalis) und Abraham Gottlob Werner." Diss. University of Tübingen.

Müller-Seidel, Walter. 1953. "Probleme neuerer Novalis-Forschung." *Germanisch-Romanische Monatsschrift*, N. S. 3, 274-92.

Striedter, Jurij. 1953. *Die Fragmente des Novalis als "Präfigurationen" seiner Dichtung*. Diss. University of Heidelberg. Rpt. Munich: Fink, 1985.

Wasmuth, Ewald. 1953. Afterword to *Novalis: Werke, Briefe, Dokumente*, 1: 557-69.

Fries, W. J. 1954. "Ginnistan und Eros: Ein Beitrag zur Symbolik in *Heinrich von Ofterdingen*." *Neophilologus* 38, 23-36.

Schrimpf, Hans-Joachim. 1956. "Novalis: Das Lied der Toten." *Die deutsche Lyrik: Form und Geschichte*, ed. Benno von Wiese. Düsseldorf, Bagel, 1: 414-29.

Haufe, Eberhard. 1957. "Die Aufhebung der Zeit in Novalis' *Heinrich von Ofterdingen*." *Gestaltung, Umgestaltung: Festschrift zum 75. Geburtstag von Hermann August Korff*, ed. Joachim Müller. Leipzig, Koehler & Amelang, 178-88.

Kluckhohn, Paul. 1958. "Neue Funde zu Friedrich von Hardenbergs Arbeit am *Heinrich von Ofterdingen*." *Deutsche Vierteljahrsschrift für Literaturwissenschaft und Geistesgeschichte* 32, 391-409.

Schulz, Gerhard. 1958. "Die Berufstätigkeit Friedrich von Hardenbergs und ihre Bedeutung für seine Dichtung und seine Gedankenwelt." Diss. University of Leipzig.

Haywood, Bruce. 1959. *Novalis: The Veil of Imagery. A Study of the Poetic Works of Friedrich von Hardenberg (1772-1801)*. 's-Gravenhage: Mouton.

Hiebel, Frederick. 1959. *Novalis: German Poet, European Thinker, Christian Mystic*. Chapel Hill: University of North Carolina Press: 1954; 2nd ed. revised.

Küpper, Peter. 1959. *Die Zeit als Erlebnis bei Novalis*. Cologne and Graz: Böhlau.

Mayer, Hans. 1959. *Von Lessing bis Thomas Mann*. Pfullingen: Neske.

Schulz, Gerhard. 1959a. "Der Bergbau in Novalis' *Heinrich von Ofterdingen*." *Der Anschnitt* 11, No. 2, 9-13.

———. 1959b. "'Der ist der Herr der Erde...' Betrachtungen zum ersten Bergmannslied in Novalis' *Heinrich von Ofterdingen*." *Der Anschnitt* 11, No. 3, 10-13.

———. 1959c. "Die Verklärung des Bergbaus bei Novalis: Betrachtungen zum zweiten Bergmannslied im *Heinrich von Ofterdingen*." *Der Anschnitt* 11, No. 4, 20-23.

Ritter, Heinz. 1961. "Die Entstehung des *Heinrich von Ofterdingen*." *Euphorion* 55, 163-95.

Träger, Claus. 1961. "Novalis und die ideologische Restauration: Über den romantischen Ursprung einer methodischen Apologetik." *Sinn und Form* 13, 618-60.

Leroy, Robert. 1963-64. "Der Traumbegriff des Novalis." *Revue des langues vivantes* 29, 232-37 and 30, 26-34.

Löffler, Dietrich. 1963. "*Heinrich von Ofterdingen* als romantischer Roman." Diss. University of Leipzig.

Mähl, Hans-Joachim. 1963. "Novalis und Plotin: Untersuchungen zu einer neuen Edition und Interpretation des 'Allgemeinen Brouillons.'" *Jahrbuch des Freien Deutschen Hochstifts*, 139-250. In Schulz 1986, 357-423.

Samuel, Richard. 1963. "Novalis: *Heinrich von Ofterdingen*." *Der deutsche Roman: Vom Barock bis zur Gegenwart*, ed. Benno von Wiese. Düsseldorf: Bagel, 1: 252-300.

Schulz, Gerhard. 1963. "Die Berufslaufbahn Friedrich von Hardenbergs (Novalis)." *Jahrbuch der deutschen Schillergesellschaft* 7, 253-312. In Schulz 1986, 283-356.

Vordtriede, Werner. 1963. *Novalis und die französischen Symbolisten*. Stuttgart: Kohlhammer.

Hilty, Palmer. 1964. Introduction to *Novalis: Henry von Ofterdingen.* New York: Ungar, 1-11.

Schulz, Gerhard. 1964. "Die Poetik des Romans bei Novalis." *Jahrbuch des Freien Deutschen Hochstifts,* 120-57. In *Deutsche Romantheorien: Beiträge zu einer historischen Poetik des Romans in Deutschland,* ed. Reinhold Grimm. Frankfurt am Main: Athenäum, 1968, 81-110.

Voerster, Erika. 1964. *Märchen und Novellen im klassisch-romantischen Roman.* Bonn: Bouvier; 2nd ed. 1966.

Ehrensperger, Oskar Serge. 1965. *Die epische Struktur in Novalis' "Heinrich von Ofterdingen."* Winterthur: Schellenberg.

Frühwald, Wolfgang. 1965. Afterword to *Novalis: Heinrich von Ofterdingen.* Stuttgart: Reclam, 229-45.

Leroy, Robert. 1965. "Die Novalis'schen Bilder der 'Nacht.'" *Revue des langues vivantes* 31, 390-403.

Mähl, Hans-Joachim. 1965. *Die Idee des goldenen Zeitalters im Werk des Novalis: Studien zur Wesensbestimmung der frühromantischen Utopie und zu ihren ideengeschichtlichen Voraussetzungen.* Heidelberg: Winter.

Hiller, Helmut. 1966. *Zur Sozialgeschichte von Buch und Buchhandel.* Bonn: Bouvier.

Conrady, Karl Otto. 1967. "Deutsche Literaturwissenschaft und Drittes Reich." *Germanistik — eine deutsche Wissenschaft: Beiträge von Eberhard Lämmert, Walther Killy, Karl Otto Conrady und Peter v. Polenz.* Frankfurt am Main: Suhrkamp, 71-109.

Rasch, Wolfdietrich. 1967. "Aspekte der deutschen Literatur um 1900." *Zur deutschen Literatur seit der Jahrhundertwende: Gesammelte Aufsätze.* Stuttgart: Metzler, 1-48.

Ritter, Heinz. 1967. *Der unbekannte Novalis: Friedrich von Hardenberg im Spiegel seiner Dichtung.* Göttingen: Sachse & Pohl.

Schlagdenhaufen, Alfred. 1967. "Klingsohr-Goethe?" *Un Dialogue des Nations: Albert Fuchs zum 70. Geburtstag.* Munich and Paris: Hueber, Klinckspieck, 121-30.

Leroy, Robert. 1968. "Novalis und das Wasser." *Revue des langues vivantes* 34, 50-57.

Schanze, Helmut. 1968. *Index zu Novalis, "Heinrich von Ofterdingen."* Frankfurt am Main: Athenäum.

Staiger, Emil. 1968. Introduction to *Novalis: Gedichte, Romane.* Zurich: Manesse, 7-48.

Heftrich, Eckhard. 1969. *Novalis: Vom Logos der Poesie.* Frankfurt am Main: Klostermann.

Ritchie, J. M. 1969. "Novalis' *Heinrich von Ofterdingen* and the Romantic Novel." *Periods in German Literature II: Texts and Contents,* ed. J. M. Ritchie. London: Wolff; American edition 1970, Chester Springs, Pa: Dufour, 117-44.

Schulz, Gerhard. 1969a. Commentary to *Heinrich von Ofterdingen. Novalis: Werke.* Munich: Beck, 688-731.

Schulz, Gerhard. 1969b. *Novalis in Selbstzeugnissen und Bilddokumenten.* Reinbek: Rowohlt.

Faber, Richard. 1970. *Novalis: Die Phantasie an die Macht.* Stuttgart: Metzler.

Mahr, Johannes. 1970. *Übergang zum Endlichen: Der Weg des Dichters in Novalis' "Heinrich von Ofterdingen."* Munich: Fink.

Molnár, Géza von. 1970. *Novalis' "Fichte Studies": The Foundations of his Aesthetics.* The Hague: Mouton.

Schanze, Helmut. 1970. "Zur Interpretation von Novalis' *Heinrich von Ofterdingen*: Theorie und Praxis eines vollständigen Wortindex." *Wirkendes Wort* 20, 19-33.

Barrack, Charles M. 1971. "Conscience in *Heinrich von Ofterdingen*: Novalis' Metaphysic of the Poet." *Germanic Review* 46, 257-84.

Link, Hannelore. 1971. *Abstraktion und Poesie im Werk des Novalis.* Stuttgart: Kohlhammer.

Glorieux, Jean-Paul. 1972. "Novalis et l'Université Française au Début du XXme Siècle: Proloque d'une renommée." *Lettres romanes* 26, 127-68.

Jacobs, Jürgen. 1972. *Wilhelm Meister und seine Brüder: Untersuchungen zum deutschen Bildungsroman.* Munich: Fink.

Kuenzli, Rudolf Ernst. 1972. "The Reception of Novalis in England and America in the Nineteenth Century." Diss. University of Wisconsin.

Peschken, Bernd. 1972. *Versuch einer germanistischen Ideologiekritik: Goethe, Lessing, Novalis, Tieck, Hölderlin, Heine in Wilhelm Diltheys und Julian Schmids Vorstellungen.* Stuttgart: Metzler.

Jay, Martin. *The Dialectical Imagination: A History of the Frankfurt School and the Institute of Social Research.* Boston and Toronto: Little, Brown and Company.

Molnár, Géza von. 1973. Another Glance at Novalis' 'Blue Flower.'" *Euphorion* 67, 272-86. In Schulz 1986, 424-49, under the title "Novalis' 'blaue Blume' im Blickfeld von Goethes Optik."

Wetzels, Walter D. 1973. "Klingsohrs Märchen als Science Fiction." *Monatshefte* 65, 168-75.

Schuller, Marianne. 1974. *Romanschlüsse in der Romantik: Zum frühromantischen Problem von Universalität und Fragment.* Munich: Fink.

Stopp, Elisabeth. 1974. "'Übergang vom Roman zur Mythologie': Formal Aspects of the Opening Chapter of Hardenberg's *Heinrich von Ofterdingen, Part II.*" *Deutsche Vierteljahrsschrift für Geistesgeschichte und Literaturwissenschaft* 48, 318-41.

Hegener, Johannes. 1975. *Die Poetisierung der Wissenschaften bei Novalis: dargestellt am Prozeß der Entwicklung von Welt und Menschheit. Studien zum Problem encyklopädischen Welterfahrens.* Bonn: Bouvier.

Heine, Roland. 1975. *Transzendentalpoesie: Studien zu Friedrich Schlegel, Novalis und E.T.A. Hoffmann.* Bonn: Bouvier.

Träger, Claus. 1975. "Ursprünge und Stellung der Romantik." *Weimarer Beiträge* 21, No. 2, 37-73. In Peter 1980a, 304-34.

Beck, Hans-Joachim. 1976. *Friedrich von Hardenbergs "Oeconomie des Styls": Die "Wilhelm Meister"-Rezeption im "Heinrich von Ofterdingen."* Bonn: Bouvier.

Grob, Karl. 1976. *Ursprung und Utopie: Aporien des Textes; Versuche zu Herder und Novalis.* Bonn: Bouvier.

Hörisch, Jochen. 1976. *Die fröhliche Wissenschaft der Poesie: Der Universalitätsanspruch von Dichtung in der frühromantischen Poetologie.* Frankfurt am Main: Suhrkamp.

Paschek, Carl. 1976. "Novalis und Böhme: Zur Bedeutung der systematischen Böhmelektüre des späten Novalis." *Jahrbuch des Freien Deutschen Hochstifts,* 138-67.

Pfotenhauer, Helmut. 1977. "Aspekte der Modernität bei Novalis: Überlegungen zu Erzählformen des 19. Jahrhunderts, ausgehend von Hardenbergs *Heinrich von Ofterdingen.*" *Zur Modernität der Romantik,* ed. Dieter Bänsch. Stuttgart: Metzler, 111-42.

Rogers, Elwin E. 1977. "Novalis' Atlantis-Erzählung: Goethe surpassed?" *German Quarterly* 50, 130-37.

Schumacher, Hans. 1977. *Narziß an der Quelle. Das romantische Kunstmärchen: Geschichte und Interpretationen.* Wiesbaden: Athenaion.

Apel, Friedmar. 1978. *Die Zaubergärten der Phantasie: Zur Theorie und Geschichte des Kunstmärchens.* Heidelberg: Winter.

Brinkmann, Richard, ed. 1978. *Romantik in Deutschland: Ein interdisziplinäres Symposion.* Stuttgart: Metzler.

Includes:

Kittler, Friedrich A. 1978. "Der Dichter, die Mutter, das Kind: Zur romantischen Erfindung der Sexualität," 102-14.

Stadler, Ulrich. 1978. "Die Auffassung vom Gelde bei Friedrich von Hardenberg (Novalis)," 147-56.

Strack, Friedrich. 1978. "Die 'göttliche' Kunst und ihre Sprache: Zum Kunst- und Religionsbegriff bei Wackenroder, Tieck und Novalis," 369-91.

Dahnke, Hans-Dietrich, et al. 1978. *Geschichte der Deutschen Literatur: 1789 bis 1830.* Berlin: Volk und Wissen Volkseigener Verlag.

Gallant, Christel. 1978. *Der Raum in Novalis' dichterischem Werk.* Berne: Lang.

Neubauer, John. 1978. *Symbolismus und symbolische Logik: Die Idee der Ars Combinatoria in der Entwicklung der modernen Dichtung.* Munich: Fink.

Becker-Cantarino, Barbara. 1979. "Priesterin und Lichtbringerin: Zur Ideologie des weiblichen Charakters in der Frühromantik." *Die Frau als Heldin und Autorin: Neue kritische Ansätze zur deutschen Literatur,* ed. Wolfgang Paulsen. Berne and Munich: Francke, 111-24.

Birrell, Gordon. 1979. *The Boundless Present: Space and Time in the Literary Fairy Tales of Novalis and Tieck.* Chapel Hill: University of North Carolina Press.

Bovenschen, Silvia. 1979. *Die imaginierte Weiblichkeit: Exemplarische Untersuchungen zu kulturgeschichtlichen und literarischen Präsentationsformen des Weiblichen.* Frankfurt am Main: Suhrkamp.

Haase, Donald P. 1979. "Romantic Facts and Critical Myths: Novalis' Early Reception in France." *Comparativist* 3, 23-31.

Kloppmann, Wolfgang. 1979. "Eine materialistische Lektüre des Bergmann-Kapitels im *Ofterdingen.*" *Romantische Utopie — Utopische Romantik,* ed. Gisela Dischner and Richard Faber. Hildesheim: Gerstenberg, 222-39.

Leroy, Robert and Eckhart Pastor. 1979. "Die Initiation des romantischen Dichters: Der Anfang von Novalis' *Heinrich von Ofterdingen.*" *Romantik: Ein literaturwissenschaftliches Studienbuch,* ed. Ernst Ribbat. Königstein: Athenäum, 38-57.

Scrase, David. 1979. "The Moveable Feast: The Role and Relevance of the *Fest* Motif in Novalis' *Heinrich von Ofterdingen.*" *New German Studies* 7, 23-40.

Kaiser, Hartmut. 1980 "Mozarts *Zauberflöte* und 'Klingsohrs Märchen.'" *Jahrbuch des Freien Deutschen Hochstifts,* 238-58.

Mahoney, Dennis F. 1980. *Die Poetisierung der Natur bei Novalis: Beweggründe, Gestaltung, Folgen.* Bonn: Bouvier.

Neubauer, John. 1980. *Novalis.* Twayne: Boston.

O'Brien, William Arctander. 1980. "Twilight in Atlantis: Novalis' *Heinrich von Ofterdingen* and Plato's *Republic.*" *MLN* 95, 1292-1332.

Peter, Klaus, ed. 1980a. *Romantikforschung seit 1945.* Königstein/Ts.: Hain; includes Introduction by Klaus Peter, 1-39.

Peter, Klaus. 1980b. *Stadien der Aufkärung: Moral und Politik bei Lessing, Novalis und Friedrich Schlegel.* Wiesbaden: Athenaion.

Stadler, Ulrich. 1980. *Die theuren Dinge: Studien zu Bunyan, Jung-Stilling und Novalis.* Berne: Francke.

Theweleit, Klaus. 1980. *Männerphantasien II: Männerkörper — Zur Psychoanalyse des weissen Terrors.* Reinbek: Rowohlt.

Cerf, Steven. 1981. "Brandes' View of Novalis." *Colloquia Germanica* 14, 114-29.

Haase, Donald P. 1981. "Nerval's Knowledge of Novalis: A Reconsideration." *Romance Notes* 22, 1-5.

Jameson, Fredric. 1981. *The Political Unconscious: Narrative as a Socially Symbolic Act.* Ithaca: Cornell University Press.

Kittler, Friedrich A. 1981. "Die Irrwege des Eros und die 'absolute Familie': Psychoanalytischer und diskursanalytischer Kommentar zu Klingsohrs Märchen in Novalis' *Heinrich von Ofterdingen.*" *Psychoanalytische und psychopathologische Literaturinterpretation,* ed. Bernd Urban and Winfried Kudszus. Darmstadt: Wissenschaftliche Buchgesellschaft, 421-70.

Stadler, Ulrich. 1981. "Novalis: *Heinrich von Ofterdingen*." *Romane und Erzählungen der deutschen Romantik: Neue Interpretationen*, ed. Paul Michael Lützeler. Stuttgart: Reclam, 141-62.

White, J. J. 1981-82. "Novalis's *Heinrich von Ofterdingen* and the Aesthetics of 'Offenbarung.'" *Publications of the English Goethe Society* 52, 90-119.

Delphendahl, Renate. 1982. "Ego-Fragmentation and Secondary Narcissism in Novalis' *Heinrich von Ofterdingen*." *Journal of Evolutionary Psychology* 3, 196-206.

Glorieux, Jean-Paul. 1982. *Novalis dans les Lettres françaises à l'Epoque et au Lendemain du Symbolisme (1885-1914)*. Louvain: Presses Universitaires de Louvain.

Hörisch, Jochen. 1982. Afterword to *Novalis: Heinrich von Ofterdingen*. Frankfurt am Main: Insel, 221-42.

Strack, Friedrich. 1982. *Im Schatten der Neugier: Christliche Tradition und kritische Philosophie im Werk Friedrichs von Hardenberg*. Tübingen: Niemeyer.

Zagari, Luciano. 1982. "'Ein Schauspiel für Eros': Nihilistische Dimensionen in Friedrich von Hardenbergs allegorischem Märchen." *Aurora* 42, 130-42.

Blackall, Eric A. 1983. *The Novels of the German Romantics*. Ithaca and London: Cornell University Press.

Eagleton, Terry. 1983. *Literary Theory: An Introduction*. Minneapolis: University of Minnesota Press.

Kurzke, Hermann. 1983. *Romantik und Konservatismus: Das "politische" Werk Friedrich von Hardenbergs (Novalis) im Horizont seiner Wirkungsgeschichte*. Munich: Fink.

Mahoney, Dennis F. 1983. "The Myth of Death and Resurrection in *Heinrich von Ofterdingen*." *South Atlantic Review* 48, No. 2, 52-66.

Ritchie, J. M. 1983. *German Literature under National Socialism*. Totowa, N.J.: Barnes & Noble.

Schreiber, Jens. 1983. *Das Symptom des Schreibens: Roman und absolutes Buch in der Frühromantik (Novalis/Schlegel)*. Frankfurt am Main: Lang.

Zeller, Bernhard, ed. 1983. *Klassiker in finsteren Zeiten 1933-1945: Eine Ausstellung des Deutschen Literaturarchivs im Schiller-Nationalmuseum Marbach am Neckar*. 2 vols. Marbacher Kataloge 38. Marbach: Deutsche Schillergesellschaft.

Phelan, Anthony. 1983-84. "'Das Centrum das Symbol des Goldes': Analogy and Money in *Heinrich von Ofterdingen*." *German Life and Letters* 37, 307-21.

Saul, Nicholas. 1984. *History and Poetry in Novalis and in the Tradition of the German Enlightenment*. London: Institute of German Studies, University of London.

Hauer, Bernhard E. 1985. "Die Todesthematik in *Wilhelm Meisters Lehrjahre* und *Heinrich von Ofterdingen*." *Euphorion* 79, 182-206.

Massey, Marilyn Chapin. 1985. *Feminine Soul: The Fate of an Ideal*. Boston: Beacon.

Murat, Jean. 1985. "Heine et Novalis: Naissance d'un Cliché." *De Lessing à Heine: Un Siècle de Relations littéraires et intellectuelles entre la France et l'Allemagne*, ed. Jean Moes and Jean-Marie Valentin. Paris: Didier-Érudition, 251-62.

Newman, Gail. 1985. "'The Visible Soul of Poetry': Women and the Poet in Novalis' *Heinrich von Ofterdingen*. Diss. University of Minnesota.

Saul, Nicholas. 1985-86. "The Motif of Baptism in three Eighteenth-Century Novels: Secularization or Sacralization?" *German Life and Letters* 39, 107-33.

Burwick, Frederick. 1986. *The Damnation of Newton: Goethe's Color Theory and Romantic Perception*. Berlin and New York: de Gruyter.

Murat, Jean. 1986. "Das Novalis-Bild der französischen Romantik: Von Madame de Staël bis Xavier Marmier." *Gallo-Germanica: Wechselwirkungen und Parallelen deutscher und französischer Literatur (18.-20. Jahrhundert)*, ed. Eckhard Heftrich and Jean-Marie Valentin. Nancy: Presses Universitaires de Nancy, 151-65.

Schulz, Gerhard, ed. 1986. *Novalis: Beiträge zu Werk und Persönlichkeit Friedrich von Hardenbergs*. 2nd ed., revised. Darmstadt: Wissenschaftliche Buchgesellschaft.

Includes:

Kittler, Friedrich. 1986. "*Heinrich von Ofterdingen* als Nachrichtenfluß," 480-508.

Molnár, Géza von. 1986. "Novalis' 'blaue Blume' im Blickfeld von Goethes Optik," 424-49.

Balmes, Hans Jürgen. 1987. Commentary and Notes to *Heinrich von Ofterdingen*. In Novalis, *Werke, Tagebücher und Briefe Friedrich von Hardenbergs*, ed. Hans-Joachim Mähl and Richard Samuel. Munich: Hanser, 3: 134-91.

Batts, Michael, Anthony W. Riley, and Heinz Wetzel, eds. 1987. *Echoes and Influences of German Romanticism: Essays in Honour of Hans Eichner*. New York: Lang.

Includes:

Reiss, Hans. 1987. "Thomas Mann and Novalis: On Thomas Mann's Attitude to Romantic Political Thought during the Weimar Republic," 133-54.

Ziolkowski, Theodore. 1987. "Hermann Hesse and Novalis: A Portrait of the Artist as a Young Dilettante," 115-32.

Behler, Ernst, and Jochen Hörisch, eds. 1987. *Die Aktualität der Frühromantik*. Paderborn: Schöningh.

Includes:

Frank, Manfred. 1987. "'Intellektuelle Anschauung': Drei Stellungnahmen zu einem Deutungsversuch von Selbstbewußtsein: Kant, Fichte, Hölderlin/Novalis," 96-126.

Fried, Jochen. 1987. "'Umschließende Sfäre': Frühromantische Mythologie und spätromantische Enttäuschung," 174-89.

Kittler, Friedrich A. 1987. "Über romantische Datenverarbeitung," 127-40.

Michel, Willy. 1987. "Der 'innere Plural' in der Hermeneutik und Rollentheorie des Novalis," 33-50.

Pott, Hans-Georg. 1987. "Der 'zarte Maßstab' und die 'sanfte Sage': Aspekte einer Metaphysik der Sprache bei Novalis und Heidegger," 63-74.

Schanze, Helmut. 1987. "Leben, als Buch," 236-50.

Stadler, Ulrich. 1987. "Hardenbergs 'poetische Theorie der Fernröhre': Der Synkretismus von Philosophie und Poesie, Natur- und Geisteswissenschaften und seine Konsequenzen für eine Hermeneutik bei Novalis," 51-62.

Boose, Lynda E. 1987. "The Family in Shakespeare Studies." *Renaissance Quarterly* 40, 707-42.

Esselborn, Hans. 1987. "Poetisierte Physik: Romantische Mythologie in Klingsohrs Märchen." *Aurora* 47, 137-58.

Hübinger, Gangolf, 1987. "Kulturkritik und Kulturpolitik des Eugen-Diederichs-Verlags im Wilhelminismus: Ausweg aus der Krise der Moderne?" *Troeltsch-Studien, Vol. 4. Umstrittene Moderne: Die Zukunft der Neuzeit im Urteil der Epoche Ernst Troeltschs,* eds. Horst Renz and Friedrich Wilhelm Graf. Gütersloh, Mohn, 92-114.

Kuzniar, Alice A. 1987. *Delayed Endings: Nonclosure in Novalis and Hölderlin.* Athens, GA: University of Georgia Press.

Mahoney, Dennis F. 1987. "Stages of Enlightenment: Lessing's *Nathan der Weise* and Novalis's *Heinrich von Ofterdingen." Seminar* 23, 200-215.

Molnár, Géza von. 1987. *Romantic Vision, Ethical Context: Novalis and Artistic Autonomy.* Minneapolis: University of Minnesota Press.

Moretti, Franco. 1987. *The Way of the World: The Bildungsroman in European Culture.* London: Verso.

Schulte-Sasse, Jochen. 1987. Foreword to Géza von Molnár, *Romantic Vision, Ethical Context: Novalis and Artistic Autonomy,* xv-xxv.

Weissenberger, Ivo. 1987. "Die Bildnisse Friedrich von Hardenbergs." *Aurora* 47, 126-36.

Hohendahl, Peter Uwe, ed. 1988. *A History of German Literary Criticism, 1730-1980.* Lincoln and London: University of Nebraska Press.

Includes:

Berghahn, Klaus L. 1988. "From Classicist to Classical Literary Criticism, 1730-1806," 13-98.

Hohendahl, Peter Uwe. 1988b. "Literary Criticism in the Epoch of Liberalism, 1820-70," 179-276.

Schulte-Sasse, Jochen. 1988. "The Concept of Literary Criticism in German Romanticism, 1795-1810," 99-177.

Jamme, Christoph, and Gerhard Kurz, eds. 1988. *Idealismus und Aufklärung: Kontinuität und Kritik der Aufklärung in Philosophie und Poesie um 1800.* Stuttgart: Klett-Cotta.

Includes:

Jamme, Christoph. 1988. "Aufklärung via Mythologie: Zum Zusammenhang von Naturbeherrschung und Naturfrömmigkeit um 1800," 35-58.

Böhme, Hartmut. 1988. "Montan-Bau und Berg-Geheimnis: Zum Verhältnis von Bergbauwissenschaft und hermetischer Naturästhetik bei Novalis," 59-79.

Kurzke, Hermann. 1988. *Novalis*. Munich: Beck.

Kuzniar, Alice. 1988. "Reassessing Romantic Reflexivity — The Case of Novalis." *Germanic Review* 63, 77-86.

Moisan, Jean. 1988. "La transcendance du héros et la problématique du métier dans *Heinrich von Ofterdingen*." *Seminar* 24, 132-50.

Pfefferkorn, Kristin. 1988. *Novalis: A Romantic's Theory of Language and Poetry*. New Haven: Yale University Press.

Ritzenhoff, Ursula, ed. 1988. *Novalis. Heinrich von Ofterdingen: Erläuterungen und Dokumente*. Stuttgart: Reclam.

Jacobs, Jürgen, and Markus Krause. 1989. *Der deutsche Bildungsroman: Gattungs-geschichte vom 18. bis zum 20. Jahrhundert*. Munich: Beck.

Kaes, Anton. 1989. "New Historicism and the Study of German Literature." *German Quarterly* 62, 210-19.

Newman, Gail. 1989. "The Status of the Subject in Novalis's *Heinrich von Ofterdingen* and Kleist's *Die Marquise von O....*" *German Quarterly* 62, 59-71.

Gold, Helmut. 1990. *Erkenntnisse unter Tage: Bergbaumotive in der Literatur der Romantik*. Opladen: Westdeutscher Verlag.

Kittler, Friedrich A. 1990. *Discourse Networks 1800/1900*. English translation of *Aufschreibesysteme 1800/1900* (Munich: Fink, 1985; 2nd ed., revised, 1987); trans. Michael Metteer, with Chris Cullens. Stanford: Stanford University Press.

Newman, Gail. 1990. "Poetic Process as Intermediate Area in Novalis's *Heinrich von Ofterdingen*." *Seminar* 26, 16-33.

Wellbery, David E. 1990. Foreword to Friedrich A. Kittler, *Discourse Networks 1800/-1900*. Stanford: Stanford University Press, vii-xxxiii.

Hardin, James, ed. 1991. *Reflection and Action: Essays on the Bildungsroman*. Columbia: University of South Carolina Press.

Includes:

Mahoney, Dennis F. 1991. "The Apprenticeship of the Reader: The Bildungsroman of the 'Age of Goethe,'" 97-117.

Jens, Walter. 1991. "A Great Festival of Peace on the Smoking Battlefields." Walter Jens and Hans Küng, *Literature and Religion: Pascal, Gryphius, Lessing, Hölderlin, Novalis, Kierkegaard, Dostoyevsky, Kafka*, trans. Peter Heinegg. New York: Paragon House, 165-82.

Kruse-Fischer, Ute. 1991. *Verzehrte Romantik: Georg Lukács' Kunstphilosophie der essayistischen Periode (1908-1911)*. Stuttgart: M & P Verlag für Wissenschaft und Forschung.

Uerlings, Herbert. 1991. *Friedrich von Hardenberg, genannt Novalis: Werk und Forschung*. Stuttgart: Metzler.

Calhoon, Kenneth S. 1992. *Fatherland: Novalis, Freud, and the Discipline of Romance*. Detroit: Wayne State University Press.

Kontje, Todd. 1992. *Private Lives in the Public Sphere: The German Bildungsroman as Metafiction*. University Park: Pennsylvania State University Press.

Kuzniar, Alice. 1992. "Hearing Woman's Voices in *Heinrich von Ofterdingen*." *PMLA* 107, 1196-1207.

Mahoney, Dennis F. 1992. "Human History as Natural History in *Die Lehrlinge zu Sais* and *Heinrich von Ofterdingen*." *Subversive Sublimities: Undercurrents of the German Enlightenment*, ed. Eitel Timm. Columbia, S.C.: Camden House, 1-11.

Pikulik. Lothar. 1992. *Frühromantik: Epoche, Werke, Wirkung*. Munich: Beck.

Roder, Florian. 1992. *Novalis: Die Verwandlung des Menschen; Leben und Werk Friedrich von Hardenbergs*. Stuttgart: Urachhaus.

Schulz, Gerhard. 1992. "Novalis: *Heinrich von Ofterdingen*." *Interpretationen: Romane des 19. Jahrhunderts*. Stuttgart: Reclam, 109-43.

Wistoff, Andreas. 1992. *Die deutsche Romantik in der Öffentlichen Literaturkritik: Die Rezensionen zur Romantik in der "Allgemeinen Literatur-Zeitung" und der "Jenaischen Allgemeinen Literatur-Zeitung" 1795-1812*. Bonn: Bouvier.

Engel, Manfred. 1993. *Der Roman der Goethezeit. Band I. Anfänge in Klassik und Frühromantik: Transzendentale Geschichten*. Stuttgart: Metzler.

Walker, Joyce. S. 1993. "Romantic Chaos: The Dynamic Paradigm in Novalis's *Heinrich von Ofterdingen* and Contemporary Science." *German Quarterly* 66, 43-49.

Uerlings, Herbert. 1994. "Novalis in Freiberg: Die Romantisierung des Bergbaus." *Romantik in Dresden*, ed. Walter Schmitz. In press.

Index